With Justice for All

Minorities and Women in Criminal Justice

❖

JANICE JOSEPH, Ph.D.

Richard Stockton College of New Jersey

DOROTHY TAYLOR, Ph.D.

University of Miami

Editors

ROSLYN MURASKIN, Ph.D.

Long Island University

Series Editor

Upper Saddle River, New Jersey 07458

Library of Congress Cataloging-in-Publication Data
With justice for all : minorities and women in criminal justice / Janice Joseph, Dorothy Taylor, editors.
     p. cm.—(Prentice Hall's women in criminal justice series)
   Includes bibliographical references.
     1. Discrimination in criminal justice administration—United States. 2. Discrimination in juvenile justice
administration—United States. 3. Discrimination in law enforcement—United States. 4. Sex discrimination
against women—United States. I. Joseph, Janice. II. Taylor, Dorothy L., 1938– III. Series.

HV9950 .W58 2002
364.973—dc21   2002074934

Publisher: Jeff Johnston
Executive Editor: Kim Davies
Assistant Editor: Sarah Holle
Production Editor: Kathleen Glidden, Stratford Publishing Services
Production Liaison: Barbara Marttine Cappuccio
Director of Production and Manufacturing: Bruce Johnson
Managing Editor: Mary Carnis
Manufacturing Buyer: Cathleen Petersen
Creative Director: Cheryl Asherman
Cover Design Coordinator: Miguel Ortiz
Cover Design: Scott Garrison
Cover Image: David Young-Wolff/Stone
Formatting and Interior Design: Stratford Publishing Services
Printing and Binding: Phoenix Book Tech Park

Pearson Education LTD, *London*
Pearson Education Australia PTY, Limited, *Sydney*
Pearson Education Singapore, Pte. Ltd.
Pearson Education North Asia Ltd., *Hong Kong*
Pearson Education Canada, Ltd., *Toronto*
Pearson Educación de Mexico, S.A. de C.V.
Pearson Education—Japan, *Tokyo*
Pearson Education Malaysia, Pte. Ltd.

Prentice
Hall

10 9 8 7 6 5 4 3 2 1
ISBN 0-13-033463-4

Dedicated to all women and minorities who have struggled
for so long to gain status so rightfully deserved when
this great nation first began.

Roslyn Muraskin, Ph.D.
Series Editor

Contents

❖

Foreword

❖

As a member of the Minorities and Women's Section of the Academy of Criminal Justice Sciences, I am pleased to write the foreword for this text. The work included herein is a needed addition to the emerging body of literature on issues surrounding minorities and women in the criminal justice system.

Post September 11, 2001, the title "Justice for All" has special meaning. These are the last three words in the Pledge of Allegiance to the Flag of the United States of America. We have seen large numbers of flags flying in all sizes throughout the country. People proudly wear them on T-shirts and hats and embroidered on all types of clothing. Flags, in the form of pins, are available in virtually every type of store one enters. "Justice for All"— these words lead us to thoughts of . . . national pride, solidarity, patriotism. Yet, when we examine our criminal justice system, we must question whether there truly is "liberty and justice for all." This text brings together snapshots of a variety of topics across the criminal justice system, allowing us, as readers, to question our assumptions and stimulating us to think about the need for change within the system and for further research on all aspects of the system as it relates to minorities and women. The emphasis of the research presented in this text is on women's issues, and many of the chapters also devote special attention to minority groups.

There has been a recent increase in the number of published articles and research papers focusing on minority populations. Yet much work remains to be done to document and explain the system responses to minority populations and the extent and type of differences in the nature and cause of crime by and against minority populations. Possibly more compelling is the need for research that documents and assists us in understanding the interaction of gender and ethnicity as we study crime and the criminal justice system. It is my hope that this volume will challenge and encourage others to continue to improve our knowledge of these important topics.

This edited volume is the result of the leadership of Drs. Joseph and Taylor in the Minorities and Women's Section of the Academy of Criminal Justice Sciences. Having known these women for several years and been the beneficiary of their friendship, I can attest to their constant efforts to mentor and support minority and women scholars in the field of criminal justice. They have each given tirelessly of their time and energies to heighten the level of attention given to the conduct of research on minorities and women within the broad range of criminal justice studies. They have specifically mentored minority students and encouraged their involvement in research and service to the field. As others reached out to them and served as their role models in the early part of their careers, Drs. Joseph and Taylor do so for young scholars today.

Mittie D. Southerland, Ph.D.
Professor and Director of Criminal Justice
Murray State University

About the Contributors

❖

Series Editor

Roslyn Muraskin, Ph.D., is professor of criminal justice at the C. W. Post Campus of Long Island University. She received her doctorate in criminal justice from the Graduate Center of the City University of New York in 1989. She holds a master's degree in political science from New York University and a bachelor's degree from Queens College. She serves as Trustee for the Northeast Region of the Academy of Criminal Justice Sciences (ACJS) and was the recipient of the Award for Excellence from the Minorities Section of the ACJS. Her publications include *It's a Crime: Women and Justice* (3rd edition, 2003), *Visions for Change: Crime and Justice in the Twenty-First Century* (3rd edition, 2001), and *Morality and the Law* (2001); and she is working on a major text in the field of Corrections, all for Prentice Hall. She serves also as the Women's Series editor for Prentice Hall. Dr. Muraskin is also the editor of *The Justice Professional,* a refereed journal published quarterly by Taylor and Francis. She is the author of numerous articles and papers, and is often quoted in the media as an expert in both women's issues and issues of criminal justice. At Long Island University, Dr. Muraskin is the Director/founder of the Long Island Women's Institute and is the Executive Director of the Alumni Chapter, both for the College of Management.

Volume Editors

Janice Joseph, Ph.D., is a professor in the Criminal Justice Program at Richard Stockton College of New Jersey. She received her Ph.D. degree from York University in Toronto, Canada. She is editor of *Journal of Ethnicity in Criminal Justice.* Her broad research interests include violence against women, women and criminal justice, youth violence, juvenile delinquency, gangs, and minorities and criminal justice. She is the author of the book *Black Youths, Delinquency, and Criminal Justice* and has published numerous articles on delinquency, gangs, domestic violence, stalking, sexual harassment, and minorities and crime.

Dorothy Taylor, Ph.D., received her Ph.D. at Florida State University. She is associate professor of criminology in the Sociology Department at the University of Miami; coordinator of the Criminology Internship Program; and program faculty member in Caribbean, African, and African-American Studies. Dr. Taylor has held the offices of trustee-at-large and secretary for the Academy of Criminal Justice Sciences. Her interests are in criminology, delinquency theories, minorities and criminality, and internships. Her current publications include The *Positive Influence of Bonding in Female-Headed African American Families,* and *Jumpstarting Your Career: An Internship Guide for Criminal Justice,* and her numerous articles have appeared in journals such as *The Journal of Black Psychology, Law and Human Behavior, Juvenile and Family Court Journal,* and the *Journal of Applied Social Psychology.*

Contributors

Delores Jones-Brown, Ph.D., is an associate professor in the Department of Law, Police Science and Criminal Justice Administration at John Jay College of Criminal Justice, City University of New York. Her research interests include the legal socialization of adolescent males, race and crime, race and criminal justice administration, sociology of law, and juvenile justice issues. She is the author of *Race, Crime and Punishment* (Chlesea House) and co-editor of *The System in Black and White: Exploring the Connections between Race, Crime, and Justice* (Praeger). Both her law degree and doctorate in Criminal Justice are from Rutgers University. She is a former post-doctoral fellow at Teachers College, Columbia University, and the National Development and Research Institutes, Inc.

John Burrows, Ph.D., is a faculty member at the School of Law, University of Wisconsin.

Timothy S. Bynum, Ph.D., is a faculty member in the School of Criminal Justice, Michigan State University.

Charles J. Corley, Ph.D., is a faculty member in the School of Criminal Justice, Michigan State University.

Lanette P. Dalley, Ph.D., is assistant professor at Minot State University, Minot, North Dakota. She received her B.S. in sociology from Montana State University (1984), an M.S.W. from Washington University–St. Louis, Missouri (1990), and a Ph.D. in criminology from Indiana University of Pennsylvania (1997). She is a licensed clinical social worker who previously served as a juvenile probation officer.

Luigi Esposito is a Ph.D. candidate at the University of Miami. His interests include social theory and race/ethnic relations. Some of his most recent articles have appeared in the *Sociological Quarterly* and the *Journal of Aging and Identity,* and he has a forthcoming article in *Studies in Symbolic Interactionism.* Along with Vincent Berdayes and John W. Murphy, he is coeditor of a forthcoming book, *The Body in Human Inquiry: Interdisciplinary Explorations of Embodiment,* to be published by Hampton Press.

Kaylene Richards Ekeh, Ph.D., is professor of criminology and criminal justice at California State University, Sacramento, in the Division of Criminal Justice.

Helen Taylor Greene, Ph.D., is associate professor in the Department of Sociology and Criminal Justice at Old Dominion University, Norfolk, Virginia. She received her Ph.D. from the University of Maryland, College Park. Her research interests include African Americans, crime and justice, community policing, police brutality, and women in policing. She is the author of numerous articles and recently co-authored *African American Criminological Thought* with Shaun L. Gabbidon, and coedited *African American Classics in Criminology and Criminal Justice,* with Shaun L. Gabbidon and Vernetta D. Young.

Elizabeth L. Grossi, Ph.D., is associate professor in the Department of Justice Administration at the University of Louisville. She holds a Ph.D. in criminology from Indiana University of Pennsylvania. Professor Grossi teaches graduate and undergraduate courses in criminological theory and corrections. Her research interests include prison boot camps, domestic violence, and program evaluation. She is actively involved in the Southern Criminal Justice Association, in which she currently serves as president. At present she is conducting research in the areas of racial profiling, gangs, and domestic violence.

Zelma Weston Henriques, Ph.D., is professor in the Department of Law and Police Science at John Jay College of Criminal Justice, City University of New York. Her major research interests are imprisoned mothers and their children; race, class, and gender issues; cross-cultural studies of crime; and human rights. She is the author of *Imprisoned Mothers and Their Children: A Descriptive and Analytical Study,* published by the University Press of America. Dr. Henriques holds a doctorate from Columbia University and was a Rockefeller Research Fellow in Human Rights at Columbia University.

David Lester, Ph.D., is a faculty member in the psychology program at the Richard Stockton College of New Jersey. He holds Ph.D. degrees from Brandeis University in psychology and from Cambridge University (U.K.) in social and political science. He has conducted research on death since the mid-1960s, and he has now published 70 books and more than 1,800 scholarly articles and notes on such topics as the fear of death, suicide, and murder. In the criminal justice field, he has written books on murder in general, serial killers, the death penalty, crime victimization, and crime with Native Americans, and coauthored a textbook on correctional counseling.

Zina T. McGee, Ph.D., is an endowed university professor of sociology at Hampton University, Hampton, Virginia, where she also serves as codirector of the Behavioral Science Research Center. She specializes in the study of violent victimization, delinquency, coping strategies, and behavioral outcomes among African American adolescents, and conducts research on the disparate treatment of black female offenders. She is a career development fellow at the National Consortium on Violence Research. Among her publications, she has authored "Patterns of Victimization and Violence among African American Youth," and she serves as institutional assessment coordinator at Hampton University.

Martin L. O'Connor, J.D., received his J.D. degree from Hofstra University. He is associate professor of criminal justice at the C. W. Post Campus of Long Island University. He was the deputy police commissioner in charge of legal affairs for both Nassau and Suffolk County Police Departments, Long Island, New York.

Wilson R. Palacios, Ph.D., is an assistant professor in the department of criminology at the University of South Florida. He holds a Ph.D. from the University of Miami, Department of Sociology. His research interests include minority risk-taking behavior, criminal justice education, and qualitative research methods.

Angel Prewitt is a faculty member in the School of Criminal Justice, Michigan State University.

Pamela Schram, Ph.D., is a faculty member in the School of Law at the University of California, Santa Barbara.

Overview

Roslyn Muraskin

❖

Women and especially minorities have long been neglected in the study of criminal justice. They are referred to in the literature as the forgotten offender. Historically, no constitutional obligation existed for all individuals to be treated alike. The government has treated disparate groups differently for too many years. Women and minorities are such groups. There are indications that significant differences have existed at all levels of male-female services by the criminal justice system. There are those (Belknap, 1996) who refer to women as "invisible." The case *Glover v. Johnson* (1979) indicated, "Keep it simple—they are only women."

Is there equality among the races and genders? Does equality with men hurt women, or is it the only way to guarantee that women are considered as equal partners? What does it mean to be equal? There is no automatic way to allow both sexes to enjoy protection unless we see a commitment to eliminate all discrimination. Gender has never been classified as a "suspect classification," and both women and minorities continue to suffer by laws established by the majority.

In the "good old days," men were considered the protector of all women. "The natural and proper timidity and delicacy which belongs to the female sex evidently unfits it for many of the occupations of civil life" (*Bradwell v. Illinois,* 1872). As women continue to struggle, as all minorities continue to struggle, they have yet to achieve all that is wanted and needed. These groups are still struggling to survive in this world of ours.

Women and minorities both deserve their dignity and the right to be treated as anyone else and by any aspect of government, including that of the criminal justice system. Are minorities to be subordinated in our country as minorities or treated as members of the human race? Progress in the realm of minority and women's issues and the criminal justice system is possible because of the continuous battle that has been fought for something called equality or parity of treatment. Traditional literature ignores the plight of women and minorities. There are those who will deprecate or ignore the point of view of these groups entirely. Public denigration is not to be socially acceptable. Attacks such as these should be a thing of the past.

According to Catharine MacKinnon, "equality in human societies is commonly affirmed but rarely practiced" (2001, p. 2). This work, dedicated to minorities and women, points out that everyone is entitled to the same consideration as everyone else. The term *minorities and women* should be set aside, and rather we should have a world where all people are considered the equal of everyone else, with all persons being endowed with the same rights and consideration as all humans. There is to be no disparate treatment in this country of individuals whose gender and whose color may be somewhat different. If we are to be the *melting pot,* then truly we should look around and understand that the criminal justice system by its very definition should be treating everyone fairly.

This volume of our women's series, *With Justice for All: Minorities and Women in Criminal Justice,* as developed by Janice Joseph and Dorothy Taylor, examines all the issues that affect these groups. As we study the issues, we hope to provide a solid basis from which to explore ourselves and the society in which we live.

REFERENCES

BELKNAP, J. (1996). *The invisible woman: Gender, crime and justice.* Belmont, CA: Wadsworth Publishing Co.
MACKINNON, C. (2001). *Sex equality.* New York: Foundation.

CASES

Bradwell v. Illinois, 83 U.S. 130 (1872).
Glover v. Johnson, 478 F. Supp. 1075 (1979).

SECTION I
Victimization

1

Domestic Violence and Asian Americans

Janice Joseph and Dorothy Taylor

Former U.S. Surgeon General C. Everett Koop stated that domestic violence is an overwhelming moral, economic, and public health burden that society can no longer bear. Most research studies focus on domestic violence in the white community. However, domestic violence knows no racial, ethnic, class, or sexual orientation boundaries. The need exists to discuss domestic violence and its intersections with race and culture because the perceptions of the problem of domestic violence vary among different cultural and racial groups. In addition, the treatment and prevention of domestic violence cannot be effective without taking into account both racial and cultural dynamics.

In this chapter we examine domestic violence within the Asian American family, and focus specifically on wife abuse and sexual abuse. We also discuss responses to domestic violence within the Asian American community. Finally, policy and future research implications are presented.

DESCRIPTION OF ASIAN AMERICANS

Asian Americans form a diverse group that originated from three major geographic areas: (1) East Asia, which includes China, Japan, and Korea; (2) Southeast Asia, which includes Cambodia, Laos, Vietnam, Myanmar, Thailand, Malaysia, Indonesia, Singapore, and the Philippines; and (3) South Asia, which includes India, Pakistan, and Sri Lanka. Their customs, traditions, values, and beliefs are rooted in political and religious systems that are thousands of years old (Oats, 1998).

3

Many Asian cultures have been influenced by the doctrines and philosophies of Buddhism, Confucianism, and Taoism. These "three teachings" serve as the religious and philosophical foundation that dominates virtually all aspects of Asian life. "Adherence to the 'three teachings' reflects a polytheistic orientation that stresses complementarity rather than conflict among Confucianism, Taoism, and Buddhism" (Chan, 1992, p. 189). Asian Americans value collectivism rather than individualism, and the family is seen as the nucleus of their communities (Chan, 1992).

The family plays a central organizing role for Asian Americans. It is the reference group that provides the individual's source of identity and emotional security throughout life (Nguyen & Williams, 1989). Families reinforce strong interdependent bonds that promote a sense of solidarity. At the same time, family functioning is regulated by clearly defined roles and rules of interpersonal conduct (Ishisaka & Takagi, 1982). The nuclear family is embedded in an extended family network that often includes grandparents, uncles, and cousins (Heras, 1985; Huang, 1989; Nagata, 1989; Tran, 1988) and in Vietnamese culture includes dead relatives (Tran, 1988). Each individual has a role and a place in the structure and the social order of the family. An individual's behavior is a reflection on one's family and one's ancestors. Therefore, Asian Americans strive to defend their family honor and to save face (that is, protect the family's reputation). Ultimately, the value of familism dictates that the family is more important than the individual (Ho, 1987; Ishisaka & Takagi, 1982; Oats, 1998).

Asian societies maintain a patrilineal family structure, in which the father or husband is the main provider for the family and the wife is responsible for the home, including rearing children and financial matters (Dung, 1984). It is the wife's duty to be a good mother. Kim (1985) suggested that a wife is basically viewed as a nonperson until she gives birth to a son, after which she gains more power as a mother and even more when she becomes a mother-in-law. The oldest males have the most authority and responsibility (Nagata, 1989; Tran, 1988). Females are expected to obey their fathers, husbands, and eldest sons (Tran, 1988). Older children are taught to care for and be responsible for younger siblings (Huang, 1989). Husbands are expected to maintain the financial welfare of the family and make most major decisions. Wives are expected to manage the finances, maintain the household, and attend to the day-to-day affairs of the children. In traditional Asian culture, the wife becomes part of the husband's family and has limited rights.

In general, Asian Americans value harmony with nature rather than mastery over nature; they see religion from a polytheistic point of view and believe the family to be more vital to the existence of the community than the individual.

For a long time, in American society, Asian Americans were considered the "model minority" (Chan, 1992). Seduced by this label, members of the Asian American community tried to suppress or mask the problems of domestic violence, sexual assault, divorce, intergenerational conflict, and community disharmony (Dasgupta, 1999). However, domestic violence is today emerging as an important issue for the Asian American community.

WIFE ABUSE

To date, there have been no nationally representative studies of Asian American partner violence (Sorenson, Upchurch, & Shen, 1996). Instead, much of the research has relied on case histories (Eng, 1995; Singh & Unnithan, 1999), clinical samples (Chan, 1987), anecdotal reports (Lai, 1986), and newspaper accounts (Chin, 1994). Consequently, estimates of wife assault have varied widely. For instance, based on his focus groups, comprised of six to ten Chinese women, Ho (1990) estimated that 20% to 30% of Chinese husbands physically abuse their wives (Ho, 1990). Although it is not possible to draw conclusions about ethnic differences based on these limited studies, interviews with victims (Ho, 1990) and community leaders (Huisman, 1996) indicate that battering is a serious problem in this population. In fact, Dasgupta and Warrier (1996), who conducted intensive interviews with 12 college-educated, professional Indian American women who had been battered, concluded that:

> Although Asian Indian immigrants have been celebrated in this country as a "model minority" our experiences of working within the community contradict this simplistic perception of the group. It is our contention that the community maintains its facade of tranquility and success by disowning problems that emerge within it. . . . A case in point is the denial of wife abuse in our community. This refusal to acknowledge the existence of woman abuse, along with our socialization into a restrictive women's role and status complicates the Asian Indian women's experience of abuse within the family. (pp. 253–254)

According to anecdotal research (Dunwoody, 1982; Lai, 1986; Rimonte, 1989), case studies (Eng, 1995; Okamura, Heras, & Wong-Kerberg, 1995), and legal accounts (Anderson, 1993; Jang, Lee, & Morello-Frosch, 1990), Asian immigrants and refugee families appear to experience more partner violence than their American-born counterparts.

Bui-Hoan and Morash (1999), in their study of Vietnamese American families, reported that the husband's patriarchal beliefs, his dominant position in the family, and conflict around changing norms and values between spouses were associated with wife abuse. They also identified economic hardship, traditional family values, beliefs in traditional female roles, and perceptions of racial discrimination as obstacles that prevented the victims from relying on the formal system to cope with the abuse.

Bhaumik (1988) examined cultural issues in violent Asian American families and found that Asian American wives who experienced abuse tended to come from families characterized by adherence to rigid Asian patriarchal attitudes. These attitudes contrast sharply with the greater freedom that women have in today's American society and suggest that cultural differences in gender-role expectations are an important factor in spouse abuse.

Ho (1990) suggested that woman battering is rooted in Asian culture, which practices the oppression of women, stressing the hierarchical position of the male as the authority in the family. Ho pointed out that the problem of woman battering among refugees and immigrants is more complex than among second- and third-generation Asian Americans because many speak little or no English, lack traditional resources, and are unfamiliar with American society.

Cultural isolation and limited family support, coupled with the lack of educational and job opportunities, limited English speaking skills, and poverty, are thought to contribute to the increased risk for partner violence (Chen & True, 1994). Asian women who enter the country illegally or through "mail order" marriages may have even greater difficulty in escaping abusive marriages. Substantial documentation of abuse, in the form of affidavits from police, medical personnel, and social service agencies, may be required from these immigrant women. The victims risk deportation even when they leave violent husbands (Anderson, 1993). Many of these women also lack a clear functioning knowledge of the English language, others lack the means to be self-sufficient, and many have left their families and friends behind, so they feel isolated amid a land of strangers. Immigrant Asian women who are unaware of the resources available to them stay much longer in abusive relationships than the nonimmigrant Asian American woman (Naresh & Surendran, 1996).

Asian American battered women are also reluctant to seek help when they are victimized. According to Chow (1989), Asian American women confront a number of cultural dilemmas in the United States, including obedience versus independence, collective or familial interest versus individual interest, and self-control versus self-expression. The traditional beliefs are based on rigid gender norms that may deter these women from viewing themselves as battered and inhibit them from seeking help. For example, in traditional Asian cultures, women are taught to obey their "male superiors." A daughter is expected to obey her father, a wife is expected to obey her husband, and a widow is expected to obey her eldest son (Chin, 1994). If a woman fails to obey her male superior, it is sometimes acceptable for him to discipline her through violent means (Yim, 1978).

Asian American women are less likely than women from other racial backgrounds to report the abuse, and those who do so usually wait until the battering has reached a crisis level (Bhaumik, 1988; Rimonte, 1989). The lack of reporting is attributed to several factors: (1) the traditional patriarchial system that believes in male supremacy, (2) the socialization process that favors the family and the community over the individual, (3) the cultural emphasis on silent suffering versus open communication, and (4) cultural norms that indirectly sanction abuse against women and tend to minimize or legitimize domestic violence in the Asian American community (Lkeda-Vogel, Lee, & Lee, 1993; Rimonte, 1989).

Mehrotra (1999) reported that battered Asian American wives use strategies of resistance to deal with the abuser. These include direct resistance, such as refusal to cook for the batterer (husband); covert acts such as spitting in their husbands' food before serving them; taking large sums of money from their husbands when they have the opportunity; refusing to have a sexual relationship with their husbands; and seeking help outside the relationship, such as calling the police and obtaining a restraining order.

SEXUAL ABUSE

Wife Sexual Abuse

Abraham (1999), in her study of sexual abuse in South Asian marriages, argued that in South Asian cultures, men are taught to control women's sexuality. Because of this sexual repression of South Asian women, sexual intercourse for women is viewed as acceptable only within the confines of marriage. Men are taught that sex is their masculine right as husbands, and marriage emphasizes sexual gratification for men and the suppression of women's sexual needs. Within the marriage, men initiate the sex act, define its nature, and determine when it ends. The wife has no say in the matter. Consequently, husbands have control over their wives sexually, and some force their wives to have sexual intercourse against their will. This is marital rape but, within the South Asian cultures, husbands are not viewed as committing an illegal offense (Abraham, 1999).

Abraham also reported that several women in her study were sexually abused by other male relatives of their husbands. Usually, these men were helping the women out of abusive marriages and took advantage of these women's vulnerability. These "significant others" assumed that the victims' economic, social, and emotional powerlessness allowed them to take such sexual liberties. Again, these women remained silent about these attacks because they have been socialized to put men's needs before their own. Abraham argued that the sexual abuse of South Asian women must be explained within a bicultural context and should also incorporate the intersection of gender, ethnicity, and class.

Yoshihama (1999) reported that the respondents in her study claimed to have experienced various types of unwanted sexual contact in their intimate relationships. Some had forced sexual intercourse when they were asleep, drunk, or drugged; when their judgment was otherwise impaired; and through the use of physical violence. One woman even reported that her partner took pictures of her during sex, and another reported unwanted use of sex toys or foreign objects.

Many of the adult victims of sexual abuse do not report the victimization. Abraham (1999) reported that many of the victims in her study did not report the incident because they have been socialized to acquiesce to the needs of their husbands and to the culture's acceptance of male dominance and women's subordination in the patriarchal order. Strong cultural norms of stoicism and saving face often prevent Asian American victims from seeking help because public emotional displays are forbidden. This code of silence is also reinforced by the feeling of shame because seeking help for personal problems is imbued with personal shame, shame of losing face with their community, and shame in the larger society. They may, therefore, seek help only in extreme cases of victimization (Quina & Carlson, 1989).

Child Sexual Abuse

The parental role is seen as more important than the marital relationship (Chan, 1992). Parents readily sacrifice their needs to look after the best interests of their children. Consequently, parents assume "the right to demand unquestioning obedience and loyalty from the child. The role of the parent is to define the law, and the duty of the child is to listen and obey" (Chan, 1992, p. 216). This ideal is referred to as filial piety, and it considers parents' authority over their children to be indisputable and their judgment to be unquestionable.

In traditional Asian American cultures, parents claim an inherent right over their children (Sue & Morishima, 1982). Loyalty, obedience, and respect are expected. Research indicates that Asian, Filipino, and Pacific Island Americans socialize their children to maintain traditional values of family cohesion, solidarity, filial piety, and a sense of obligation to the family (Huang, 1989; Sluzki, 1979; Wong, 1987). Emphasis is also placed on the character development of the child (Wong-Kerberg, 1993). A variety of child-rearing strategies are used, including modeling desired behavior (Nguyen & Williams, 1989), didactic teachings (Chan, 1992), physical discipline during the earlier years (Union of Pan Asian Communities, 1982), rewards, and the use of shame (Sue & Sue, 1982).

Where data are available, the reported incidence of child sexual abuse for Asian American populations appears to be low. However, Korbin (1991) stated that "the absence of published or documented cases of child sexual abuse does not necessarily mean an absence of the problem" (p. 68). In fact, according to Okamura, Heras, and Wong-Kerberg (1995), their experiences working with Asian American families have led them to believe that the actual incidence of child sexual abuse is much higher than is reported. In a survey of 33 Asian, Pacific Island, and Filipino professional and paraprofessional human service providers in a community-based agency, Okamura (1992) found that only 15% of the respondents reported that sexual child abuse did not occur in their communities, and a further 24% reported that they did not know if sexual abuse occurred in their communities. Fifteen percent agreed that "it is acceptable in my culture for fathers or uncles to check on a girl's body, including the vaginal area, for medical reasons," and 35% agreed with the statement, "It is acceptable in my culture or among members of my culture for a baby boy to have his genitals kissed and fondled by family members as expressions of joy that it is a boy child." Ima and Hohm (1991) found that 50% of the Asian Pacific sexual abuse cases involved incest perpetrated by fathers, compared with only 36% in a national study.

An Asian American victim of child abuse may not disclose his or her victimization because of personal shame that is due to the nature of the abuse. It is rare for an Asian child to disclose sexual abuse directly. Adult Asian women who were sexually abused as children or adolescents, for example, typically suffer in silence for years about their abuse, telling no one and accepting it as fate (Hicks, 1993). Because loss of virginity brings dishonor to self and family, female victims may deny trauma or reframe the abuse in a more socially acceptable way (Cole, Espin, & Rothblom, 1992).

In the Asian American culture, victims of child sexual abuse are not always perceived as victims (Rao, Di Clemente, & Ponton, 1992). Children are frequently not believed when they disclose their sexual victimization. When the child discloses abuse, the family frequently directs anger toward the child. The family perceives the disclosure as putting the entire family's reputation at risk because anything brought to bear outside the family, especially a complaint from a child against an adult of a sexual transgression, threatens family unity. Because of the sexual nature of the abuse, parents may feel discomfort, embarrassment, and shame to such an extent that they try to protect both the child's and family's reputations by adamant denial. Some parents will firmly maintain that the abuse did not occur. Some parents will contend that the child is lying and pressure the child to recant (Okamura, Heras, & Wong-Kerberg, 1995). Rao, Di Clemente, and Ponton (1992) found in their retrospective study comparing Asian sexual child abuse cases with other populations that Asian family members were the least supportive of the victim. Compared with blacks, whites, and Hispanics, Asian mothers or primary caretakers were half as likely to report the abuse to authorities. Most Southeast Asian parents in Wong's (1987) sexual abuse prevention program revealed that they do not believe sexual abuse to be a problem and that a family member would not sexually abuse a child.

The dynamics of shame and denial are usually followed by blaming and accusations of betrayal. If the parents come to acknowledge the abuse, many will blame the child. Children are held responsible for "being at the wrong place at the wrong time" or for being a "bad child" and somehow responsible for attracting the sexual advances. If the perpetrator is a parent or family member, blaming allows the guilty party to save face. If a child is removed from the home or a parent is ordered out of the home by court order, the child may be blamed for the disruption and breakup of the family. A nonoffending parent often will align with the offending parent against the child in an attempt to preserve the family's respectability in their community. The child victim suffers under the cultural taboos and is seen as "damaged goods" and undesirable for marriage into any family (Okamura, Heras, & Wong-Kerberg, 1995).

INTERVENTION AND COMMUNITY ADVOCACY

Intervention programs and strategies are designed to control the behavior of the perpetrator and to stop future occurrences. In other cases, intervention programs and strategies are used to help the victims and offenders lead nonviolent and safe lives. In this section of the chapter, we focus on the legal and social service approaches to domestic violence in Asian American families.

Law Enforcement Intervention Strategies

Asian Americans are reluctant to involve outside agencies in family matters, especially law enforcement officers. One of the reasons for this is the traditional reliance of Asian Americans on the private resolution of conflicts, which excludes police involvement. In addition, there is often a great fear of authority figures, especially among recent immigrants from autocratic or war-torn Asian countries. However, some efforts have been made by law enforcement agencies to overcome the barriers between Asian communities and police departments. Cultural awareness training has been implemented as a means of improving police officers' understanding and treatment of Asian Americans. Interpreters have been hired where numbers warrant it. Some police departments across the country are making efforts to make their officers more accessible to the Asian American communities. San Diego and Oakland, California, for example, have established Asian advisory committees that act as liaisons between the police departments and the Asian communities. San Diego and Los Angeles have introduced civilian community service officers who work out of storefront offices in the Asian communities. Their role is to act as buffers between the two communities by taking reports, attending community events, offering crime prevention and counseling programs, and providing similar community-oriented services (Perry, 2000).

Community Advocacy

Community Organizations. Understanding and sensitivity to cultural issues are sometimes lacking when professionals try to assist Asian American victims of domestic violence. It is understandable that many Asian Americans would prefer to go to organizations whose staff can speak their language, understand their problems, and sympathize better with their situation. Consequently, in the last decade, Asian Americans have established organizations in their communities to meet the needs of victims of domestic violence. These organizations are of two types: the temple and cultural organizations and feminist organizations.

The temple and cultural organizations focus on advocacy and are there to preserve the ties of the family (Naresh & Surendran, 1996). One such organization is the Muslims against Family Violence (MAFV), which endeavors to eliminate domestic violence in the San Francisco Bay Area Muslim community by promoting a comprehensive educational campaign and enhancing community awareness of this important issue (Muslims against Family Violence, 1999). There is also a Union of Pan Asian Communities in San Diego that works with child abuse victims and families from the Asian Pacific and Filipino American communities. Its range of services includes prevention, treatment, advocacy, outreach, and aftercare support. It is staffed with a multidisciplinary team of mental health professionals and para-professionals that is culturally competent and trained in child maltreatment (Okamura, Heras, & Wong-Kerberg, 1995). A Southeast Asian sexual abuse prevention program has been established in King County, Washington. This program uses outreach and community support and involvement to develop appropriate materials for distribution (Wong, 1987).

The South Asian Women's Organizations (SAWO) and Asian Women's Self Help Association (ASHA) are local support groups designed to reinforce cultural values. These organizations serve the needs and concerns of South Asian women and their children. They provide victims of domestic violence with psychological, social, legal, and economic support. Most important, they raise public awareness of the problem of domestic violence in the South Asian American communities (Abraham, 1995; Preisser, 1999). Their goal is to preserve the family structure and the marriage bond and make things work (Naresh & Surendran, 1996).

The second type of Asian American organization is the feminist organizations committed to women empowerment and liberation (Naresh & Surendran, 1996). Feminist organizations have led the fight for abused and exploited South Asian women, both in the home and in the workplace. The first such organization, Manavi, was founded by six New Jersey women. Since its inception ten years ago, approximately 20 such organizations have expanded throughout the United States and Canada. A small network has been created between Sakhi in New York, Apna Ghar in Chicago, Asha in Maryland, Narika, Sahara, and Maitri in California, and related organizations. They serve as information resources, guides, and support for victims of domestic violence. They also make women's issues more visible in the South Asian community as well as in the national forum. With publicity campaigns, issue forums, and occasional conferences, these organizations hope to gain public support and recognition. Despite the lack of resources, limited funds and space, community opposition, and the inescapable shortage of full-time staff, these organizations have made tremendous strides in the women's struggle. As they become more established, they should become further valued by the community (Naresh & Surendran, 1996).

Conferences.   In California in 1997, the Asian Women's Shelter, in collaboration with several other community organizations and with support from the state health department, organized a statewide conference on domestic violence in the Asian American communities. The conference was attended by more than 400 Asian community service providers and activists. Since then, additional efforts have addressed domestic violence, including a Korean conference in Los Angeles, a South Asian conference in New York, and a broader pan-Asian conference in Ohio. Through these conferences, community interest in eliminating domestic violence has increased (Asian Institute on Domestic Violence, 1999).

Institute on Domestic Violence.   In 1998, the Asian community launched the Asian Institute on Domestic Violence to deal with domestic violence in the Asian American and Pacific Islander American communities. The Asian Institute on Domestic Violence was created in Chicago at a meeting attracting more than 80 ethnically diverse experts on various aspects of domestic violence. The Asian Institute on Domestic Violence hopes to eliminate domestic violence in Asian communities by building supportive networks, increasing awareness and prevention of domestic violence, identifying and expanding resources, and informing and promoting research and policy. Professionals such as violence experts, shelter workers, health educators, and policy activists who provide service to the Asian American communities want to ensure that policy makers, service providers, and others do all they can to ensure that Asian Americans, especially women and children, can live free of family violence and find culturally appropriate services if they do face abuse (Asian Institute on Domestic Violence, 1999).

IMPLICATIONS FOR POLICY AND RESEARCH

Policy Implications

Asian Americans are reluctant to involve outside agencies in domestic matters for several reasons: (a) cultural, (b) institutional, and (c) stereotypical notions about Asian Americans. They face cultural barriers that impede seeking help through formal and informal avenues. Asians fear dishonor and "losing face" (Ho, 1990), and so they are reluctant to seek help (Kanuha, 1994). An understanding and appreciation of cultural values is important in examining domestic violence among Asian Americans, who place a strong value on the family, including extended family members.

There are institutional barriers as well that make it difficult for ethnic minorities to access necessary services (Rodriguez & O'Donnell, 1995). Agencies may be ill equipped to handle the needs of Asian American clients. They may lack translators and bicultural and bilingual professionals, reading material in the client's native language, or ethnically sensitive treatment programs (Eng, 1995; Fontes, 1995). The structural barriers include rules against treating non-English-speaking or immigrant clients, geographic distance from minority communities, prohibitive fee structures, and inflexible or inconvenient hours of operation (Eng, 1995; Fontes, 1995).

There are racial stereotypes. The stereotyped view of violence as more normal among minority groups than among whites has posed barriers to the intervention and prevention of domestic violence in minority communities. These stereotypes may contribute to victim blaming, which in turn reduces the likelihood of help seeking by minority women (Rasche, 1988). Moreover, the fear of reinforcing stereotypes, coupled with community and family loyalty, may encourage some women to hide their abuse. For example, one battered Korean American woman feared that her coworkers would believe that "there was something wrong with Korean people" if they learned of her abuse (Richie & Kanuha, 1993, p. 291). Community leaders may also fear that discussing minority partner violence will reinforce negative stereotypes. The concern about maintaining a positive community image of minorities may contribute to community denial of domestic violence and discourage women from seeking help within their own communities (Eng, 1995).

Some of the programs for abused women are located outside minority neighborhoods. A national survey of 142 domestic partner violence treatment programs found that more than half (55%) of the programs were located in white neighborhoods, 15% did not provide training on ethnic minority issues, 70% did not have manuals or literature concerning culturally sensitive practice methods, and 61% did not have a bilingual counselor (Williams, 1994). When these institutional barriers were removed, community agencies reported an increase in ethnic minority clients (Rimonte, 1989).

Huisman (1996) interviewed 18 service providers whose clientele included battered Asian American women and found that several needs specific to Asian American women were not addressed. He reported that language was a major constraint for these women. Many programs did not have staff members or translators available to address the diversity of Asian American communities.

Based on these problems faced by victims of domestic violence in the Asian American community, social agencies should provide:

- More culturally sensitive training for their personnel in order to meet the needs of Asian American victims. Those agencies and communities that have instituted such strategies and programs should be applauded, but culturally sensitive training should be required for all law enforcement officers, clergy, youth workers, and other professionals who work with Asian Americans.
- More culturally specific detection, intervention, prevention, and treatment programs for Asian Americans. Agencies, such as battered women's shelters and crisis centers, may perpetuate the subordination and marginalization of minority groups such as Asian Americans by adopting strategies and policies that are inappropriate for Asian American clients. Agencies serving the needs of Asian Americans need, therefore, to develop culturally sensitive programs for Asian Americans who have been victimized.
- Translators for Asian American victims who face language barriers. The language barriers limit Asian American women's access to information. Because of the number of different languages spoken by Asian Americans, community programs should have staff members or translators available to address the diversity of Asian American communities.
- Programs that are more accessible to Asian Americans. Some immigrant communities are isolated from access to human service programs and resources, which increases their vulnerability to domestic violence. Accessible and affordable programs should be available to Asian American victims of domestic violence.

Domestic violence is self-perpetuating and will not stop without intervention and prevention. The Asian American community has a vital part to play in the prevention of domestic violence. The Asian American community should:

- Establish intervention and prevention programs to combat domestic violence in Asian American communities. Although some programs (as discussed earlier) have been established, many more are needed.
- Prevent domestic violence through early intervention for families at risk for domestic violence. Certain social institutions, organizations, and individuals, such as the church, family, friendship networks, and social leaders in the Asian American communities, must play an active role in preventing domestic violence.
- Condemn domestic violence in their communities by encouraging victims to leave abusive relationships or seek justice for the violence against them. Most important, Asian Americans have to begin to acknowledge certain behaviors as violent behaviors. If such behaviors are not recognized as violent, these behaviors will continue, and prevention of such behaviors will be extremely difficult.

IMPLICATIONS FOR FUTURE RESEARCH

Ho (1990) reported that domestic violence in the Asian American community has been ignored by researchers and health officials because it rarely comes to the attention of the authorities, probably because Asian Americans consider family problems a private matter.

Because of the paucity of informatin, first, there needs to be more research on Asian Americans and domestic violence. By ignoring Asian Americans in their research on domestic violence, researchers are missing substantial information in the overall understanding of domestic violence among all people of color. In addition, research on domestic violence should be examined within the framework of ethnicity and culture.

Second, the existing measures used in research on Asian Americans have been designed to study white populations and may not be applicable to Asian Americans. The use of research instruments developed for white Americans may lead to false and inaccurate conclusions about Asian Americans. What are needed are tools of measurement and assessment that adequately capture the cultural experiences of Asian Americans. This will become vitally important as the number of Asian Americans increases in American society.

Third, there is a serious gap in the knowledge of domestic violence among different Asian American groups. Though Asian Americans share a common heritage, there are differences between the various Asian American groups. Researchers need to compare domestic violence experiences across Asian American groups rather than just comparing them as a whole with the white population or other racial and ethnic groups. Data on racial and ethnic commonalities and differences among Asian Americans are crucial in the planning, development, and implementation of strategies and programs designed to combat domestic violence against Asian Americans.

Research on Asian Americans also lacks studies within the Asian American groups in which different experiences in victimization within an Asian American group is studied. For example, are risk factors or experiences similar across age, socioeconomic status, or religious strata for Japanese, Chinese, or Cambodians? There are probably differences, but only research studies can reveal them. This is a challenge for future research.

SUMMARY

Domestic violence is a problem that affects everyone, irrespective of race, ethnicity, sexual orientation, or religion. Domestic violence in the Asian American community has gone unnoticed for a very long time, largely because it was not recognized as such and because the general society viewed Asian Americans as the "model minority." However, things have changed, and attention is being focused on domestic violence in the Asian American community.

Asian American victims of domestic violence face several obstacles when they seek service from mainstream social agencies. To better serve the needs of this group of clients, service providers need a better understanding of the Asian American community and more comprehensive culturally sensitive training for their personnel.

There has been some community advocacy among Asian Americans, and several communities have established their own social agencies to serve the needs of Asian American victims of domestic violence. Despite these efforts, more such agencies are needed in the Asian American community. More important, leaders and members of the Asian American community have to recognize and acknowledge that domestic violence is unacceptable and should not be tolerated. There is also a need for more scholarly research on Asian Americans and domestic violence.

DISCUSSION QUESTIONS

1.   What factors are related to domestic violence in Asian American families?

2.   Why are Asian American women reluctant to report their victimization?

3.   Discuss two responses of Asian Americans to child abuse.

4.   Why are Asian Americans reluctant to involve outside agencies in family conflict?

5.   Describe the Asian Institute on Domestic Violence.

REFERENCES

ABRAHAM, M. (1999). Sexual abuse in South Asian immigrant marriages. *Violence against Women, 5*(6), 591–618.

ABRAHAM, M. (1995). Ethnicity, gender, and marital violence. *Gender and Society, 9*(4), 450–468.

ANDERSON, M.J. (1993). A license to abuse: The impact of conditional status on female immigrants. *The Yale Law Journal,* 102, 1401–1430.

ASIAN INSTITUTE ON DOMESTIC VIOLENCE. (1999). Available at: http://www.apiahf.org/programs/DV.html.

BHAUMIK, M. (1988). *A study of wife abuse in two cultures: The American and the Asian American.* Unpublished doctoral dissertation, University of California–Los Angeles.

BUI-HOAN, N. & MORASH, M. (1999). Domestic violence in the Vietnamese immigrant community: An exploratory study. *Violence against Women, 5*(7), 769–795.

CHAN, C.S. (1987). Asian American women's psychological response to sexual exploitation and cultural sterotypes. *Women and Therapy, 6*(4), 33–38.

CHAN, S. (1992). Families with Asian roots. In E.W. Lynch & M.J. Hanson (Eds.), *Developing cross-cultural competency: A guide for working with young children and their families* (pp. 181–257). Baltimore, MD: Paul H. Brookes.

CHEN, S.A., & TRUE, R.H. (1994). Asian/Pacific Island Americans. In L. D. Eron, J. H. Gontry, & J. P. Schleyel (Eds.), *Reason to hope: A psychological perspective on violence and youth* (pp.145–162). Washington, DC: American Psychological Association.

CHIN, K. (1994). Out of town brides: International marriage and wife abuse among Chinese immigrants. *Journal of Comparative Family Studies, 25,* 53–69.

CHOW, E.N. (1989). The feminist movement: Where are all the Asian American women? In Asian Women United of California (Eds.), *Making waves: An anthology of writings by and about Asian American women* (pp. 362–377). Boston, MA: Beacon.

COLE, E., ESPIN, E., & ROTHBLOM, E. (1992). *Refugee women and their mental health.* Binghamton, NY: Harrington Park Press.

DASGUPTA, S.D. (1999). Guest editor's introduction. *Violence against Women, 5*(6), 587–590.

DASGUPTA, S.D., & WARRIER, S. (1996). In the footsteps of Arundhati: Asian Indian women's experiences of domestic violence in the United States. *Violence against Women, 2,* 238–259.

DUNG, T.N. (1984). Understanding Asian families: A Vietnamese perspective. *Children Today, 13,* 10–12.

DUNWOODY, E. (1982). Battering in Indochinese refugee families. *Response to Victimization of Women and Children, 5*(5), 1–12.

ENG, P. (1995). Domestic violence in Asian/Pacific Island communities. In D. L. Adams (Ed.), *Health issues for women of color: A cultural diversity perspective* (pp. 78–88). Thousand Oaks, CA: Sage.

FONTES, L.A. (1995). *Sexual abuse in nine North American cultures: Treatment and prevention.* Thousand Oaks, CA: Sage.

HERAS, P. (1985). Cultural considerations in the assessment and treatment of child sexual abuse. *Journal of Child Sexual Abuse, 1*(3), 119–124.

HICKS, G. (1993, February 18). Ghosts gathering: Comfort women issue haunts Tokyo as pressure mounts. *Far Eastern Economic Review, 156*(7), pp. 32–37.

HO, C.K. (1990). An analysis of domestic violence in Asian American communities: A multicultural approach to counseling. In L.S. Brown & M.P.P. Root (Eds.), *Diversity and complexity in feminist therapy* (pp. 129–150). New York: Haworth Press.

HO, M. (1987). *Family therapy with ethnic minorities.* Newbury Park, CA: Sage.

HUANG, L.N. (1989). Southeast Asian refugee children and adolescents. In J.T. Gibbs, L.N. Huang, & Associates (Eds.), *Children of color* (pp. 30–66). San Francisco, CA: Jossey-Bass.

HUISMAN, K.A. (1996). Wife battering in Asian American communities. *Violence against Women, 2*(3), 260–283.

IMA, K., & HOHM, C.F. (1991). Child maltreatment among Asian and Pacific Islander refugees and immigrants. *Journal of Interpersonal Violence, 6*(3), 267–285.

ISHISAKA, H. & TAKAGI, C. (1982). Social work with Asian and Pacific Americans. In J. Green (Ed.), *Cultural awareness in human services* (pp. 121–156). Englewood Cliffs, NJ: Prentice Hall.

JANG, D., LEE, D., & MORELLO-FROSCH, R. (1990). Domestic violence in the immigrant and refugee community: Responding to the needs of immigrant women. *Response to Victimization of Women and Children, 13*(4), 2–7.

KANUHA, V. (1994). Women of color in battering relationships. In L. Comas-Diaz & B. Greene (Eds.), *Women of color: Integrating ethnic and gender identities in psychotherapy* (pp. 428–454). New York: Guilford Press.

KIM, S.C. (1985). Family therapy for Asian Americans: A strategic-structural framework. *Psychotherapy, 22,* 342–348.

KORBIN, J.E. (1991). Cross-cultural perspectives and research directions for the 21st century. *Child Abuse & Neglect, 15*(Suppl. 1), 67–77.

LAI, T.A. (1986). Asian women: Resisting the violence. In M.C. Burns (Ed.), *The speaking profits us: Violence in the lives of women of color* (pp. 8–11). Seattle, WA: Center for the Prevention of Sexual and Domestic Violence.

LKEDA-VOGEL, L., LEE, T., & LEE, J. (1993, October). Domestic violence. *Korean American Journal,* 9–11.

MEHROTRA, M. (1999). The social construction of wife abuse. *Violence against Women, 5*(6), 619–640.

MUSLIMS AGAINST FAMILY VIOLENCE. (1999). Available at: http://www.mpac.org/mafv/.

NAGATA, D.K. (1989). Japanese American children and adolescents. In J.T. Gibbs, L.N. Huang, & Associates (Eds.), *Children of color* (pp. 87–113). San Francisco, CA: Jossey-Bass.

NARESH, H., & SURENDRAN, A. (1996). Silence: Domestic violence. Available at: www.columbia.edu/cu/zamana/sangam/fall96/Silence.html.

NGUYEN, N.A., & WILLIAMS, H. (1989). Transition from east to west: Vietnamese adolescents and their parents. *American Academy of Child and Adolescent Psychiatry, 28*(4), 505–515.

OATS, G.C. (1998). Cultural perspectives on intimate violence. In N.A. Jackson & G.C. Oats (Eds.), *Violence in intimate relationships: Examining sociological and psychological issues* (pp. 225–243). Woburn, MA: Butterworth-Heinemann.

OKAMURA, A. (1992). *Ethnicity and physical disability.* Paper presented at the San Diego Conference on Responding to Child Maltreatment, San Diego, California.

OKAMURA, A., HERAS, P., & WONG-KERBERG. L. (1995). Asian, Pacific Island, and Filipino Americans and sexual child abuse. In L.A. Fontes (Ed.), *Sexual abuse in nine North American cultures: Treatment and prevention* (pp. 67–96). Thousands Oaks, CA: Sage.

PERRY, B. (2000). Perpetual outsiders: Criminal justice and the Asian American Experience. In the Criminal Justice Collective of Northern Arizona University (Ed.), *Investigating difference: Human and cultural relations in criminal justice* (pp. 99–110). Boston, MA: Allyn and Bacon.

PREISSER, A.B. (1999). Domestic violence in South Asian communities in America: Advocacy and Intervention. *Violence against Women, 5*(6), 684–699.

QUINA, K., & CARLSON, N.L. (1989). *Rape, incest, and sexual harassment.* Westport, CT: Praeger.

RAO, K., DI CLEMENTE, R.J., & PONTON, L.D. (1992). Child sexual abuse of Asians compared with other population. *Journal of the American Academy of Child and Adolescent Psychiatry, 31,* 880–886.

RASCHE, C.E. (1988). Minority women and domestic violence: The unique dilemmas of battered women of color. *Journal of Contemporary Criminal Justice, 4,* 150–171.

RICHIE, B.E., & KANUHA, V. (1993). Battered women of color in public health care systems: Racism, sexism, and violence. In B. Blair & S. E. Cayleff (Eds.), *Wings of gauze: Women of color and the experience of health and illness* (pp. 288–299). Detroit, MI: Wayne State University Press.

RIMONTE, N. (1989). Domestic violence among Pacific Asians. In Asian Women United of California (Ed.), *Making waves: An anthology of writings by and about Asian American women* (pp. 327–473). Boston, MA: Beacon.

RODRIGUEZ, O., & O'DONNELL, M. (1995). *Help-seeking and use of mental health services by the Hispanic elderly.* Westport, CT: Greenwood.

SINGH, R.N., & UNNITHAN, N.P. (1999). Wife burning. *Violence against Women, 5*(6), 641–653.

SLUZKI, C. (1979). Migration and family conflict. *Family Process, 18*(4), 379–390.

SORENSON, S.B., UPCHURCH, D.M., & SHEN, H. (1996). Violence and injury in marital arguments: Risk patterns and gender differences. *American Journal of Public Health, 86,* 35–40.

SUE, D., & SUE, D. (1982). *Counseling the culturally diverse: Theory and practice.* New York: John Wiley.

SUE, S., & MORISHIMA, J.K. (1982). *The mental health of Asian Americans.* San Franscisco, CA: Jossey-Bass.

TRAN, T.V. (1988). The Vietnamese American family. In C.H. Mindel, R.W. Habenstein, & R. Wright (Eds.), *Ethnic families in America* (pp. 276–299). New York: Elsevier.

UNION OF PAN ASIAN COMMUNITIES. (1982). *Pan Asian child rearing practices: Filipino. Japanese, Korean, Samoan, Vietnamese.* San Diego, CA: Pan Asian Parent Education Project, Union of Pan Asian Communities.

WILLIAMS, O.J. (1994). Domestic partner abuse treatment programs and cultural competence: The results of a national survey. *Violence and Victims, 9*(3), 287–296.

WONG, D. (1987). Parenting child sexual abuse among Southeast Asian refugee families. *Children Today, 16*(6), 18–22.

WONG-KERBERG, L. (1993, May). *Children's memories: Current knowledge, implications for effective intervention—cultural perspectives.* Paper presented at the California Consortium for the Prevention of Child Abuse, Giarretto Institute, Berkeley, CA.

YIM, S.B. (1978). Korean battered wives: A sociological and psychological analysis of conjugal violence in Korean immigrant families. In H.H. Sunoo & D.S. Kim (Eds.), *Korean women in a struggle for humanization* (pp. 171–199). Memphis, TN: Association of Korean Christian Scholars in North America.

YOSHIHAMA, M. (1999). Domestic violence against women of Japanese descent in Los Angeles: Two methods of estimating prevalence. *Violence against Women, 5*(8), 869–897.

2

Sexual Aggression against Female College Students

Janice Joseph

There was a time when college was seen as a sanctuary, a place where teaching, learning, and social exchange took place in an environment that posed minimal danger to the physical safety and security of students. Today, colleges are no longer the ivory towers of the past. They are plagued by all kinds of crimes and violence. The purpose of this chapter is to present data on the nature and extent of sexual aggression against women on a small college campus. Also discussed is the legal response to sexual aggression on college campuses, with recommendations as to how colleges can deal effectively with sexual aggression.

REVIEW OF THE LITERATURE

Many studies have documented the prevalence of rape and lesser forms of sexual aggression in the college population, most in the last decade. In a national study, Koss, Gidycz, and Wisniewski (1987) surveyed 6,159 men and women enrolled in 32 universities about their experiences with rape, attempted rape, and sexual coercion. Their results showed that 27.5% of college women reported an experience during their college years that met a legal definition of rape and that 7.7% of college men reported perpetrating an act that met the legal definition of rape.

Muehlenhard and Linton (1987) conducted a study of 635 college men and women to explore sexual aggression in dating situations. Their findings showed that 77.6% of the women had experienced some form of sexual aggression and 14% had engaged in unwanted sexual intercourse. For the men, 57.3% reported involvement in some form of sexual aggression, and 7.1% reported engaging in unwanted intercourse. Meilman, Riggs, and Turco (1990) also reported findings from a randomly selected sample of campus males and females about unwanted sexual experiences. Of the females, 33.2% reported being victims of unwanted attempted intercourse, and 11.5% reported unwanted completed intercourse during their college years.

Alcohol and Sexual Aggression

Several investigators have explored the relationship between alcohol consumption and sexual aggression on college campuses. Results from several empirical studies have documented strong associations between alcohol consumption and sexual aggression on campus (Crowe & George, 1989; Commission on Substance Abuse at Colleges and Universities, 1994; Abbey, Ross, McDuffie, & McAuslan, 1996; Meilman, 1993). Miller and Marshall (1987) found that 60% of the women who engaged in unwanted sexual intercourse reported that they had been using alcohol or other drugs when coerced. Koss and Dinero (1989) reported that alcohol use was one of the four primary predictors associated with a college woman's chances of being raped. They reported that, of those men and women reporting attempted unwanted sexual experiences, slightly over half said that alcohol was involved. Nicholson and associates (1998) in their study on alcohol and unwanted sexual activity on college campuses found that alcohol continues to be a factor in sexual violence on college campuses.

REPORTING SEXUAL AGGRESSION

Victims of sexual aggression rarely report their experiences to campus or local law enforcement authorities (Koss & Oras, 1982; Koss et al., 1987; Miller & Marshall, 1987). In many cases, these crimes are not recognized as such by victims, even when their descriptions of the assault met the definition of rape (Koss et al., 1987; Muehlenhard & Linton, 1987). One explanation for the underreporting of sexual aggression could be that, when women have been assaulted while under the influence of alcohol, they tend to feel more responsible for the attack than do women who were sober (Kanin, 1985). Other explanations involve the victims' feelings of guilt, shame, and helplessness, particularly when the women knew their assailant (Miller & Marshall, 1987). When the assailant is a friend or date, not only has the woman's body been violated but also her trust in others has been betrayed and her faith in her own judgment has been shaken. Women may not report the assault because they may feel that nothing can be done.

THE STUDY

Methodology

The data were collected in 1998 from a small Northeastern college. Sexual aggression on college campuses is a sensitive topic that students are often reluctant to discuss. To get a significant number of students to participate in the survey and to generate a good response rate, the questionnaire was administered in the classroom. Nineteen classes from various disciplines, including criminal justice, business, sociology, and social work, were selected nonrandomly to participate in the survey. Once the purpose and the goals of the study were explained to the students, they signed an informed consent form before completing the questionnaire.

They were told that participation in the survey was completely voluntary and anonymous and that all the information they provided would be kept strictly confidential. Additionally, students were told that they did not have to answer any question that they did not want to and that they could stop filling out the questionnaire at any time. The respondents were also informed that the content of the questionnaire might be psychologically disturbing, and they were given a list of telephone numbers of on-campus services to contact, should they become upset during or after the survey.

Measuring Instrument

A 65-item instrument was administered about the nature and extent of sexual aggression on the campus. The questionnaire was developed after considerable study of similar instruments used in other research. A pretest of a draft was administered to a group of students, and additional changes were made on the basis of the pretest results. The respondents were asked about their perceptions of sexual aggression, their experiences with sexual aggression as victims and perpetrators, the involvement of alcohol in sexually aggressive incidents, the reporting of sexual assault to authorities, and demographic information.

Measures

Sexual aggression was defined as unwanted sexual activities and included kissing, hugging, petting, attempted rape, rape, and other forms of unwanted touching in an intimate way. *Unwanted* was defined as those situations in which the person did not want to engage in the sexual experience and communicated this is some way (said "no," said she did not want to do it, or struggled), felt intimidated, or was forced to engage in the behavior. These definitions are consistent with the legal definitions of sexual contact and rape and center on the lack of consent. Sexual aggression was measured on a 9-point scale, ranging from kissing against a person's will to unwanted sexual intercourse.

A *victim* was defined as any recipient of the act of aggression, whether male or female, and a *perpetrator* was a person, male or female, who engaged in sexually aggressive acts against others. The study focused on the sexual experiences of the respondents since the time they began study at the college and incidents that occurred on the college campus.

Sample

The nonrandom sample was 502 students at a small Northeastern college. Of these, 52% were male and 48% were female. Twenty-nine percent were between the ages of 19 and 21, 58% were between 22 and 24, and 13% were 25 and older. Forty-six percent were in the social sciences, 36% in natural sciences, 15% in professional studies, and 2% in fine arts. Ninety-one percent were full-time and 9% part-time. Eighty-seven percent were white, 10% African American, and 3% Hispanic. Sixty-one percent were juniors, 24% were

TABLE 2.1 Demographic Characteristics by Gender

	Males (%)	Females (%)	Chi-Square (χ^2)	Degrees of Freedom
Age				
19–21 years	49	31		
22–24 years	41	53		
25 years and older	10	16	8.0*	2
Ethnic/Racial Background				
Whites	92	80		
Blacks	5	17		
Hispanics	3	3	8.6*	2
College Status				
Freshman	22	5		
Sophomore	24	24		
Junior	52	71		
Senior	2	0	16.5**	3
Respondent's Major				
Social science	50	45		
Natural science	29	42		
Professional studies	19	11		
Other	2	2	n.s.	3

  *Significant at .05.
**Significant at .01.

sophomores, 13% were freshmen, and 2% were seniors. The gender differences in Table 2.1 show that there were significant differences between the males and females with regard to age, race and ethnicity, and college status.

DATA ANALYSIS AND FINDINGS

Perceptions of Sexual Aggression

The survey examined 16 perceptions about sexual aggression, especially about rape. The responses were measured on a 4-point scale: (1) "agree," (2) "strongly agree," (3) "disagree," and (4) "strongly disagree." Table 2.2 indicates that the perceptions of the males regarding sexual aggression are different from those of the females. Significantly more males than females agreed with all the statements. The greatest significant differences between the males and females were for the statements "It is not rape if the woman behaves

TABLE 2.2 Responses to the Following Statements and Gender Percentages Agreeing with Statement

	A Males (%)	B Females (%)	Males		Females		G F Value
			C Mean	D S.D	E Mean	F S.D	
It is okay to kiss a person against his or her will while on a date.	32	3	1.7	.47	2.0	.15	21.3***
It is okay to touch a person's thighs without permission while on a date.	30	3	1.7	.46	2.0	.19	18.0***
A woman who experiences sexual aggression deserves it if she decides to go to a man's house late at night.	29	3	1.7	.45	1.9	.18	16.2**
Rape is committed by strangers.	32	3	1.7	.47	2.0	.18	19.6***
Women who did not fight back haven't been raped.	50	9	1.5	.50	1.9	.29	30.9***
It is rape, only if she is a virgin.	31	3	1.7	.46	2.0	.18	18.0***
Good girls don't get raped.	31	6	1.8	.47	1.9	.23	15.1**
It is not rape if the woman behaves seductively.	51	7	1.4	.50	1.9	.25	39.5***
Most date "rapes" that are reported are reported because the woman wants to get back at the man.	57	10	1.4	.50	1.9	.31	39.4***
A woman who goes to a man's apartment on the first date implies that she is willing to have sex.	33	4	1.6	.47	1.9	.20	20.3***
In most cases, when a woman was raped, she was asking for it.	34	3	1.7	.47	2.0	.16	23.7***
When a woman says "no," she really means "yes."	34	4	1.7	.47	2.0	.15	23.9***
A woman should be responsible for preventing sexual aggression against her.	45	8	1.5	.50	1.9	.26	29.1***
The degree of the woman's resistance should be the major factor in determining rape.	52	13	1.5	.50	1.9	.34	25.9***
There is no such thing as date rape.	42	12	1.5	.49	1.9	.32	15.8**

*Significant at .05.
**Significant at .01.
***Significant at .001.

seductively and suggestively" (F = 39.5; $p < .001$) and "Most date 'rapes' that are reported are reported because the woman wants to get back at the man" (F = .39.4; $p < .001$). The least difference between the males and females was in their responses to the statements "Good girls don't get raped" (F = 15.1; $p < .01$) and "There is no such thing as date rape" (F = 15.8; $p < .01$). It is clear that males and females view sexually aggressive behaviors differently.

Nature of the Sexual Aggression

Victims of Sexual Aggression.   The data indicated that significantly more females (43%) than males (4%) reported experiencing sexual aggression ($X^2 = 50.9$; $p < .001$). Table 2.3 also shows that significantly more females than males experienced all forms of sexual aggression listed in the survey.

Rape Incidents.   The respondents were also asked if they had ever been a victim of the most serious form of sexual aggression—rape. Table 2.3 shows that significantly ($X^2 = 34.3$; $p < .001$) more females (21%) than males (7%) reported being the victim of rape. The data also indicate that the rape victims were likely to be white, 19–21 years old, juniors in college, and majoring in social science. In 94% of the rape cases, the victims were acquainted with the perpetrator. In 74% of the cases, there was consensual intimacy before the sexual attack. In 95% of the cases, there was one perpetrator, in 3% of the cases there were two perpetrators, and in 2% of the cases three. All victims stated that they made it clear to the offender that they did not want to have sexual intercourse.

Sixty-seven percent of the rape victims reported that they were threatened, and 48% said that actual force was used. Of those victims on whom force was used, 18% reported that they were hurt and required medical attention. Eighty-one percent stated that the rape experience had affected them psychologically. Many of the victims were afraid to walk alone, and they became very distrustful of others.

Male Perpetrators of Sexual Aggression.   Table 2.3 also shows significant differences between the males and females with regard to their perpetrating sexual aggression against another. Males were significantly more likely than females to be the perpetrators of sexual aggression (28% vs. 3%). Eighty-two percent of the perpetrators stated that they knew the victim, 60% said that they were interacting socially, and only 8% believed that what they did was sexual violence.

Characteristics of the Sexually Aggressive Incidents

Ninety percent of all sexually aggressive incidents occurred on dates, and 82% of the victims and perpetrators were acquaintances. Sixty-two percent of these rapes took place in the perpetrator's on-campus residence, 28% in the victim's on-campus residence, and 10% in places such places as a classroom or a car.

This study explored the relationship between alcohol and sexual aggression by asking the victims if they or the perpetrators were intoxicated at the time of the incident. The results indicated that 61% of the victims reported that they had used alcohol prior to the sexually aggressive incident and that 76% of the perpetrators had used alcohol prior to

TABLE 2.3   Sexually Aggressive Behaviors and Gender

	Males (%)	Females (%)	Chi-Square (χ^2) (df = 1)
Victims of unwanted sexual aggression	7	21	34.2***
Kiss against your will	35	49	3.7*
Touched breast/chest against your will	28	53	19.4**
Touched thigh against your will	9	47	40.1***
Removed outer garment against your will	5	42	43.2***
Removed underwear against your will	3	35	33.9***
Touched genitals against your will	2	34	38.1***
Victim of rape	7	21	34.0***
Perpetrator of sexual aggression	28	3	25.6***

*Significant at .05.
**Significant at .01.
***Significant at .001.

the attacks. However, only 14% of the victims and 36% of the perpetrators reported that they were intoxicated at the time of the sexually aggressive acts.

Reporting Sexual Aggression.   Only 26% of the victims reported the sexual aggression against them to the college campus police, local agencies, or another person. Of those who reported their experiences, 73% reported it to a friend or relative, 13% to the police, and 14% to another person. Fifty-eight percent of those who did not report it stated that they felt that it was their fault, 13% did not report the act because of fear of revenge, and 25% said that no one would believe them.

Discussion

The overall number of female respondents who reported experiencing some sort of sexual aggression (43%) was higher than the number of males reporting involvement in sexual aggression against women (28%). There are several possible explanations for this discrepancy. The sample is not one of couples, so it is possible that more female victims than male perpetrators were sampled, or that some men are frequent offenders. A second, and probably more likely explanation for the male–female discrepancy is that men and women do have different perceptions of sexual aggression and sex role expectations. Indeed, the data in Table 2.2 show that men and women have different perceptions of sexually aggressive behaviors.

Although women are fearful of walking alone on campus at night, it is not in these settings that the sexual aggression took place. The data clearly indicate that sexual aggression is part of the normal social environment of college life. The strategies of limiting one's activities at night or changing one's lifestyle would, therefore, be useless to college female students for protecting themselves against male sexual aggression.

Limitations of the Study

First, the results of this study are based on a sample from a small college, and so the results may not be applicable to all colleges. The results should, therefore, be taken cautiously. However, the results can give some insights into the problems of sexual aggression on college campuses and can form the groundwork for further research.

Second, the sample is primarily of white students with very few minority students. Thus, the experiences of minority students could not be analyzed because of the lack of racial and ethnic diversity among the respondents did not allow a complex analysis of sexual aggression among racial or ethnic groups. However, the small number of minority students in the sample reflected the small number of minority students enrolled in this institution.

LEGAL RESPONSE TO VIOLENCE ON CAMPUS

Federal Response

In 1990, the first legislation regarding sexual assault and violence against women on college campuses was passed in the Student-Right-to-Know and Campus Security Act. The act requires colleges and universities to report, investigate, and prevent sex offenses that occur on campuses. It also requires institutions to provide information on policies related to the reporting of other criminal actions, campus security, and law enforcement. Additionally, the law mandates that colleges and universities disclose the results of campus disciplinary proceedings to victims of violent crimes (Student-Right-to-Know and Campus Security Act, 1990).

The Campus Security Act was intended to encourage colleges and universities to put more emphasis on campus safety and on crime prevention. There are, however, some problems with how this act is interpreted and followed. One problem is the inconsistency in the way colleges and universities report their violent crime statistics. For example, a university may report predictions of crimes instead of actual crimes (Hunnicutt, 1998). There is confusion in reporting statistics on "forcible" and "nonforcible" sex offenses. Some institutions continue to report only rape (Lewis & Farris, 1997). Many institutions withhold or underreport crime statistics to promote the image of a safe, secure campus environment (Hunnicutt & Kushibab, 1998). Furthermore, the crime-reporting obligations of student services could jeopardize the confidentiality between counselors and students (Lederman, 1994).

Another federal law regarding violence on Campus is the 1991 campus Sexual Assault Victim's Bill of Rights. This bill, commonly known as the Ramstad Amendment and signed into law in 1992, amended the Higher Education Act of 1992. This law requires colleges and universities to adopt policies and procedures to prevent and deal with sexual offenses once they have occurred. The Ramstad Amendment requires institutions of higher learning to develop and distribute a campus sexual assault policy that describes (1) educational programs to promote awareness of rape, acquaintance rape, and other sex offenses;

(2) institutional sanctions for sex offenses, both forcible and nonforcible; and (3) procedures informing victims of the name of the person who should be contacted after an assault and the importance of retaining evidence. The law requires institutions to notify the victim of the option of reporting sexual assault to law enforcement officers. Finally, campus authorities must notify victims about available counseling services and offer options of changing academic schedules and living arrangements necessitated by the sexual assault (Smith & Fossey, 1995).

State Response

The states have responded to violence on college campuses by enacting laws dealing with hate crimes, sexual assault and rape, and hazing, as well as stricter penalties for alcohol and drug violations. These laws have resulted in an increased number of cases in criminal and civil courts (Hunnicutt & Kushibab, 1998).

Although a college or university may seem to be an insular environment, its employees and students are subject to state criminal laws. States have laws prohibiting various forms of sexual aggression against women (sexual contact, sexual assault, and rape), and these laws can be enforced against perpetrators who violate the law on college campuses.

Traditionally, states acknowledged sovereign immunity for public colleges and universities, whereby a state college or university could not be held liable for most forms of wrongful conduct. However, most states have abolished the doctrine of the sovereign immunity, and so a state-operated institution can be held accountable under tort theory. Consequently, the number of lawsuits against colleges and universities on the basis of negligence and other wrongful conduct by the institution has increased. These lawsuits often allege that the institutions failed to maintain adequate security and exercise reasonable care to protect students from foreseeable harm (Hunnicutt & Kushibab, 1998).

IMPLICATIONS

Policy Implications

Some colleges and universities have revised their policies and student codes to reflect the new requirements of federal or state laws. The University of North Carolina at Chapel Hill, the University of Washington, Princeton University, the University of Michigan at Ann Arbor, and Arizona State University have reviewed and revised their policies to meet the requirements mandated by federal and state laws in response to violence on campus (Hunnicutt & Kushibab, 1998). These universities have taken positive steps to deal with violence on campus, but many colleges and universities are not doing enough to deal with the problem of sexual aggression on their campuses.

The results of the present study clearly show that there is a problem on college campuses with regard to sexual aggression. The results show also that alcohol is an important factor in these sexually aggressive behaviors. Recognition that the problem exists is the first step colleges can take toward resolving sexual aggression. Efforts to reduce sexual aggression should include the total college environment, with a strong emphasis on violence prevention and safety for both men and women.

Recommendations

All colleges and universities, including those with no history of sexual aggression, should:

1. Enact a policy addressing sexual aggression. Colleges should adopt a policy that condemns and prohibits sexual aggression. Such a policy should also explain the process by which victims may file complaints. Sexual aggression policies have little or no effect unless they are widely publicized. They should be brought to the attention of the college community regularly—at orientation, in student handbooks, on campus bulletin boards, during general meetings, and in brochures, videos, and posters.

2. Establish formal procedures for handling sexual aggression. Every college and university should have clear procedures for handling complaints of sexual aggression of any kind. Because of their nature, sexually aggressive incidents should receive high priority. Top-level administrators should monitor the handling of these cases and give special attention to developing strategies for averting additional episodes of sexual violence.

3. Encourage the reporting of these incidents. Unless incidents of sexual aggression are reported, college officials can do little about them. Because victims fear revictimization and being accused of lying, they seldom report these incidents. Establishing a telephone hot line (with emphasis placed on confidentiality) can help victims take the first step.

4. Discipline perpetrators of sexually aggressive incidents. Treating sexually aggressive incidents as childish pranks trivializes the incidents and the profound effect they have on both the victim and the larger community. Individuals found to have engaged in such incidents should be disciplined appropriately. Moreover, the outcome of such incidents should be published.

5. Provide assistance for victims. To minimize the potential trauma of sexual violence incidents, support services should be made available to victims. These should include advocacy, counseling, and peer support. Training should be provided to resident advisors, campus security, student life personnel, and other staff to help them to respond sensitively to the needs of victims.

6. Provide information on alcohol use and abuse. For example, a mandatory course can be created on the issue of alcohol. Colleges also need to restrict the use of alcohol on the college campus and be more aggressive in the enforcement of alcohol policies and laws.

7. Educate students about appropriate and inappropriate behavior, including information on what legally constitutes sexual aggression, sexual assault, and rape; the importance of a woman's consent; and avoiding risky situations. One format for such information is a required course for freshmen.

8. Collect data on sexually aggressive incidents. A system should be established on every campus to identify, classify, and compile information on sexually aggressive incidents. Data on such incidents can be evaluated during regular assessment of the campus environment and the possible need for intervention.

By sharing the data with the campus community, the administration can show its ongoing commitment to dealing with the problem. Victims will feel encouraged to report incidents, even when their perpetrators cannot be identified

9. Establish a task force to deal with sexual aggression. The level of awareness can be increased by creating a task force to counter sexual violence on the campus. Such a task force should be composed of students, staff, faculty, and administrators. This task force can monitor and guide the university's response to sexually aggressive incidents, provide advocacy for victims, develop publicity materials to encourage reporting, and sponsor educational programs aimed at reducing sexual aggression. To be effective, the task force must be given adequate financial support.

10. Educate the college campus about sexual aggression. Educating the community about sexual aggression should be a high priority for colleges and universities. From orientation on, students should receive clear and repeated messages that discourage sexual aggression. To this end, the university should sponsor speakers, workshops, and seminars.

These strategies provide a guideline as to what can be undertaken for an integrated approach to sexual aggression on college campuses.

Implications for Future Research

Beyond documenting sexual aggression against women in college, what is needed is a thorough examination of male aggression in general against college females. Such an examination would place sexual aggression within institutional and interactional contexts. It would also address the continuum of sexually aggressive behaviors against women on college campuses. As the nature of the relationship between men and women changes, so, too, would the contexts and situations in which men display aggressive behavior toward women. These social situations need to be studied.

There is also a need for comparative studies to identify different patterns of sexual aggression on college campuses. The social atmosphere and environment may vary significantly between colleges, a factor that may have substantial impacts on the rate of sexual aggression and the reporting of such aggression. Researchers should try to identify these various patterns through comparative studies.

In the existing social literature, the institution's tolerance of men's violence is often neglected. The collegiate response to male violence needs to be explored. It appears that some institutions minimize male violence against women if the perpetrators are athletes. The extent to which these practices increases sexual violence against women needs to be addressed in future research.

Finally, there is a need to evaluate prevention and intervention programs designed to deal with sexual aggression and violence on college campuses. Very often programs are instituted to prevent unacceptable behaviors, but these programs are not evaluated to determine their effectiveness. Social scientists need to investigate the extent to which preventive programs are effective in curtailing sexual aggression on college campuses.

SUMMARY

The data from this study indicate that sexual aggression against women occurred on this college campus and that men and women have different perceptions of sexual aggression. The data also show that incidents occurred in situations where the woman had agreed to interact socially with the man.

It is much easier to describe the problem than to identify solutions for dealing with sexual aggression. However, those who provide leadership on college campuses have to realize that sexual aggression and violence can and do occur on college campuses in this country. Clearly, the college campus is not a tranquil sanctuary for students, faculty, and staff. No college campus is immune from any kind of violence, and so colleges and universities need to take the necessary precautions to prevent and control all forms of violence. Colleges and universities have a legal obligation to protect students, faculty, and staff and to provide a safe environment for them.

DISCUSSION QUESTIONS

1. Discuss two reasons why victims of sexual aggression on college campuses rarely report their victimization.

2. Discuss the relationship between alcohol and sexual aggression on college campuses.

3. Describe the Student-Right-to-Know and Campus Security Act.

4. Describe the Sexual Assault Victim's Bill of Rights.

5. What is sovereign immunity?

REFERENCES

ABBEY, A., ROSS, L.T., McDUFFIE, D., & McAUSLAN, P. (1996). Alcohol and dating risk factors for sexual assault among college women. *Psychology of Women Quarterly, 20,* 147–169.

COMMISSION ON SUBSTANCE ABUSE AT COLLEGES AND UNIVERSITIES. (1994). *Rethinking rites of passage: Substance abuse on America's campuses.* New York: Columbia University, Center on Addiction and Substance Abuse.

CROWE, L.C., & GEORGE, W.H. (1989). Alcohol and human sexuality: Review and integration. *Psychological Bulletin, 105,* 374–386.

HUNNICUTT, K.H. (1998). Women and violence on campus. In A.M. Hoffman, J.H. Schuh, & R.H. Fenske (Eds.), *Violence on campus: Defining the problems, strategies for action* (pp. 149–167). Gaitherburg, MD: Aspen.

HUNNICUTT, K.H., & KUSHIBAB, P. (1998). The legal response to violence on campus. In A.M. Hoffman, J.H. Schuh, & R.H. Fenske (Eds.), *Violence on campus: Defining the problems, strategies for action* (pp. 273–299). Gaitherburg, MD: Aspen.

JOHNSTON, L.D., O'MALLEY, P.M., & BACHMAN, J.G. (1992). *Smoking, drinking, and illicit drug use among American secondary school students, college students, and young adults, 1975–1991. Volume II: College Students and Young Adults.* Rockville, MD: U.S. Department of Health and Human Services, National Institute on Drug Abuse.

KANIN, E.J. (1985). Date rapists. *Archives of Sexual Behavior, 14,* 219–231.

KOSS, M.P., & DINERO, T.E. (1989). Discriminant analysis of risk factors for sexual victimization among a national sample of college women. *Journal of Consulting and Clinical Psychology, 57,* 242–250.

KOSS, M.P., GIDYCZ, C.A., & WISNIEWSKI, N. (1987). The scope of rape: Incidence and prevalence of sexual aggression and victimization in a national sample of higher education students. *Journal of Consulting and Clinical Psychology, 55*(22), 162–170.

KOSS, M.P., & ORAS, C.J. (1982). Sexual experience survey: A research instrument investigating sexual aggression and victimization. *Journal of Consulting and Clinical Psychology, 50,* 455–457.

LEDERMAN, D. (1994). College must list crimes reported to counselors, U.S. says. *Chronicle of Higher Education, 40*(35), A32.

LEWIS, L., & FARRIS, E. (1997). *Campus crime and security at postsecondary education institutions,* NCES 97–402. Washington, DC: Department of Education, National Center for Education Statistics.

MEILMAN, P.W. (1993). Alcohol-induced sexual behavior on campus. *American Journal of College Health, 42,* 27–31.

MEILMAN, P.W., RIGGS, P., & TURCO, J.H. (1990). A college health service's response to sexual assault issues. *American Journal of College Health, 39,* 145–147.

MILLER, B., & MARSHALL, J.C. (1987). Coercive sex on the university campus. *Journal of College Student Personnel, 28,* 38–47.

MUEHLENHARD, C.L., & LINTON, M. (1987). Date rape and sexual aggression in dating situations: Incidence and risk factors. *Journal of Counseling Psychology, 34,* 186–196.

NICHOLSON, M., WANG, M.Q., MANEY, D., YUAN, J., MOHNEY, B.S., & ADAME, D.D. (1998). Alcohol related violence and unwanted sexual activity on the college campus. *American Journal of Health Studies, 14*(1), 1–10.

SMITH, M.C., & FOSSEY, R.W. (1995). *Crime on campus: Legal issues and campus administration.* Phoenix, AZ: American Council on Education.

STUDENT-RIGHT-TO-KNOW AND CAMPUS SECURITY ACT OF 1990, 20 U.S.C §1001, 1990 Amendments. Public Law 101–542, Title 1, §101.

3

The Response of the United States Supreme Court to Sexual Harassment

Martin L. O'Connor

Sexual harassment is a significant problem in our society, and our court system is struggling with a vast array of legal issues pertaining to harassment. Although legal claims for workplace sexual harassment have their genesis in statutes created by Congress and the guidelines of the Equal Employment Opportunity Commission, the law of sexual harassment has, for the most part, been created by the courts. The term *sexual harassment* was not even coined until 1975 (Belknap & Erez, 1997, p. 143), and some 11 years later the U.S. Supreme Court decided its first sexual harassment case. In 1998 and 1999, the Supreme Court accepted and decided five major cases dealing with sexual harassment. The following pages attempt to sketch the response of the U.S. Supreme Court to sexual harassment.

In 1986, the U.S. Supreme Court decided its first case dealing with sexual harassment. One might ask, What took so long? Although the discriminatory behavior that we now know as sexual harassment has existed for centuries, this behavior did not become an actionable legal claim until recent years. Sexual harassment legal claims have their genesis in the Civil Rights Act of 1964. In this law, Title VII provides that it is an unlawful employment practice for an employer:

(1) to fail or refuse to hire or discharge an individual, or otherwise to discriminate against any individual with respect to his compensation, terms, conditions, or privileges of employment, because of such individual's race, color, religion, sex, or national origin; or

(2) to limit, segregate, or classify his employees or applicants for employment in any way which would deprive or tend to deprive any individual of employment opportunities or otherwise adversely affect his status as an employee, because of such individual's race, color, religion, sex or national origin. (42 U.S.C. section 2000e–2(a) (1988))

The Civil Rights Law of 1964 was not designed to address sex discrimination, and the word *sex* was added to the legislation at the last minute on the floor of the House of Representatives by opponents of the measure in an attempt to prevent its passage (110 Cong. Rec. 2577–84, 1964). Hence, there is little legislative history to guide the courts or the Equal Employment Opportunity Commission (EEOC), which was created as the primary enforcement agency for Title VII. Although Title VII prohibited discrimination based upon gender, the earliest cases that found their way into court alleging sexual harassment were unsuccessful, and the courts held there was no such claim as sexual harassment under Title VII (*Tomkins v. Public Service Electric & Gas Co.,* 1976; *Miller v. Bank of America,* 1976; *Corne v. Bausch and Lomb, Inc.,* 1975; *Barnes v. Train,* 1974). Following these cases, Catharine MacKinnon published a compelling article arguing that the courts should consider sexual harassment as a form of discrimination and an actionable legal claim (MacKinnon, 1979). In 1980, the EEOC issued guidelines defining sexual harassment and establishing parameters for unacceptable behavior in the workplace. The EEOC determined that harassment on the basis of sex is a violation of section 703 of Title VII and defined sexual harassment as:

Unwelcome sexual advances, requests for sexual favors, and other verbal or physical conduct of a sexual nature constitute sexual harassment when

(1) submission to such conduct is made either explicitly or implicitly a term or condition of an individual's employment,

(2) submission to or rejection of such conduct by an individual is used as the basis for employment decisions affecting such individual, or

(3) such conduct has the purpose or effect of unreasonably interfering with an individual's work performance or creating an intimidating, hostile, or offensive working environment. (EEOC Guidelines on Discrimination Because of Sex, 29 C.F.R.Sec. 1604.11 (a), 1981)

These guidelines recognize two forms of sexual harassment. First, in the quid pro quo form of sexual harassment, a supervisor may condition an employee's job status or rewards on an employee's submission to unwelcome sex-related behavior. Basically, quid pro quo involves an employer using his or her authority to extort sexual favors. Because supervisors usually have sufficient power to extort sexual favors and subordinates do not, only supervisors are capable of quid pro quo sexual harassment. Of course, employer liability may also exist when supervisors base employment decisions upon an employee's refusal to submit. The second type of sexual harassment recognized by these guidelines is the most frequent form of sexual harassment, the "hostile environment." In the typical hostile environment case, a victim suffers a number of sex-related inquiries, jokes, slurs, propositions, touching, or other forms of abuse. For this behavior to violate Title VII, it must be so severe or pervasive that it alters the conditions of the victim's employment and creates a hostile or abusive work environment. Supervisors and fellow employees can engage in hostile environment sexual harassment.

A number of studies have demonstrated that sexual harassment in the workplace is a serious problem in the United States. For example, 53% of working women report having encountered behavior they describe as sexual harassment (Gutek, 1985). In 1995, the results of a survey of 1.7 million civilian employees in the executive branch of the federal government revealed that in the last two years 44% of the women and 19% of the men experienced some unwanted sexual attention. In addition, 37% of the female respondents said that they had experienced unwanted sexual teasing, jokes, remarks, and questions (U.S. Merit System Production Board, 1995).

By the early 1980s, virtually all federal courts began to recognize sexual harassment as a bona fide legal claim. Eleven years after the term *sexual harassment* was coined and six years after the EEOC wrote its first guidelines on the subject, a bank teller named Mechelle Vinson was the first plaintiff to find her sexual harassment claim on the docket of the U.S. Supreme Court.

MERITOR SAVINGS BANK V. VINSON (1986)

In 1974, Mechelle Vinson was hired as a teller trainee at the Meritor Savings Bank in Washington, D.C. She was quickly promoted to teller, head teller, and by 1978 assistant branch manager. In September 1978, Mechelle notified her supervisor that she was taking sick leave for an indefinite period. Two months later, she was fired for using excessive sick leave. Shortly thereafter, Vinson filed a lawsuit against her former supervisor, Sidney Taylor, and the bank, alleging that she had been subjected to sexual harassment by Taylor in violation of Title VII. At trial, Vinson testified that during her probationary period, her supervisor, Taylor, treated her in a fatherly way and made no sexual advances. Shortly thereafter, he invited her to dinner, made sexual advances, and suggested that they go to a motel. At first, Vinson refused the advances, but because she feared losing her job, she eventually agreed to engage in sex with Taylor. She estimated that she was compelled to have sexual intercourse with Taylor 40 or 50 times while employed at the bank and that he raped her on a few occasions. In addition, she testified that Taylor fondled her during working hours, exposed himself to her, and even entered the women's restroom while she was there alone. Vinson testified that because she was afraid of Taylor she never filed a complaint pursuant to the bank's complaint procedures and that the actions of Taylor stopped when she started going steady with her boyfriend in 1977.

Taylor denied all of the allegations and the district court entered a judgment in favor of the supervisor and the bank, deciding that no sexual harassment occurred. The district court concluded that Vinson's promotions were obtained upon merit alone, that she had not been required to grant Taylor any sexual favors to obtain them, and that any sex she may have engaged in with her supervisor was voluntary. In holding that the bank was not liable, the court noted the bank's express policy against discrimination and stated that neither Mechelle Vinson nor any other employee had ever lodged a complaint about sexual harassment against Taylor and that the bank could not be held liable if it had no notice of a supervisor's actions. The U.S. Court of Appeals for the District of Columbia reversed, concluding that Mechelle Vinson had stated a claim for sexual harassment under Title VII based upon a "hostile environment" and that an employer is strictly liable for discriminatory acts by supervisors. The U.S. Supreme Court agreed to hear the case, and it affirmed the judgment of the Court of Appeals but differed significantly in its decision regarding the issue of employer liability. The Court, citing EEOC guidelines, ruled that Title VII covers sexual harassment discrimination and that it includes not only quid pro quo harassment but also a hostile environment. The *Meritor* Court held that Title VII provides an employee with the right "to work in an environment free from discriminatory intimidation, ridicule and insult."

Meritor is a very important case because for the first time the U.S. Supreme Court placed its imprimatur on Title VII sexual harassment claims that had developed in the lower courts and recognized that sexual harassment is a form of discrimination covered by Title VII. Although the Court was critical of the bank's grievance procedure because it was incomplete and did not address sexual harassment, it did hold that the Court of Appeals erred in concluding that employers are always automatically liable for sexual harassment by their supervisors. In hostile environment cases, the Court said that the harassment must be sufficiently "severe or pervasive to alter the conditions of the [victim's] employment." Unfortunately, the Court refused to issue a definitive ruling regarding employer liability and suggested that agency principles must be applied to determine employer liability. The *Meritor* Court left to lower courts the task of elucidating the elements of sexual harassment claims and forging a coherent analysis. Specifically, the Court failed to indicate whether sexual harassment should be measured or evaluated from the perspective of the "reasonable person," "reasonable woman," or "reasonable man." The Court's recourse to the arcane principles of agency law to determine employer liability is regrettable. Agency law has been criticized because many judges and lawyers do not have a grasp of agency law principles and agency law is "not a simple set of basic principles that find easy application in many contexts" (Phillips, 1991, p. 1271). Therefore, how can employers analyze agency law principles to protect themselves from liability in sexual harassment cases? Some can argue that the Court is not to blame for this situation because of the decision of Congress to define *employer* in Title VII to include "any agent of the employer." Whoever is at fault begs the question. Agency principles merely muddy the water of employer liability in sexual harassment cases and provide very little, if any, legal guidance.

In *Meritor,* the Court of Appeals found that testimony about the provocative dress of the plaintiff had no place in the sexual harassment litigation. Chief Justice Rehnquist, writing for the unanimous Court, disagreed and suggested that a plaintiff's speech and dress is "obviously relevant" to the issue of whether the defendant's conduct was welcome. The problem with this approach is that it focuses upon the behavior of the plaintiff and not the defendant, which is reminiscent of defense tactics in rape cases before rape shield laws were created to protect victims. Since *Meritor,* Rule 412 of Federal Rules of Evidence dealing with the federal "rape shield" law has been amended to apply to civil as well as criminal cases involving sexual misconduct or harassment. Rule 403 requires a court to balance the probative value of the evidence against its potential prejudice. Notwithstanding Rehnquist's view regarding relevancy, it would seem that speech and dress in most sexual harassment cases would be of little relevance, highly prejudicial, and therefore inadmissible. Finally, the Court did not decide in *Meritor* whether the victim of sexual harassment must suffer "psychologically," as some lower courts have held. Hence, lower courts continued to grapple with the psychological impact issue until the U.S. Supreme Court agreed in 1993 to review another sexual harassment case.

HARRIS V. FORKLIFT SYSTEMS, INC. (1993)

Theresa Harris worked as the manager of an equipment rental company from April 1985 to October 1987. Her immediate supervisor was Charles Hardy, who was also the company president. Hardy often insulted Harris because of her gender and frequently made her the target of sexual innuendo. Hardy told Harris on several occasions, in the presence of other employees, "You're a woman, what do you know?" and "We need a man as a rental manager." In addition, he told her that she was a "dumb ass woman" and, in front of others, suggested that she go with him "to the Holiday Inn to negotiate a raise." Hardy occasionally asked Harris and other women to get coins from his pants pocket, and he threw objects on the ground in front of Harris and other women and asked them to pick them up. In mid-August 1987, Harris complained to Hardy about his conduct. Hardy expressed surprise that Harris was offended, claimed he was joking, and apologized. He also promised that he would stop, and on the basis of this assurance, Harris stayed on the job. However, a month later, Hardy began anew, and while Harris was arranging a deal with one of the company's customers, Hardy, in front of other employees, said, "What did you do, promise the guy . . . some [sex] Saturday night?" Shortly thereafter, Harris quit her job and brought a sexual harassment lawsuit against Hardy based on the theory of a hostile work environment.

The district court, even though it found Hardy to be a "vulgar man," concluded that Hardy's conduct did not create a hostile environment under Title VII because Theresa Harris failed to prove she had suffered serious damage to her psychological well-being. The court of appeals affirmed, and the case was appealed to the U.S. Supreme Court. Justice O'Connor, less than one month after oral argument, writing for a unanimous Court, reversed the court of appeals and held that a victim of sexual harassment does not have to "demonstrate psychological injury" to recover under Title VII for sexual harassment. The Court said that for a plaintiff to state a sexual harassment claim, the "sexually objectionable environment must be both objectively and subjectively offensive" so that a "reasonable person" would find the environment hostile or abusive, and so would the victim of the alleged harassment. The objective standard appears to limit sexual harassment claims by protecting the employer from hypersensitive employees. The subjective test provides for the perceptions of the harassment victim. The Court's decision requires proof of harm; yet, a plaintiff does not have to demonstrate that he or she had "a nervous breakdown" before Title VII is violated. The benefit of this approach is that it helps to focus attention on the behavior of the harasser rather than on the target or victim of the harassment. The *Harris* Court also adopted the "reasonable person" standard without commenting on the "reasonable woman" standard that has been adopted by several federal circuit courts of appeal. Hence, one may argue that the Supreme Court has implicitly overruled the "reasonable woman." standard. On remand, Forklift was ordered to institute a sexual harassment policy, and Theresa Harris was awarded $151,435 plus interest, costs, and attorney fees. Forklift appealed but withdrew the appeal when the case was settled for an undisclosed sum.

The *Harris* Court noted that there is "no mathematically precise test" that will tell us whether an environment is "hostile" or "abusive." To make a determination regarding whether the environment is hostile in violation of Title VII, the Court said that one must look at the "frequency of the discriminatory conduct; its severity; whether it is physically threatening or humiliating, or a mere offensive utterance; and whether it unreasonably interferes with an employee's work performance." In effect, the Court took a middle path between making actionable any conduct that is merely offensive and requiring the conduct to cause a severe psychological injury. In his concurring opinion, Justice Scalia expressed concern that some of the words and phrases used in the Court's decision, "that the conduct must be severe or pervasive enough to create an objectively hostile or abusive work environment that a reasonable person would find hostile or abusive," are so vague that "as a practical matter [the Court's decision] lets virtually unguided juries decide whether sex-related conduct engaged in by an employer is egregious enough to warrant damages." However, Justice Scalia noted, "be that as it may, I know of no alternative."

CLINTON V. JONES (1997)

Can the president of the United States be sued for sexual harassment while in office?

In 1994, a woman from Arkansas filed a sexual harassment lawsuit in the Federal District Court in Arkansas against the president of the United States. Plaintiff Paula Jones alleged that when President Clinton was the governor of Arkansas, he had an Arkansas State Police officer summon Jones to the then-governor Clinton's hotel room in Little Rock. Jones alleged that shortly after she entered the hotel room, Clinton exposed himself and made "abhorrent" sexual advances to her and that her rejection of those advances led to punishment by her supervisors in the state job she held at the time. President Clinton denied the charges and promptly advised the district court that he would file a motion to dismiss on presidential immunity and other grounds. The district court denied the dismissal on immunity grounds but ordered any trial stayed until the Clinton presidency ended. Both sides appealed to the U.S. Supreme Court, which held that the district court "abused its discretion . . . in deferring trial until the president leaves office." The Federal District Court ". . . has jurisdiction to decide this . . . [sexual harassment] . . . case . . . [and] . . . like every other citizen who properly invokes that jurisdiction [Paula Jones] has a right to an orderly disposition of her claim." Hence, the U.S. Supreme Court held that a sexual harassment case against a sitting president of the United States could not be delayed and must go forward.

ONCALE V. SUNDOWNER OFFSHORE SERVICES, INC. (1998)

Some 19 years after Catharine MacKinnon wrote her compelling article proposing sexual harassment as a legal claim, the U.S. Supreme Court decided to review no less than four sexual harassment cases during the 1998 term of the Court. The first of these cases involved same-sex sexual harassment.

In October 1991, Joseph Oncale was working for Sundowner Offshore Services on an oil platform in the Gulf of Mexico. He was employed as a roustabout on an eight-man crew. On several occasions, Oncale was forcibly subjected by some crew members to humiliating actions and physically assaulted in a sexual manner, and one crew member threatened to rape him. Oncale's complaints to supervisory personnel produced no remedial action and the company's safety compliance clerk told Oncale that the crew members picked on him, too, and then he called Oncale a name "suggesting homosexuality." Oncale eventually quit, indicating as his reason for leaving "sexual harassment and verbal abuse." Shortly thereafter, Oncale sued his employer under Title VII, alleging that he had been discriminated against because of his sex. The district court dismissed the suit, and the Fifth Circuit affirmed, holding that there is no cause of action under Title VII for same-sex sexual harassment. The U.S. Supreme Court unanimously reversed and ruled that discrimination in the form of same-sex sexual harassment is actionable under Title VII. The Court noted that in racial discrimination cases, there is no reason to presume that a person would not discriminate against members of his own race. Therefore, the Court found that nothing in the statutory language of Title VII or in precedents precluded a claim of same-sex sexual harassment but cautioned that Title VII is "not a general civility code for the American workplace." The Court noted that:

> We have emphasized . . . that the objective severity of harassment should be judged from the perspective of a reasonable person in the plaintiff's position, considering all of the circumstances. . . . In same-sex (as in all) harassment cases, that inquiry requires careful consideration of the social context in which the particular behavior occurs and is experienced by its target. . . . The real social impact of workplace behavior often depends on a constellation of surrounding circumstances, expectations and relationships which are not fully captured by a simple recitation of the words used or the physical acts performed. Common sense, and an appropriate sensitivity to social context, will enable courts and juries to distinguish between simple roughhousing among members of the same sex, and conduct which a reasonable person in the plaintiff's position would find severely hostile or abusive.

The Court said that these standards are necessary so that courts and juries do not mistake "male on male horseplay or intersexual flirtation for discriminatory conditions of employment." The evaluation of whether there is an actionable "hostile environment" should be made by the reasonable person in the plaintiff's position, giving careful consideration to the social context in which the behavior occurs. For example, the Court noted that in a football player's working environment, the coach may "smack a player on the buttocks as he heads off the field," but this same behavior "experienced by the coach's secretary back at the office" may be quite different. The Court said that "common sense, and an appropriate sensitivity to social context, will enable courts and juries to distinguish between simple teasing or roughhousing among members of the same sex, and conduct which a reasonable person in the plaintiff's position would find severely hostile or abusive."

Since Oncale was decided, one federal judge has written that in borderline cases of sexual harassment, juries and not federal judges may be more appropriate to decide factual issues.

> Whatever the early life of a Federal Judge, he or she lives in a narrow segment of the enormously broad American socioeconomic spectrum, generally lacking the current real life experience required in interpreting subtle sexual dynamics of the workplace based on nuances, subtle perceptions, and implicit communications . . . a jury made up of a cross-section of our heterogeneous communities provides the appropriate institution for deciding whether borderline situations should be characterized as sexual harassment and retaliation. . . ." (Jack B.

Weinstein, Federal District Judge sitting on the Second Circuit Court of Appeals in *Galagher v. Delaney,* p. 342, 1998)

This is an extraordinary statement commenting upon the experience of members of the federal judiciary. If this view is adopted by other federal courts, there may be fewer summary judgments in sexual harassment cases, more trials, protracted litigation, and greater pressure on employers to settle sexual harassment claims.

FARAGHER V. CITY OF BOCA RATON (1998)

Beginning in 1985, Beth Ann Faragher worked part-time during the summer as a lifeguard for the Parks Department of the City of Boca Raton, Florida. The city employed about 40 lifeguards, six of whom were women. Bill Terry, David Silverman, and Robert Gordon were Faragher's immediate supervisors. Terry had authority to hire new lifeguards, supervise all aspects of a lifeguard's work, deliver oral reprimands, and make a record of such discipline. After five years of part-time work, Faragher resigned in 1990. Two years after her resignation, she brought a sexual harassment lawsuit against Terry, Silverman, and the City of Boca Raton, asserting that her supervisors discriminated against her by creating a "sexually hostile atmosphere" in her work environment. Faragher asserted that she and other female lifeguards were repeatedly subjected to uninvited and offensive touching and lewd remarks, and women were spoken of in offensive terms. Specifically, she alleged that Terry once said that "he would never promote a woman to the rank of Lieutenant," and Silverman said, "Date me or clean the toilets for a year." During a five-year period, "Terry repeatedly touched the bodies of female employees . . . would put his arm around [Faragher] with his hand on her buttocks . . . [and] . . . made contact with another female lifeguard in a motion of sexual simulation . . . [and] . . . once commented disparagingly about Faragher's shape." During an interview with a woman he hired as a lifeguard, Terry said that "female lifeguards have sex with their male counterparts . . . [will you] . . . do the same. . . ." Silverman behaved in similar ways and "once tackled Faragher and commented that but for a physical characteristic he found unattractive, he would readily have sexual relations with her, and another time, he pantomimed oral sex."

Faragher did not complain to higher management about Terry and Silverman. Although she spoke of their behavior to Gordon, she did not regard these discussions as formal complaints. Other female lifeguards had similar conversations with Gordon, and Gordon responded to one of these female lifeguards that "the City just doesn't care. . . ." Two months before Faragher resigned, another female lifeguard wrote a letter to the city's personnel director to complain that Terry and Silverman had harassed her and other female lifeguards. The city investigated the complaint. On finding that Terry and Silverman had behaved improperly, it reprimanded them and required them to choose between a suspension without pay and forfeiture of annual leave. The district court found that Terry and Silverman had discriminated against Faragher, and the court also said that the city was liable because the harassment was so pervasive that the city "had knowledge or constructive knowledge" and that Terry and Silverman were acting as agents of the city when they committed their harassing acts. On appeal, the Eleventh Circuit affirmed the judgment finding sexual harassment by the two supervisors, but reversed the judgment against the city because Terry and Silverman were not acting within the scope of their employment when they engaged in harassment and were not aided in their actions by an agency relationship, and the city had no constructive knowledge of the harassment by virtue of its pervasiveness or Gordon's actual knowledge.

At the outset, the Supreme Court noted that it was taking this case because the lower courts had struggled since *Meritor* to derive manageable standards to govern employer liability. In *Faragher,* the U.S. Supreme Court not only reversed the judgement of the court of appeals that was in favor of the employer but also, in an extraordinary exercise of its power, sent the case back to the district court with a directive that a judgment be entered in Faragher's favor. The Court held that the city of Boca Raton was liable for the acts of Terry and Silverman and with respect to employer liability said:

> An employer is subject to vicarious liability to a victimized employee for actionable hostile environment created by a supervisor (with immediate or successively higher) authority over an employee. When no tangible employment action is taken, a defending employer may raise an affirmative defense to liability or damages, subject to proof by a preponderance of the evidence. The defense comprises two necessary elements: (a) that the employer exercised reasonable care to prevent and correct promptly any sexually harassing behavior, and (b) that the plaintiff employee unreasonably failed to take advantage of any preventive or corrective opportunities provided by the employer or to avoid harm otherwise. . . . No affirmative defense is available, however, when the supervisor's harassment culminates in a tangible employment action, such as discharge, demotion, or undesirable reassignment.

Because the city of Boca Raton had failed to disseminate its sexual harassment policy to beach employees and lifeguards, the city made no attempt to keep track of the conduct of its beach supervisors, and the city's sexual harassment policy did not include any provision that the harassing supervisors could be bypassed in registering complaints, the Court ruled as a matter of law that the city of Boca Raton could not be found to have exercised reasonable care in preventing the supervisor's misconduct. In essence, the Court threw out the laissez-faire "see-no-evil" defense that some employers were raising with respect to sexual harassment claims. Employers who do not proactively take steps to prevent and stop sexual harassment in the workplace can no longer comfortably say, "I am not responsible because I did not know of the sexual harassment." The Court's decision makes it clear that the way for employers to avoid liability for sexual harassment is to have in place a comprehensive sexual harassment policy and to train its employees with respect to that policy. In addition, an employer must carefully monitor the work environment, adopt a zero-tolerance policy regarding sexual harassment, and take swift action to enforce the harassment policy as appropriate.

BURLINGTON INDUSTRIES V. ELLERTH (1998)

Kimberly Ellerth quit her job after 15 months as a salesperson at Burlington Industries because she had been subjected to constant sexual harassment by one of her supervisors, Ted Slowik. Slowik was a midlevel manager who had the authority to hire and fire but was not a policy maker. In the summer of 1993, while on a business trip, Slowik invited Ellerth to the hotel lounge, an invitation Ellerth felt compelled to accept because Slowik was her boss. When Ellerth gave no encouragement to remarks Slowik made about her breasts, he told her to "loosen up" and warned, "[y]ou know, Kim, I could make your life very hard or very easy at Burlington." Several months later, when Kim was being considered for promotion, Slowik expressed reservations during the promotion interview because she was not "loose enough." The comment was followed by his reaching over and rubbing her knee. Ellerth did receive the promotion, but, when Slowik called her to announce it, he told Ellerth that "you're going to be out there with men who work in factories, and they certainly like women with pretty butts/legs." During telephone calls, Slowik asked Ellerth what she was wearing and once said, "Are you wearing shorter skirts yet, Kim, because it would make your job a whole heck of a lot easier." A short time later, Ellerth's immediate supervisor cautioned her about returning telephone calls to customers in a prompt fashion. In response, Ellerth quit. Ellerth never suffered negative job consequences at Burlington, and she was, in fact, promoted once. Ellerth did not inform anyone in authority of Slowik's comments, even though Burlington had a sexual harassment policy in place. Subsequently, Ellerth filed a sexual harassment lawsuit against Slowik and her employer, Burlington Industries. The district court granted a summary judgment in favor of Burlington. The Seventh Circuit Court of Appeals reversed, in a decision that produced no fewer than eight separate opinions regarding when an employer is liable for the sexual harassment of its employees. The opinions had no consensus or controlling rationale, so the 12-judge panel produced a per curiam opinion pleading for a U.S. Supreme Court decision that would "bring order to a chaotic field of practice." Hence, the U.S. Supreme Court accepted the case to clarify the law in sexual harassment cases regarding employer liability.

The U.S. Supreme Court said that the plaintiff in *Burlington* had attempted to couch her claim in terms of a quid pro quo rather than a hostile environment claim because the lower courts had held that it was the appropriate standard regarding the harassment that had occurred. If the plaintiff established a quid pro quo claim, the employer would be subject to vicarious liability. The Supreme Court concluded that these distinctions were irrelevant for the purposes of determining whether an employer should be liable for the actions of its supervisors. The Court found that Ellerth's claim involved *unfulfilled threats* and decided it should be treated as a hostile environment claim, which requires showing severe or pervasive conduct. The Supreme Court accepted the district court's finding that the conduct alleged by Ellerth was severe and pervasive, and it affirmed the Seventh Circuit's decision reversing the grant of summary judgment. The Court noted on remand that Burlington would have an opportunity to assert and prove that it had taken care to prevent and correct promptly any sexually harassing behavior and that Ellerth had unreasonably failed to take advantage of any preventive or corrective opportunities provided by Burlington to avoid the harassment. It is clear that *Burlington* stands for the proposition that "unfulfilled threats" can be the subject of sexual harassment claims under Title VII, and the employee does not have to suffer "tangible employment action" before a sexual harassment claim is actionable. In *Burlington* and *Faragher,* the Court tried to justify its *Meritor* agency principle's rationale. By tortured reasoning, the Court is still clinging to its agency principles for sexual harassment liability. However, it appears that the new two-pronged test that the Court has created in regard to employer liability presents much clearer guidance to lower courts and employers than the murky agency concepts the Court referred to in *Meritor.*

GEBSER V. LAGO VISTA INDEPENDENT SCHOOL DISTRICT (1998)

In 1991, Alida Star Gebser was an eighth grade student at the Lago Vista middle school in Texas. She joined a school book discussion group led by a teacher, Frank Waldrop. Waldrop often made sexually suggestive comments to the students. When Gebser entered high school and was assigned to classes taught by Waldrop, he began to direct more of his sexually suggestive comments to Gebser. He subsequently initiated sexual contact with Gebser and kissed and fondled her. Eventually, the two engaged in sexual intercourse on numerous occasions and even had sexual intercourse during class time, although never on school property. Gebser did not report this relationship to school officials, even though she realized Waldrop's conduct was improper, because "she wanted to continue having him as a teacher." More than a year after this relationship began, parents began to complain to the high school principal about Waldrop's comments in class. At a meeting between the parents, the principal, and the teacher, Waldrop indicated that he did not believe that he made offensive remarks but apologized to the parents and said it would never happen again. The principal did not report the parents' complaints to the school superintendent. Several months later, the police discovered Waldrop and Gebser engaging in sexual intercourse, and Waldrop was arrested. The school district terminated Waldrop's employment, and the state of Texas revoked his teaching license. The school district had not promulgated or distributed a grievance procedure for lodging sexual harassment complaints, nor had it issued a formal antiharassment policy. Gebser and her mother filed suit against the school district and Waldrop, raising claims under Title IX of the Education Amendment of 1972. The district court granted a summary judgment in favor of the school district and remanded the claims against Waldrop to the state court. The district court opined that:

> The Title IX statute "was enacted to counter policies of discrimination . . . in federally funded education programs" and only if school administrators have some kind of notice of gender discrimination and fail to respond in good faith can the discrimination be interpreted as a policy of the school district."

Gebser and her mother appealed to the Fifth Circuit Court of Appeals on the Title IX claim and the court affirmed the lower court decision. It held that a school district could not be held vicariously liable under Title IX for a teacher's sexual harassment of a student based on common law of agency theories. Gebser and her mother argued that the school district should be held liable for the tortious acts of its employee because, even if these acts were outside the scope of his employment, the teacher was aided in accomplishing the tort by the existence of an agency relationship and his position of authority within the school. The U.S. Supreme Court in a 5–4 decision said that the school district was not liable for this sexual harassment by Waldrop. The majority of the Court reasoned that, absent further direction from Congress, Title IX does not create a private right of action, and a damages remedy will not lie against a school district "unless an official who at a minimum has authority to address the alleged discrimination and to institute corrective measures has actual knowledge of the discrimination . . . and fails to adequately respond." Unlike Title VII cases, the Supreme Court said that a school district cannot be held liable for the acts of its employees pursuant to the common law principles of agency. The Court noted that because Title VII includes a phrase "any agent," the principles of agency law apply. Because Title IX has no comparable phrase, the Court concluded that the statutory language of Title IX is not consistent with the notion of liability for a school district based on traditional principles of common law agency. The result of *Gebser* is that the laissez-faire "see-no-evil" defense that the Court effectively jettisoned in the *Faragher* and *Burlington* Title VII cases is alive and well in Title IX school district sexual harassment cases.

In *Gebser,* four justices (Stevens, Souter, Ginsburg, and Breyer) vigorously dissented. The dissenting judges stated that when Congress creates a statute such as Title IX, there is a presumption that "Congress intends to authorize all appropriate remedies," which would include the right of a child and a parent to bring a discrimination lawsuit against a school district for the sexual misconduct of its teachers. The dissenters noted that the U.S. Department of Education recently issued policy guidance "stating that a school district is liable under Title IX if one of its teachers was aided in carrying out sexual harassment of students by his or her position of authority with the institution." The dissenters further noted that "as long as school boards can insulate themselves from knowledge about this sort of conduct, they can claim immunity from damages." It seems clear that *Gebser* provides no encouragement to school districts to promulgate comprehensive sexual harassment policies and root out discrimination. In fact, this decision may result in some school districts further insulating themselves from knowledge of sexual harassment so that they can avoid vicarious liability for their harassing employees.

AURELIA DAVIS V. MONROE COUNTY BOARD OF EDUCATION ET AL. (1999)

Less than one year after the *Gebser* decision, the U.S. Supreme Court decided another school sexual harassment case. The mother of LaShonda Davis brought a Title IX lawsuit against the Monroe County Board of Education, alleging that her fifth-grade daughter had been the victim of sexual harassment by another student. LaShonda was allegedly the victim of a prolonged pattern of sexual harassment by one of her classmates. According to the complaint, the classmate attempted to touch LaShonda's breasts and genital area and made vulgar statements such as "I want to get in bed with you" and "I want to feel your boobs." The harassing classmate engaged in this conduct on numerous occasions, and each time LaShonda reported the conduct to her mother and her classroom teacher. The classroom teacher assured LaShonda's mother that the school principal had been informed of the harassing conduct. No disciplinary action was taken against the harassing student, and the sexual harassment continued for several months in both academic and physical education classes. On several occasions, the harassing student rubbed his body against LaShonda. LaShonda alleged that she suffered significantly during the many months of harassment, and her previously high grades dropped as she became unable to concentrate on her studies. Her parents discovered that LaShonda was so depressed over the harassment that she had written a suicide note. When LaShonda's parents asked the school principal what action the school intended to take against the harassing student, the principal allegedly stated, "I guess I'll have to threaten him a little bit harder." At the time of the harassment, the Monroe County Board of Education had not instructed its personnel on how to respond to peer sexual harassment and had not established a policy dealing with the issue. The harassment finally stopped when criminal charges were brought against the harassing student, and he pleaded guilty to a charge of sexual battery.

The civil complaint alleged that the school board is the recipient of federal funds for purposes of Title IX, that the persistent sexual advances and harassment by LaShonda's fifth-grade classmate interfered with her ability to attend school and perform her studies, and that the deliberate indifference of the school officials to the unwelcome sexual advances created an intimidating, hostile, and offensive environment. The school board contended that Title IX only proscribes misconduct by recipients of federal funds, not third parties, and that they cannot be liable for the misconduct of third parties over whom they have little control. The district court dismissed the Title IX claim on the grounds that student-on-student sexual harassment provides no ground for a private lawsuit by a parent against a school district. The court of appeals sitting en banc affirmed. The U.S. Supreme Court granted certiorari to decide under what circumstances a recipient of federal educational funds can be liable for student-on-student sexual harassment.

The Supreme Court in a 5–4 decision reversed the court of appeals and held that under Title IX a private right of action against a school board may lie when there is deliberate indifference to sexual harassment of which the board has actual knowledge and the harassment is so severe, pervasive, and objectively offensive that it can be said to deprive the victim of access to educational opportunities or benefits. The Court agreed that the recipient of federal funds under Title IX can be liable for only its own misconduct, and the Court noted that in this case the parents of LaShonda Davis were not attempting to hold the school board liable for the actions of the fifth-grader. However, the Court noted that the school board may be liable for its "decision to remain idle in the face of known student-on-student harassment in its schools." The Court said that the deliberate indifference must at a minimum cause students to undergo harassment or "make them . . . vulnerable to it," and the recipient of federal funds under Title IX can be liable only when it has authority to take remedial action to correct the harassment. The Court noted that the alleged harassment took place during school hours on school grounds, frequently in the classroom, and thus under the "operation of the funding recipient . . . [and] . . . the nature of the State's power over public school children is custodial . . . permitting a degree of supervision and control that could not be exercised over free adults."

Justice Kennedy filed a strong dissenting opinion, in which Chief Justice Rehnquist and Justices Scalia and Thomas joined. The dissenters argued that only when states receive clear notice of the conditions attached to federal funds can they be held liable and that here there was no clear notice to the school board that a private right of action by third parties would be permissible under Title IX. The dissenters argued that federal control of discipline in our nation's schools is "contrary to our traditions and inconsistent with the sensible administration of our schools." The dissenters questioned whether the alleged conduct by this fifth-grader constituted sexual harassment because there was "no power relationship between the harasser and the victim." In addition, the dissenters suggested that the majority was creating a situation in which there would be a significant increase in lawsuits against school districts because simply alleging a decline in school grades may be enough to survive a motion to dismiss a lawsuit, and "almost every child at some point has trouble in school because he or she is being teased by his or her peers." The dissenters stated that there is a great deal of teasing in schools. An overweight child may skip gym classes because other children tease her about her size, a student may refuse to wear glasses to avoid taunts of "four eyes," or a child may refuse to go to school because a bully calls him "scaredy-cat"; in many of these cases, the teasing detracts from students' ability to learn. The dissenters noted that a "female plaintiff who pleads only that a boy called her offensive names, that she told a teacher, that the teacher's response was unreasonable, that her school performance suffered as a result, appears to state a successful claim."

In response, the majority argued that the dissent misinterpreted its decision and that school districts are not facing sweeping liability. Rather, the majority stated that in a school setting "students often engage in insults, banter, teasing, shoving, pushing, and gender specific conduct that is upsetting to students subjected to it." However, the majority notes that "damages are not available for simple acts of teasing and name-calling among school children . . . [and] . . . damages are only available where the behavior is so severe, pervasive, and objectively offensive that it denies its victims the equal access to education that Title IX is designed to protect."

Notwithstanding the fearful views of the dissenting justices, it seems clear that the majority rule in *Davis* provides sufficient protection for school districts to address and correct the dizzying array of immature behavior that may occur in schools without the continual threat of a federal lawsuit. Simple, daily, adolescent behavior will not be sufficient to commence a legal action. In fact, the harassing student behavior will have to be severe and pervasive, have a significant impact on the student, and be virtually ignored by the school district before a lawsuit may be successful under Title IX. In this case, the conduct by the fifth-grader was so severe and pervasive that it led to a criminal conviction. The major impact of *Davis* is that school districts will have to educate both its employees and its students about sexual harassment and adopt a zero-tolerance policy toward sexual harassment in schools. In addition to avoiding expensive liability, school districts will reap other benefits from strong sexual harassment policies, even if an investigation reveals that harassment did not occur. These benefits include an improved school environment for teachers and students, a periodic evaluation of harassment policies, and the ability to discover problems and address them before they become actionable sexual harassment.

CONCLUSION

Although sexual harassment law has its genesis in the Civil Rights Act of 1964 and EEOC guidelines, most of the sexual harassment law has been created by the judicial branch of government. Every plaintiff (Vinson, Harris, Jones, Faragher, Ellerth, Oncale) who has brought a Title VII sexual harassment lawsuit to the U.S. Supreme Court has received a favorable ruling. In *Vinson, Harris, Jones,* and *Oncale,* the decisions of the U.S. Supreme Court were unanimous. In *Burlington,* only Justice Thomas dissented, and in *Faragher* there were two dissenting justices (Thomas, Scalia). The Supreme Court has been so responsive to plaintiffs in Title VII workplace sexual harassment cases that some business interests are complaining that "antibias laws are creating a more hostile environment for employers" (*Forbes,* 1998, p. 154) and that the Court is "exaggerating the benefits of anti-harassment policies and willfully refusing to acknowledge their costs" (*New Republic,* 1998, p. 8). Although sexual harassment law is now well established, the law is still growing because sexual harassment claims are fact-sensitive, and many legal issues are still unresolved. The U.S. Supreme Court's decision in *Meritor* and its progeny have been indispensable to the advancement of workplace sexual harassment protection. However, policing employee sexual relationships is a difficult task, and sometimes the line between voluntary and involuntary is not easy to ascertain. No one can expect a workplace that is forever free of envy, jealousy, personal grudges, sexual banter, and horseplay. There is no litmus test that can tell us precisely when innocuous banter becomes sexual harassment. The commonsense social context and the "reasonable person" standard adopted in *Harris* may be well suited for sexual harassment claims because they embrace feminine as well as masculine perspectives.

The issue of sexual harassment is no longer on the back burner. It is a major public policy issue, in part because of the decisions of the U.S. Supreme Court. The courts in the country have provided much guidance and reflection regarding the elements of sexual harassment claims. Now it is up to Congress to revisit the substantive provisions of Title VII and make sure that the various standards and elements of the law of sexual harassment that have been created by the judiciary are sufficient to help in ridding our workplaces of sexual harassment. Congress should immediately revisit the discrimination provisions of Title IX in light of the *Gebser* decision to provide no employer liability unless there is actual notice to high-ranking staff of the employer. Sexual harassment that occurs in the workplace does not differ substantially from sexual harassment that may occur in schools. Members of the Supreme Court may say that they were interpreting a statute in the *Gebser* Title IX case and were bound by the terms of that statute, which, according to the majority, limited the liability of a school district that had done little if anything to root out sexual harassment. Nevertheless, it is mindless not to incorporate the employer liability standards of Title VII, or other appropriate liability standards, into Title IX cases. If the Supreme Court is unwilling or unable to incorporate these liability standards, then Congress should quickly amend the statute to achieve this result. There is no doubt that strong antiharassment laws created by Congress can influence employer action and employer liability, and there is much truth in the old adage that "money talks."

Finally, no matter what substantive or procedural changes are made in the law to benefit victims of discrimination, if sexual harassment is to be significantly reduced or eliminated, gender power balances in our society must be changed, and the values underlying the law of sexual harassment (equal treatment, nondiscrimination, and fair play) must be internalized by all who function in our workplaces.

DISCUSSION QUESTIONS

1. Describe the two forms of sexual harassment recognized by the Equal Employment Opportunity Commission (EEOC).

2. Why was *Meritor Savings Bank v. Vinson* (1986) considered such a significant case?

3. Explain the "empty threat" claim.

4. Of the eight sexual harassment cases presented, which were considered quid pro quo, and why?

5. What substantive or procedural changes have been made in the law to benefit victims of sexual discrimination since 1964?

CASES

Aurelia Davis v. Monroe County Board of Education et al. 67 U.S.L.W. 4329 (1999).

Barnes v. Train, 13 FEP Cases 123 (1974).

Burlington Industries v. Ellerth, 118 S.Ct. 2257 (1998).

Clinton v. Jones, U.S.L.W. 4372 (1997).

Corne v. Bausch & Lomb, Inc., 390 F. Supp. 161 (1975).

Faragher v. City of Boca Raton, 118 S.Ct. 2275 (1998).

Gebser v. Lago Vista Independent School District, 118 S.Ct. (1989).

Gallagher v. Delaney et al., 139 F. 3d 338 (1998).

Harris v. Forklift Systems, Inc., 114 S.Ct. 367 (1993).

Miller v. Bank of America, 418 F. Supp. 233 (1976).

Meritor Savings Bank, FSB v. Mechelle Vinson et al., 106 S.Ct. 2399 (1986).

Oncale v. Sundowner Offshore Services, Inc., et al., 118 S.Ct. 998 (1998).

Tomkins v. Public Serv. Elec. & Gas Co., 422 F. Supp. 553 (1976).

REFERENCES

BELKNAP, J., & EREZ, E. (1997). Redefining sexual harassment: Confronting sexism in the 21st century. *Justice Professional, 10*(2), 143.

FORBES, (1998, May 4). "A wild card gets wilder." 154.

GUTEK, B.A. (1985). *Sex and the workplace.* San Francisco: Jossey-Bass.

MACKINNON, C.A. (1979). *Sexual harassment of working women! A case of discrimination.* New Haven: Yale University Press.

NEW REPUBLIC (1998, July 20). Anti-expressionism, p. 8

PHILLIPS, M.J. (1991). Employer sexual harassment liability under agency principles: A second look at *Meritor Savings Bank, FSB v. Vinson. Vanderbilt Law Review, 44,* 1229–1269.

U.S. MERIT SYSTEMS PROTECTION BOARD (1995, October). *A survey of civilian employees in the executive branch 1980–1987.* Office of Merit Systems Review and Studies. Washington DC: U.S. Government Printing Office.

SECTION II
Police

4

Police Arrest Decisions

Preliminary Results from Kentucky's Multiagency Approach to Domestic Violence

Elizabeth L. Grossi

In this chapter, I examine the factors associated with the arrest of domestic violence offenders in a midsize city in Kentucky. Using data from all domestic violence police reports for 1999, I address two questions. First, which victim, offender, and situational characteristics are associated with an officer's decision to arrest in domestic violence cases? Second, were these factors consistently associated with arrest both before and after officers underwent department-wide domestic violence training? The results indicate that victim injuries, drugs or alcohol use, the existence of an emergency protective order, and gender of both the victim and the offender were associated with increased likelihood of arrest in domestic violence cases.

BRIEF REVIEW OF THE LITERATURE

One of the more salient issues relating to the criminal justice system's response to domestic violence is the police officer's decision to arrest offenders. Over the past several years, a number of researchers have directly and indirectly examined police officers' decisions to arrest (Feder, 1998). In addition, a number of studies have examined the effects of manda-

This project was supported by Grant No. 98-WE-VX-0018 awarded by the Violence against Women Office, Office of Justice Programs, U.S. Department of Justice. Points of view of this document are those of the author and do not necessarily represent the official policies of the U.S. Department of Justice.

tory arrest and pro-arrest domestic violence policies and laws on sentencing and recidivism (Bourg & Stock, 1994; Feder, 1997; Jones & Belknap, 1999; Lanza-Kaduce, Greenleaf, & Donahue, 1995; Robinson, 1999). More recently, some studies have focused on the potential negative effects of police involvement in domestic violence cases (Miller, 1989; Rasche, 1995). Despite the evolving research and public policy debates concerning the "best practice" for responding to domestic violence, many questions remain concerning police officers' decisions to arrest offenders, the effects of the arrest on the victim, and the impact of arrest on offender recidivism.

Despite these concerns, numerous jurisdictions have imposed pro-arrest or mandatory arrest policies for domestic violence cases. Jones and Belknap (1999) attributes the rise in pro-arrest policies to three factors. The first relates to judicial decisions regarding the failure of police to protect battered women. The second reason concerns the increased efforts of organized groups to lobby for more effective police response to domestic violence incidents. Third, research following the Minneapolis project (Sherman & Berk, 1984), which indicated that arrest was an effective deterrent to domestic violence, has prompted many jurisdictions to alter their policies to reflect a more proactive response to domestic violence. In turn, these factors have led to considerable changes in the way police enforce domestic violence statutes.

A number of researchers have attempted to identify factors that contribute to law enforcement officers' decision to arrest the perpetrator in domestic violence cases. In previous research, factors that influence arrest decisions included the nature and extent of the victims' injuries (Berk & Loseke, 1981; Buzawa & Austin, 1993; Kane, 1999; Mignon & Holmes, 1995), the victims' desire for arrest (Buzawa & Austin, 1993; Buzawa & Buzawa, 1995; Feder, 1999), prior police contacts with perpetrator (Smith & Klein, 1984; Waaland & Keeley, 1985; Websdale, 1998), use of drugs and/or alcohol by perpetrator (Berk & Loseke, 1981; Jones & Belknap, 1999; Mignon & Holmes, 1995), gender, race, marital, and socioeconomic status of victim and perpetrator (Bachman & Coker, 1995; Erez, 1986; Ferraro, 1989; Fyfe, Klinger & Flavin, 1997; Smith & Visher, 1981), police attitudes toward women (Belknap, 1996; Feder, 1997, 1999), offender presence at scene (Berk & Loseke, 1981; Feder, 1999), and departmental policies relating to arrest in domestic violence incidents (Feder, 1999; Jones & Belknap, 1999).

Feder (1999) identifies four groups of factors associated with the police response to domestic violence: police, offender, victim, and situational characteristics. Of these, situational factors (i.e., victim injury, victim's preference for arrest, and the offender's presence) are the most consistent and influential in determining the response of police (Feder, 1999). The current study examines three of the four groups identified by Feder (1999)—situational, victim, and offender characteristics and their relationship with the police officers' decision to arrest.

THE KENTUCKY PROGRAM

In 1998, a midsize police department in Kentucky became the primary partner in a grant awarded by the Violence against Women Office. A number of state and local agencies in the metropolitan area were also funded as part of the federal grant. Specifically, the key agencies involved in the grant were the city police, county attorney, state attorney, a nonprofit agency operating rape crisis and domestic violence programs, the local probation and parole office, and a local university.

The project involved a multidisciplinary approach to domestic violence that intended to improve the accountability and supervision of domestic violence offenders and provide more extensive services to victims of domestic violence. The key components were (1) providing domestic violence awareness and investigation training to all police officers, (2) placing an interdiction team of a police detective, victim advocate, and probation and parole officer in each of the five police districts, (3) providing an additional detective and victim advocate for district teams and prosecutors to assist with processing and keeping track of felony domestic violence cases, and (4) offering workshops to publicize the grant and gain community interest and support for the program.

During the winter of 1999, the teams were assembled, and each team member received three days of intensive domestic violence training. The topics addressed during these training sessions included case investigation, victim advocacy, crime scene processing, departmental policies, legal issues related to domestic violence, community resources available to victims of domestic violence, and the general provisions of the grant. The teams were placed in each of the five police districts in February 1999. Each team was responsible for reviewing domestic violence reports and conducting follow-up visits with victims within 24 to 48 hours. The purpose of the follow-up visit was to provide additional referrals and references, to assist victims in obtaining emergency protective orders (EPOs), and to continue the investigation.

In June 1999, all sworn and civilian employees of the police department were required to undergo four hours of domestic violence training. The training was conducted by several local prosecutors, detectives, and victim advocates, many of whom had completed the three-day training earlier in the year. The four-hour training session was a condensed version of the earlier training provided to the interdiction teams. The training focused on conducting more thorough investigations of domestic violence crimes (i.e., detailed reports, photographs of injuries and property damage, and statements and cooperation from victims and witnesses). In essence, the training was designed to provide officers with the skills to develop cases that could be successfully prosecuted without reliance on the victim's participation at trial.

In addition to the training sessions, designated agency representatives attended periodic grant partner meetings through the duration of the grant. These meetings, led by police representatives, gave each grant partner timely, firsthand information regarding the progress of the grant, as well as the opportunity to identify key issues or obstacles for their agency or those that were directly related to the agency's ability to interface with other grant partners.

METHODS

As previously noted, data for this study come from a larger ongoing project. The current research design involves the collection of all domestic violence-related police reports processed for the period January 1 to December 31, 1999. In all, the department processed more than 2,700 domestic violence reports for the 1999 calendar year. For the purposes of this chapter, only those cases where the perpetrator was at the scene when police arrived were chosen (N = 1,325). These cases were selected for analysis as the data collection efforts to date include data from the initial police report only and do not indicate if a subsequent arrest was made. Collection of these data is in progress but not complete, and inclusion at this point would not provide an accurate representation of police follow-up activity.

One of the more difficult issues relating to the crime of domestic violence is defining the term. A number of prominent scholars have addressed the issue of defining domestic violence, but a precise definition remains elusive. Belknap (1996) discusses the difficulties related to differentiating between violence perpetrated against women by an intimate male partner (e.g., women battering) from other terms such as *domestic violence* and *spouse abuse.* She examines the historical literature and notes the legal as well as political reasons that have contributed to the difficulty in developing precise definitions of concepts such as women battering, intimate abuse, and courtship violence. In addition, definitions often vary by jurisdiction, regardless of any philosophical or political issues. For the purposes of this chapter, the statutory definition of domestic violence is used for the geographic region under study.

According to the Kentucky Revised Statutes (KRS 403.720), "*domestic violence and abuse* means physical injury, serious physical injury, sexual abuse, assault, or the infliction of fear of imminent physical injury, serious physical injury, sexual abuse, or assault between family members or members of an unmarried couple." Furthermore, the KRS defines *family member* as "a spouse, including former spouse, a parent, a child, a stepchild, or any other person related by consanguinity or affinity within the second degree; and member of an unmarried couple means each member of an unmarried couple which allegedly has a child in common, any children of that couple, or a member of an unmarried couple who are living together or have formerly lived together." Both KRS definitions are used in this chapter.

DISCUSSION OF KEY FINDINGS

A breakdown of victim, offender, and general information about the relationship between the victim and the offender is presented in Table 4.1. The majority of offenders were male (75%), nonwhite (58%), and 40 years of age or younger (77%). Likewise, the majority of victims were women (77%), nonwhite (53%), and 40 or younger (77%). The relationships between the offender and the victim varied, although most cases involved spouses (25%) or former spouse (1%), unmarried individuals with a child in common (19%), and unmarried persons with no children in common (32%). In the majority of cases, an emergency protective order had not been previously issued (90%), and children were present in about half (47%) of all cases. The majority of calls to police were reported by the victim (56%), although others reporting domestic violence offenses include the victim's family (13%), neighbors (12%), and the perpetrator (6%). Use of drugs or alcohol by either victim or perpetrator was noted in some cases, although the detection of alcohol use (43%) was higher than drug use (6%).

The factors associated with arrest were analyzed before and after the domestic violence training. Group 1 (N = 658) contains domestic violence cases processed by the police from January 1, 1999, through June 30, 1999. Group 2 (N = 661) cases occurred from July 1, 1999, through December 31, 1999. Again, the cases included in this analysis are

TABLE 4.1   Offender and Victim Variables

Variable	N	(%)
Victim gender (N = 1,324)		
Male	309	23.3
Female	1,015	76.7
Victim race (N = 1,322)		
White	622	47.0
Nonwhite	700	53.0
Victim age (N = 1,316)	X = 32.8 s.d. 12.13	
Offender gender (N = 1,324)		
Male	990	74.8
Female	334	25.2
Offender race (N = 1,324)		
White	562	42.4
Nonwhite	762	57.6
Offender age (N = 1,311)	X = 32.1 s.d 11.49	
Victim–offender relationship (N = 1,315)		
Spouse	327	24.9
Former spouse	15	1.1
Unmarried, child in common	251	19.1
Unmarried, other	415	31.6
Child/stepchild	82	6.3
Parent/grandparent	113	8.6
Sibling	74	5.6
Other	38	2.9
Outstanding EPO (N = 1,299)		
Yes	141	10.9
No	1,158	89.1
Children present (N = 1,161)		
Yes	550	47.4
No	611	52.6
Caller status (N = 1,292)		
Victim	726	56.2
Perpetrator	74	5.7
Family member	171	13.2
Neighbor	159	12.3
Other	162	12.5

continued

TABLE 4.1   (*continued*)

Variable	N	(%)
Drugs involved (N = 1,116)		
Yes	70	6.3
No	589	52.8
Unknown	457	40.9
Alcohol involved (N = 1,238)		
Yes	537	43.4
No	447	36.1
Unknown	254	20.5

only those where the perpetrator was present when police arrived at the scene. Variables in the analysis were victim and perpetrator race (nonwhite; white), victim and perpetrator gender, caller status (victim; other), outstanding protective order (yes; no), victim injured (yes; no), injury visible (yes; no), involvement of drugs or alcohol (yes; no; unknown), children present (yes; no), use of weapon (hands/feet; gun, knife, or other), and the outcome of the police response (arrest; no arrest). In addition, we studied the relationship between the perpetrator and the victim. For this measure, we created two groups. The first group is cases with a spousal (current or previous) or partnered relationship. The second group is cases involving parents, children, siblings, extended family, and the like.

When an offender was present upon police arrival at the scene, an arrest was made about 69% of the time. The most common charge for those arrested was aggravated assault (48%), followed by simple assault (13%) and violation of an EPO (7%). About 31% of the cases involved other charges such as terrorist type of threatening, criminal mischief, harassment, disorderly conduct, and weapons charges. The majority of offenders were charged with one offense; however, roughly 19% were charged with two crimes, and slightly more than 12% were charged with three or more. In most instances, the victim was injured (63%), and the injury was visible to police in about half of all cases (51%). In addition, medical attention was accepted by the victim in slightly more than 16% of all cases. The primary weapon used by domestic violence offenders was a hand, foot, or both (75%), and only a few cases involved a gun (3%) or a knife (5%). The most common injuries for domestic violence cases were soreness or redness (25%), bruises or swelling (18%), cuts (13%), and scratches (12%). (See Table 4.2.)

For arrests both before and after mandatory domestic violence training, the police officers' decision to arrest appears to be associated with similar, if not identical, factors. First, the rate of arrest before and after the police training was similar. Arrest resulted in 68.7% of all cases occurring before the police underwent the mandatory training and in 69.9% of all cases after training. At first, it may appear odd that the percentage of cases resulting in arrest did not increase significantly after the officers received training on domestic violence, but this rate of arrest is higher than that reported in most studies. For

TABLE 4.2   Situational Variables

Variable	N	(%)
Arrest (N = 1,321)		
Yes	916	69.3
No	405	30.7
Initial charge (N = 1,100)		
Aggravated assault	633	47.8
Violation of EPO	79	7.2
Simple assault	147	13.4
Terroristic threatening	17	1.5
Harassment	4	0.4
Criminal mischief	8	0.7
Disorderly conduct	6	0.5
Weapons charge	2	0.2
Other	116	10.5
No charge	88	8.0
Number of charges (N = 1,101)		
None	88	8.0
One	89	61.1
Two	90	18.7
Three or more	134	2.2
Victim injured (N = 1,320)		
Yes	825	62.5
No	495	37.5
Injury visible (N = 1,311)		
Yes	672	51.3
No	639	48.7
Medical attention (N = 1,308)		
Yes	212	16.2
No	786	60.1
Refused	310	23.7
Weapon used (N = 1,098)		
Hands or feet	822	74.9
Knife	59	5.4
Gun	30	2.7

continued

TABLE 4.2   (*continued*)

Variable	N	(%)
Weapon used (N = 1,098) (*continued*)		
Other	89	8.1
None	98	8.9
Nature of injury (N = 1,142)		
Soreness or redness	286	25.0
Bruises or swelling	287	17.7
Cuts	145	12.7
Scratches	135	11.8
Bruises and cuts	22	1.9
Bites	15	1.3
Broken bones	7	0.6
Other	30	2.6
No injury	300	26.3

example, Jones and Belknap (1999) note that arrest rates range from 4% to 12% in jurisdictions without pro-arrest policies and that rates are slightly higher (15–30%) in jurisdictions with pro-arrest polices.

Table 4.3 illustrates the results of the chi-square analysis of individual and situation factors and their relationship to police officers' decisions to arrest. Police are more likely to arrest, both before and after training, when the victim is injured. More than 85% (before) and 86% (after) of the cases result in arrest when the victim is injured, as compared with 39% (before) and 43% (after) of the cases in which the victim is not injured. Further, the decision to arrest also is associated with the visibility of the injury. Arrest occurs in roughly half of all domestic violence cases when an injury is not visible; however, arrest, both before and after training, occurs in at least 86% of the cases with visible injuries.

Another factor associated with the police officers' decision to arrest that was evident both before and after the domestic violence training was the use of drugs and/or alcohol. More than 80% of the cases involving alcohol resulted in arrest. This relationship was evident for both before and after groups. A similar association was found with drug use in that more than 75% of the cases involving drug use resulted in arrest. In addition, arrest was more likely when the police officers were uncertain about the use of drugs and/or alcohol than when they were certain that either drugs or alcohol was not involved.

A third factor consistently related to the likelihood of arrest was the existence of an outstanding emergency protective order. The data for both before and after training indicate that arrest occurs in 88% (before) and 94% (after) of the cases where a protective order has been issued. Although on some levels this finding seems obvious, the increase is notable in that it may indicate changes in attitudes of police regarding the utility of protective orders. Perhaps

TABLE 4.3   Factors Associated with Cases Resulting in Arrest

Variable	Before N (%)	After N (%)
Victim race		
Nonwhite	248 (68.3)	244 (73.1)
White	204 (69.2)	217 (66.8)
Victim gender[3]		
Female	349 (69.5)	369 (72.5)
Male	103 (66.0)	93 (61.2)
Offender race		
Nonwhite	269 (69.0)	268 (72.6)
White	183 (68.3)	194 (66.4)
Offender gender[2]		
Female	98 (59.8)	111 (65.7)
Male	354 (71.7)	351 (71.3)
Victim injured[1]		
No	95 (39.4)	108 (43.0)
Yes	357 (85.6)	351 (86.5)
Injury visible[1]		
No	153 (49.4)	173 (53.1)
Yes	296 (86.5)	282 (86.0)
Weapon		
Hands/feet	331 (76.6)	311 (80.4)
Gun/knife/other	70 (81.2)	69 (75.3)
Drugs involved[1]		
No	156 (57.4)	197 (62.7)
Yes	29 (76.3)	24 (75.0)
Unknown	203 (76.6)	150 (78.1)
Alcohol involved[1]		
No	105 (51.2)	138 (57.5)
Yes	212 (80.6)	221 (81.3)
Unknown	111 (74.0)	74 (71.2)
Outstanding protective order[1]		
No	385 (66.4)	380 (66.3)
Yes	55 (88.7)	74 (93.7)
Children present		
No	198 (67.8)	221 (69.9)
Yes	187 (68.2)	189 (69.0)
Caller status		
Victim	239 (66.6)	246 (67.2)
Other	203 (71.0)	203 (73.3)

[1]$p < .01$ for both before and after training cases
[2]$p < .01$ for before training cases only
[3]$p < .01$ for after training cases only

after training, officers were more knowledgeable about departmental policies and state laws regarding emergency protective orders and thus more likely to (1) make efforts to determine if an EPO was previously issued and (2) take action (i.e., arrest) if an EPO was in effect.

Thus far, three factors were consistently related to the likelihood of arrest for cases occurring before, as well as after, officers underwent domestic violence training: victim injury, existence of an EPO, and drug and alcohol use. This pattern failed to emerge when we examined other variables of interest, with the exception of gender of both the victim and offender. An examination of the victim's gender reveals that, before training, 69.5% of the cases involving women victims and 66% of the cases involving male victims resulted in arrest—a difference that failed to achieve statistical significance. However, after the police completed training, the rate of arrest in cases with male victims is much l[ower tha]n that for female victims. For those cases processed after the training, only 61.2% [of ca]ses with male victims resulted in arrest, whereas 72.5% of the cases with female v[ictims r]esulted in arrest. In essence, the rate for male victims declined while the rate f[or fema]le victims increased ($X^2 = 7.116$; $p < .01$).

A similar pattern emerges when the offender's gender is examine[d. More] than 71% of the cases involving male offenders resulted in arrest for cases proces[sed bef]ore police underwent training, while only 59.8% of cases involving female offe[nders r]esulted in arrest. This difference was less notable and failed to achieve statistica[l significa]nce for the cases processed after police completed training. The rate of arrest for [male offe]nders was the same as the rate for the pretraining cases (71%); however, the rate [of arrest]t for cases involving female offenders increased from less than 60% to 65.7% ($X^2 = 8.113$; $p < .01$). Thus, differences existing between the rate of arrest for male and female offenders before the officers underwent training were less pronounced for cases occurring after training— officers were arresting more women. At this point, it is premature to suggest that this increase is due to dual arrest practices of police or an actual increase in female offending; however, both explanations clearly warrant further examination.

CONCLUSIONS

The findings suggest that arrest decisions in Kentucky are related to many of the factors found in previous studies, with minor variations. In the current study, police officers' decisions to arrest were related to the use of drugs or alcohol, a history of conflict between the offender and the victim (e.g., issuance of EPO), and the presence of a visible injury. This finding parallels the findings of other studies and suggests that when violence is defined as "serious" by the police, an arrest may be more likely. Also, the higher rates of arrest for incidents involving drug or alcohol use may indicate that officers' concerns about the potential for an escalation in violence may prompt an arrest. The relationship between the existence of a previously issued emergency protective order and arrest is less straightforward. On one hand, police may be more likely to arrest when an EPO has been issued because they have a duty to do so. On the other hand, the higher rate of arrest for incidents that do not involve EPOs may be due to an increased awareness among officers of the potential for escalation of abuse over the course of the victim–offender relationship (Morton, Runyan, Moracco, & Butts, 1998). In this case, the police would be acting as intervention agents by attempting to deter or at least delay subsequent violence. Unfortunately, an

analysis of this type would require substantial additions to the current data and is beyond the scope of this chapter

The findings related to the gender of both the offender and the victim clearly warrant additional study. Researchers have noted a recent practice among police officers of arresting both the offender and the victim. Dual arrests result when both the victim and the offender are arrested, regardless of the circumstances of the violent incident (Martin, 1997). The dual arrest appears to provide officers with a means of resolving the current situation but fails to provide the victim with any sense of empowerment or resolution. Instead, the victim and offender are temporarily disengaged, and the potential for continued and possibly more lethal violence remains. Clearly, the process of dual arrest requires considerable examination to ensure that pro-arrest policies of police are not simply providing a quick-fix response to domestic violence by arresting both parties.

In sum, this study examined the changes in arrest patterns for domestic violence cases. It appears that officers' decisions to arrest remained fairly stable despite the efforts to increase arrests and to sensitize officers to the dynamics of domestic violence. However, the training may have a more substantial impact on later stages of the criminal justice process; that is, it could be that the effects of the training are most evident in the prosecution and sentencing of these cases. Perhaps officers, while maintaining the traditional approach to arrest, altered their methods of collecting evidence to build cases against the offender that would be based on more than the victim's statement. The domestic violence training, while including a thorough review of departmental policies and existing domestic violence laws, also included a substantial amount of information regarding the prosecution of domestic violence cases. Indeed, the final analysis must include an outcome measure of conviction rates and factors associated with successful convictions. Also, this study examined only those cases where the offender was present at the scene when police arrived and does not include data regarding subsequent arrests made by the police. The inclusion of these data would provide a more precise and complete understanding of the impact of the domestic violence training.

DISCUSSION QUESTIONS

1. Describe the two main issues regarding the relationship between police arrest decisions and Kentucky's multiagency approach to domestic violence.

2 Discuss the effects of mandatory arrest and pro-arrest domestic violence policies and/or laws on sentencing and recidivism.

3. Why is police discretion to arrest domestic violent offenders considered to be a serious criminal justice problem?

4. Discuss and evaluate the key components of the multidisciplinary approach to domestic violence. What are the pros and cons of such a proposal as set forth?

5. Discuss the issue of dual arrest. What are the advantages or disadvantages of this "quick-fix"?

REFERENCES

BACHMAN, R., & COKER, A. (1995). Police involvement in domestic violence: The interactive effects of victim injury, offender's history of violence, and race. *Violence and Victims, 10*(2), 91–106.

BELKNAP, J. (1996). *The invisible woman: Gender, crime, and justice.* Belmont, CA: Wadsworth.

BERK, S.F., & LOSEKE, D. (1981). "Handling" family violence: Situational determinants of police arrest in domestic disturbances. *Law and Society Review, 15*(2), 317–346.

BOURG, S., & STOCK, H. (1994). A review of domestic violence arrest statistics in a police department using a pro-arrest policy: Are pro-arrest policies enough? *Journal of Family Violence, 9*(2), 177–189.

BUZAWA, E., & AUSTIN, T. (1993). Determining police response to domestic violence victims. *American Behavioral Scientist, 36*(5), 610–623.

BUZAWA, E., & BUZAWA, C. (1985). Legislative trends in the criminal justice response to domestic violence. In A. Lincoln & M. Straus (Eds.), *Crime in the family* (pp. 134–147). Springfield, IL: Charles C. Thomas.

BUZAWA, E., HOTELING, G., & KELIN, A. (1999). What happens when a reform works? The need to study unanticipated consequences of mandatory processing of domestic violence. *Journal of Police and Criminal Psychology, 13*(2), 43–54.

EREZ, E. (1986). Intimacy, violence, and the police. *Human Relations, 39*(3), 265–281.

FEDER, L. (1997). Domestic violence and police response in a pro-arrest jurisdiction. *Women and Criminal Justice, 8*(4), 79–98.

FEDER, L. (1998). Police handling of domestic and nondomestic calls: Is there a case for discrimination? *Crime and Delinquency, 44*(2), 335–349.

FEDER, L. (1999). Police handling of domestic violence calls: An overview and further investigation. *Women and Criminal Justice, 10*(2), 49–67.

FERRARO, K. (1989). Policing women battering. *Social Problems, 36*(1), 61–74.

FYFE, J., KLINGER, D., & FLAVIN, J. (1997). Differential police treatment of male-on-female spousal violence. *Criminology, 35*(3), 455–473.

JONES, D.A., & BELKNAP, J. (1999). Police responses to battering in a progressive pro-arrest jurisdiction. *Justice Quarterly, 16*(2), 249–273

KANE, R. (1999). Patterns of arrest in domestic violence encounters: Identifying a police decision-making model. *Journal of Criminal Justice, 27*(1), 65–79.

LANZA-KADUCE, L., GREENLEAF, R., & DONAHUE, M. (1995). Trickle-up report writing: The impact of a proarrest policy for domestic disturbances. *Justice Quarterly, 12*(3), 525–542.

MARTIN, M. (1997). Double your trouble: Dual arrest in family violence. *Journal of Family Violence, 12*(2), 139–157.

MIGNON, S., & HOLMES, W. (1995). Police responses to mandatory arrest laws. *Crime and Delinquency, 41*(4), 430–442.

MILLER, S. (1989). Unintended side effects of pro-arrest policies and their race and class implications for battered women: A cautionary note. *Criminal Justice Policy Review, 3*(3), 299–317.

MORTON, E., RUNYAN, C., MORACCO, K., & BUTTS, J. (1998). Partner homicide–suicide involving female homicide victims: A population-based study in North Carolina. *Violence and Victims, 13*(2), 91–106.

RASCHE, C. (1995). Minority women and domestic violence: The unique dilemmas of battered women of color. In B. Price & N. Sokoloff (Eds.), *The criminal justice system and women* (pp. 246–261). New York: McGraw-Hill.

ROBINSON, A. (1999). Conflicting consensus: Public reaction to a domestic violence pro-arrest policy. *Women and Criminal Justice, 10*(3), 95–120.

SHERMAN, L., & BERK, R. (1984). The specific deterrent effects of arrest for domestic assault. *American Sociological Review, 49,* 261–272.

SMITH, D., & KLEIN, J. (1984). Police control of interpersonal disputes. *Social Problems, 31*(4), 468–481.

SMITH, D., & VISHER, C. (1981). Street-level justice: Situational determinants of police arrest decisions. *Social Problems, 29*(2), 167–177.

WAALAND, P., & KEELEY, S. (1985). Police decision making in wife abuse: The impact of legal and extralegal factors. *Law and Human Behavior, 9*(4), 355–366.

WEBSDALE, N. (1998). *Rural woman battering and the criminal justice system: An ethnography.* Thousand Oaks, CA: Sage.

5

Where Is Mayberry?

Community-Oriented Policing and Officers of Color

Wilson R. Palacios

This chapter examines how proponents of community-oriented policing (COP) have failed to assess empirically the impact, if any, of recent hiring practices involving applicants of color. Although some scholars (Feinman, 1994; Miller, 1998, 1999) have explored the issue of gender and policing, for the most part, COP scholars have ignored the social construction of applicants' race and ethnicity (Holdaway, 1997). In doing so, many in the field of police studies have missed the opportunity to examine the intersection of police officers' racial–ethnic identity, gender, allegiance to the police subculture, and the communities they serve. Such a contextualization would be appropriate, because there is a concerted effort throughout many law enforcement jurisdictions to hire more police officers of color.

Law enforcement recruitment patterns are changing (Reaves & Goldberg, 2000), and local and state jurisdictions and agencies are attempting to fill their ranks with law enforcement officers of color. However, this "token" hiring mechanism has been implemented under the assumption that greater racial–ethnic representation within the ranks of law enforcement will improve the profession's public image with communities of color. For many in law enforcement, the COP model represents the ideal recruitment strategy for repairing such historically strained relationships. However, in the rush to improve such relationships, the policing profession has neglected the antagonisms between police officers of color and the general law enforcement community. The time has come for some sensitive but important questions to be asked.

How a COP officer's race-ethnicity and gender affect the manner in which he or she works in communities of color is an important issue. Little is known about how Latino police officers manage to traverse their working and cultural identities in the field. In addition, little is known about the similarities and/or differences between Latino, African American/black, Asian, and Native American male and female police officers. For instance, does one's cultural identity supersede one's professional reference group? How do such police officers invoke masculine and feminine scripts, such as machismo, in their policing behavior? Furthermore, although it is known that there are within group differences in overall language and behavioral patterns among people of color, exactly how these differences manifest themselves in policing behavior is not known.

Another issue is whether there are attitudinal differences between African American police officers hired in the past 15 years and those officers hired prior to the implementation of COP. Scholars and practitioners must accept the fact that contemporary police officers will more often be people of color. Therefore, the need for a new theoretical and research framework becomes even more critical as police jurisdictions across the nation blindly rush to fill job vacancies.

A NEW APPROACH TO POLICING THE COMMUNITY

Society is experiencing a new era in policing, and COP is the hallmark of this law enforcement transition. As Cordner (1997) noted, "Community policing has evolved from a few small foot patrol studies to the preeminent reform agenda of modern policing" (p. 451). This model emphasizes service, community, and localized problem solving over the traditional incident-driven approach to policing (see Kelling & Moore, 1988; Peak & Glensor, 1996). Guided by the premise of maintaining order (Kelling & Wilson, 1982; Skogan, 1990), COP depends on the ability of the police, as an organization, to reorient operations, maintain a geographic focus, and tailor preventive measures to local problems, such as gang graffiti, abandoned houses, loitering, truancy, street-level drug dealing, and public intoxication (Cordner, 1997; Kelling & Coles, 1996).

Therefore, according to Kelling and Coles (1996), "Community policing must necessarily take a variety of forms, since individual communities or even districts within cities will emphasize different elements to reflect discrete local needs, traditions, and values" (p. 158). Kelling and Coles outlined the basic fundamentals of community policing as follows:

1. Belief in the broad function of policing (maintaining public order)
2. The view of citizens as collaborators with law enforcement officers
3. The use of mentoring rather than supervising of police personnel in the field
4. An emphasis on specific tactical patrols and assignments
5. Assistance to citizens in solving problems
6. An increase in the overall quality of life for citizens

So, whether as a process by which crime control is shared with the community or as a means of developing communication with local residents and community leaders (Fielding, 1995), community policing represents a significant departure from traditional reactive policing (see Kennedy & Moore, 1997; Miller, 1999). In the end, while COP remains many things to many people, its working paradigm focuses on citizen input, problem-oriented policing, and personalized service (Cordner, 1997).

The impetus for this new approach to policing evolved from public antagonisms between law enforcement officers and the communities in which they serve. The traditional model of policing alienated local residents, especially those in communities of color (Kelling, 1988; Kelling & Moore, 1988; Kennedy & Moore, 1997; Miller, 1999; Peak & Glensor, 1996). Kennedy and Moore (1997) suggested that, "despite overall coherence and commonsense validity, this reform strategy has come to be viewed over the past ten to fifteen years with increasing dissatisfaction by both practitioners and scholars" (p. 472).

The COP model was designed as a countermeasure to the "reform strategy" of policing. With its focus on service, this policing alternative emphasized accountability by initiating programmatic and tactical changes, thereby empowering local residents, businesses, and frontline patrol officers. By adopting this friendly style of policing, the police were able to forge a positive working relationship with the community. Sparrow (1988) noted that "the concept of community policing envisages a police department striving for an absence of crime and disorder and concerned with, and sensitive to, the quality of life in the community" (p. 1). Moreover, such an approach to policing would both directly and indirectly help communities achieve long-term goals, such as reduction of disorder, fear, and crime (Miller, 1999). The COP model represented a theoretical shift, as well as a working paradigm, in which both crime control and prevention are priorities (Kelling & Moore, 1988).

The philosophy, vernacular, and method made the COP model extremely popular. All individuals, regardless of race, ethnicity, class, and gender, want to live in safer communities without fear. They just want to proceed with the task of living and forging productive and successful lives for themselves and their significant others. According to a report by the Council of Economic Advisers (1998), "A safe environment is important for stable childhood development, good health, and successful involvement in education and the job market. No single summary measure can capture the difficulties crime creates in the lives of individuals and communities" (p.50). Therefore, in theory, the COP model has broad appeal.

The popularity of the COP model (see Fielding, 1995; Friedman, 1992; Skogan & Hartnett, 1997) was situated in this common desire. Its approach allowed the model to crescendo (Manning, 1997) into what many police researchers see as a revolutionary approach to policing (Cordner, 1997; Kelling, 1988) and led some (Kennedy & Moore, 1997) to envision it as a police movement, although the exact nature of the movement actually depends on whom one asks (Zhao & Thurman, 1997).

Since the passage of the 1994 Crime Control Act, many local police jurisdictions and municipalities have incorporated some aspects of the *movement* into their hiring decisions, departmental restructuring, resource allocations, and community-enhancement efforts (Kennedy & Moore, 1997). Manning (1997) referred to COP as a "presentational strategy" in that no one department is able to adopt all the ideal strategies of the model. Moreover, what ultimately made COP an attractive alternative to the "professional-strategic model" was that it was touted as a viable mechanism for repairing historically strained relationships between the police and communities of color (Peak & Glensor, 1996; Walker, Spohn, & DeLone, 2000; Williams & Murphy, 1990).

POLICING COMMUNITIES OF COLOR

Historically, communities of color and law enforcement have had a paradoxical relationship (Moore & Pachon, 1985; Williams & Murphy, 1990). Although they are most in need of police services, communities of color also remain the most alienated (DeGeneste & Sullivan, 1997; Moore & Pachon, 1985). For many people of color, the police represent a force that has traditionally sustained discriminatory and racist social policies (Williams & Murphy, 1990). According to Williams and Murphy (1990), "Frustrated and angry, many blacks came to see the police as symbolizing the entire system, those institutions and resources that had been so unresponsive to their needs" (p. 11). This feeling of conflict and alienation is not limited to police interactions. Despite 30 years of progressive social justice programs (such as Affirmative Action, DARE, and Head Start), the lives of many residents are situated in a social environment that appears to be more racially and ethnically segregated (Massey and Denton, 1993) and violent (Walker, Spohn, & DeLone , 2000) than in the past.

Massey and Denton (1993) suggested that "despite the optimism of the early 1970s, a comprehensive look at trends and patterns of racial segregation within large metropolitan areas in the ensuing decade provides little evidence that the residential color line has diminished in importance" (p. 81). Furthermore, although the country can be a bit more optimistic about the lowering crime rate (Rand, 1998), communities of color persistently endure a higher rate of criminal victimization (Bastian & Taylor, 1994).

A review of trend data (1973–1997) revealed that the rates of property crime for African American households consistently exceed those for white households (see Council of Economic Advisers, 1998; Walker et al., 2000). Moreover, trend data on personal victimization (robbery and aggravated assault) reveals higher rates for African Americans: "For the two most serious (non-murder) violent crimes, the likelihood of victimization is much higher for African Americans than for whites" (Walker et al., 2000, p. 32). According to the National Crime Victimization Survey, the rate of robbery for African Americans is three times the rate for whites—14 versus 4.8 per 1,000—and the rate for Latinos is about 43% higher than that for non-Hispanics (Walker et al., 2000).

The rate of victimization is even more astounding for deaths by homicide. The stark reality is that a child is murdered every two hours in the United States, and "the risk of being murdered by a gun has increased for all young people since the mid-1980s" (Children's Defense Fund, 1994, p. 64). Homicides are the second leading cause of fatalities among adolescents in the United States, accounting for 22% of all deaths for youth ages 14 to 25 in 1991 (Sells & Blum, 1996). The homicide rate for males is 400% higher than for females (see Council of Economic Advisers, 1998). Furthermore, African American males face the greatest likelihood of death by homicide (114.9 per 100,000) when compared to whites (see Children's Defense Fund, 1994; Walker et al., 2000), followed by Latinos (48.9), American Indians (26.6), Asians (15.6), and non-Hispanic whites (6.4) (Council of Economic Advisers, 1998).

Moreover, homicide is the leading cause of death for African American males and females aged 15 to 24—123.1 per 100,000 (Bastian & Taylor, 1994; Council of Economic Advisers, 1998; Sells & Blum, 1996). The homicide rate is more than 700% higher for African American youths than for white youths (Sells & Blum, 1996). This trend continues despite the national downward trend in both property and personal victimization rates (Council of Economic Advisers, 1998).

In addition to violent crime, communities of color have had to contend with major shifts in residential migration patterns in the past 20 years. These shifts have forced many to reconsider the "black–white dichotomy" (see Hawkins, 1995; McKean, 1996; Myers, Cintron, & Scarborough, 1994) that is normally used to situate the study of race and criminality in this country. What is often rather difficult for some to accept is that the U.S. population is changing along racial and ethnic lines. Large cities, such as New York, Los Angeles, Houston, and Miami, are faced with a burgeoning number of foreign-born residents (DeGeneste & Sullivan, 1997; Vargas, 1997). For example, in 1994, Miami was 50% Latino, and the remaining residents were African Americans and whites (21% and 29%, respectively) (DeGeneste & Sullivan, 1997).

The proportion of Latinos in the United States has increased by 50%, and "through high birth rates and immigration, Latinos are projected to surpass African Americans as America's largest racial minority population" (Vargas, 1997, p. 3). The estimated 29.7 million people of Hispanic origin represent 11.1% of the U.S. population (Reed & Ramirez, 1997). This Latinization of America (Rodriguez, 1996; Vargas, 1997), particularly in cities such as Miami and Houston, has created tension and conflict between competing racial and ethnic groups that law enforcement officers are ultimately brought in to deal with (DeGeneste & Sullivan, 1997).

Southern California has also seen the effects of "acculturation in reverse" (Padilla, 1995). According to a 1990 study (DeGeneste & Sullivan, 1997), nearly 40% of the residents of the city of Los Angeles were foreign born, and Latinos and Asians constituted half the city's population; furthermore, the population of South Central Los Angeles was about 60% Latino and 35% African American. DeGeneste and Sullivan (1997) added that "by 2010 California will become one of the world's most ethnically varied places. Nonwhites will become the majority" (p. 2). Vargas (1997) stated that "a third of the new immigrants entering the United States through California makes this state America's new Ellis Island" (p. 2).

Such significant demographic transformations have occurred within a weakening and displaced infrastructure (Carnoy, 1994; Council of Economic Advisers, 1998; Wilson, 1996). For many racial and ethnic minorities, reduced access to medical and mental health care, housing, education, employment, and job training (Council of Economic Advisers, 1998) translates into a social reality that is demoralizing and alienating, to say the least. These social dislocations or "quiet riots" (Harris & Wilkins, 1988) engender conflict, racial and ethnic antagonisms, exclusion, social segregation, and xenophobia (DeGeneste & Sullivan, 1997; Moore & Pachon, 1985; Portes & Bach, 1985). As a result, cultural and ethnic identity has taken on a whole new meaning, as various groups compete for limited resources (see Foner, 1987; Portes & Bach, 1985).

Racial and ethnic consciousness becomes heightened and leads to "ethnic resilience" (Portes, 1995), and being labeled Jamaican, Haitian, Cuban, Mexican, Ecuadorian, Colombian, or African American thus takes on an economic, political, and social meaning, such as "situational Latino ethnicity," which Padilla (1995) succinctly defined as "an intergroup identity reflecting a consciousness such as language and an awareness of being different from other social groups in the United States" (p. 441).

Unfortunately, in the midst of scarcity, the police are often at the intersection of individual and group needs, existing racial and ethnic antagonisms, economic inequities, and political strife. Under these conditions, community policing takes on a whole new meaning for both the line officer and the community resident. Williams and Murphy (1990) argued that "unfortunately, our police, and all of our other institutions, must contend with many bitter legacies from that larger history. The history of American policing strategies cannot be separated from the history of the Nation as a whole" (p. 13).

NEW WINE IN AN OLD BOTTLE: COMMUNITY POLICING AND COMMUNITIES OF COLOR

The policing community is quick to justify its existence by professing to be the "frontline" defense in the fight against crime. At one level, this statement is correct. In particular, for many people of color, the police are the only government representatives they have or will ever come in contact with. However, what the police must come to terms with and respond to is that, at the least, America is changing demographically (higher rates of immigration coupled with a younger population of specific racial and ethnic groups). This change is unavoidable, and the manner in which police officers *do* policing must change accordingly. Policing in the new millennium requires police personnel to confront both directly and indirectly many of the social stressors previously outlined. "Only by acknowledging a primary role in preventing and mediating conflict in the community can police begin to remediate long-standing and emerging tensions" (DeGeneste & Sullivan, 1997, p. 15).

Initially, the COP model was considered to be a viable law enforcement tool for redefining relationships with communities of color (Peak & Glensor, 1996). This was essentially the basic appeal of the model (Williams & Murphy, 1990) and, as was previously argued, its overall "presentational strategy" (Manning, 1997). However, despite more than 20 years of numerous COP initiatives, such relationships have improved only moderately. For instance, the continual use of "perceptual cues" or "racial hoaxes" (Russell, 1998; Skolnick, 1994) by law enforcement personnel have sustained, if not increased, the volatility between the police and communities of color (Escobar, 1999; Flowers, 1988; Jackson, 1994; Peak & Glensor, 1996).

Furthermore, the use of such perceptual markers creates a working culture that inevitably supports "police racism"—a complex and situational phenomenon arising from different situations and varying according to spatial and temporal events that often occur in police work (Chan, 1997). Despite the popularity of the COP model and its basic tenets of community empowerment, police accountability, operational reform, and service, there remains a working police culture that informally supports the old ways of policing (Burris & Whitney, 1999; Chan, 1997; Miller, 1999). "Regardless of rules and guidelines, inappropriate behavior on the streets still occurs" (Williams & Murphy, 1990, p. 12).

The tragedy of Amadou Diallo and the storm of protest against the New York City Police Department for this and lesser known cases (see Vives, 1999) serve as an unfortunate reminder of what the COP model was supposed to curtail. Roane (2000) noted that police jurisdictions from New Orleans to Newark have modeled New York City's aggressive policing style in the hopes of duplicating that city's dramatic decrease in overall crime (for a review of the New York model, see Silverman, 1999). But such popularity has not been without fallout. "As officers have been pushed to make more stops, the claims of police abuse, the lawsuits, and the investigations into whether cops unfairly target minorities have mounted" (Roane, 2000, p. 25). This type of alleged police misconduct is not limited to New York City (Mangat, 1999; White, 1999).

Allegations of racial profiling have been made in New Jersey, California, Illinois, and Florida (Bhatia, 1999; House, 1999; Miller, 1999), and the Los Angeles Police Department's Rampart Division became embroiled in the largest corruption scandal in that department's history (Roane, 2000). Harris (1997) contended that "the stopping of black drivers, just to see what officers can find, has become so common in some places that this practice has its own name—driving while black" (p. 546). However, this practice is certainly not limited to African Americans, as Latino motorists in New Jersey have learned (see Davis, 1997).

Davis (1997) stated that "when people of color experience injustices that are tolerated and even sanctioned by courts and other criminal justice officials, they develop distrust and disrespect for the justice system. The use of race-based pretextual traffic stops tears a hole in the fabric of our constitution by allowing discriminatory behavior to invade the criminal justice system" (p. 442). Similarly, Escobar (1999) noted that "the Los Angeles Police Department's increasing focus on a linkage between race and criminality has resulted in continual tensions between that police department and the Mexican American community" (p. 132). Although many of these cases have been made public and hence may lead to some police reform measures, law enforcement's credibility will remain tenuous within communities of color unless true change occurs from within.

Furthermore, such cases only illustrate why such zero-tolerance policies and/or "hyper law enforcement" practices perpetuate the continuation of police–resident antagonisms, especially in communities of color (Miller, 1999; Scheingold, 1999; Skogan, 1990). Scheingold (1999) contended that "the broader vision of community policing must incorporate a complex understanding of the composition of all neighborhoods, one that transcends the easy divisions of good and bad, the manageable and the intractable" (p. 189).

Community policing programs have generated years of federally funded research and the allocation of extra funds for hiring additional police personnel. They also allowed local law enforcement departments to purchase sophisticated police "hardware" (e.g., modern telecommunications equipment, patrol cars, and crime-mapping software and computers) and evaluate local policing initiatives (e.g., truancy programs and curfew ordinances). They have also served as an influential political platform by creating the National Institute of Justice Office of Community Oriented Policing Services. However, community policing has failed to build a constituency base in communities of color (Duffee, Fluellen, & Roscoe, 1999; Scheingold, 1999).

RACE AND ETHNICITY AND THE COP MODEL: A FORCED MARRIAGE

Although there are exceptions (see Carter, 1983; Perez-McCluskey, 1998; Williams & Murphy, 1990), the issue of race and ethnicity has been conspicuously limited in any discussions of the COP model. For instance, a December 1996 meeting of a consortium of police scholars and practitioners in Washington, D.C., on methods of designing and implementing measures of police organizational performance (Langworthy, 1999) covered a variety of key areas:

1. The impact domain—how intended police effects on the environment can be measured
2. The process domain—how the police can know if they are doing their work as they should
3. The community assessment domain—how the performance of the police can be monitored by the public
4. Organizational health—how police departments can determine if their employees are satisfied with their work
5. Community context—how police organizations can monitor changes in the work environment that impede or promote their ability to achieve organizational goals

For each area identified by the participants (see Langworthy, 1999), a multitude of performance indicators, such as the following, were included:

• Local arrest and recidivism statistics
• Resident satisfaction surveys
• Local incarceration statistics
• Victimization surveys
• Survey and observational measures of disorder
• Assessment of citizens' encounters with the police
• Quality of life index
• Police integrity index and instruments

The obvious benefit of this meeting was the identification of a variety of tangible performance measures to be used in empirically evaluating future community-based policing initiatives (Langworthy, 1999). However, there were few explicit discussions of race and ethnicity within any context.

The failure to address or situate the COP model within a racial and/or ethnic context was clearly out of step with the current hiring practices of local law enforcement departments (Bureau of Justice Statistics, 1999; Peak, 1997), the popularity of COP strategies (Dunham & Alpert, 1997), the continual problems between law enforcement and communities of color, and projections of a younger and larger Latino population by 2010 (Marger, 1997; Rodriguez, 1996). The only context in which race and/or ethnicity is ever considered is in the hiring process of law enforcement officers.

In the aggregate, the hiring of racial and ethnic minority and women police officers has received considerable attention in the literature (see Bayley, 1994; Felkenes, 1992; Hooper, 1992; Peak, 1997; Polombo & Demarais, 1992; Walker, 1983, 1985; Walker et al., 2000). According to a 1999 Bureau of Justice Statistics (BJS) report, racial and ethnic minorities, as an aggregate, constituted only 19% of the full-time sworn officers in sheriffs' departments in 1997. As a group, minority sheriffs' officers experienced a continual 3% increase in personnel between 1987 and 1997. African American and Latino officers experienced a marginal 2% increase in their ranks (Bureau of Justice Statistics, 1999).

As of June 1997, about 22% of the full-time sworn police personnel employed by local police departments were members of racial or ethnic minorities (Reaves & Goldberg, 2000). However, the BJS (1999) report did not provide within- or between-group comparisons of various minority law enforcement officers. In general, such federal reports present limited aggregate data on Latino and women police officers (Walker et al., 2000). Therefore, some commentators (e.g., Walker & Turner, 1992; Walker et al., 2000) have advocated the use of the Equal Employment Opportunity (EEO) Index as a better measure of such hiring efforts and of enhanced employment opportunities for racial and ethnic minority police officers than figures in the BJS and other federal reports.

The EEO Index compares the percentages of police officers from various minority groups with the percentages of these groups in the local population. The utility of the EEO Index is that it permits comparisons across police departments (Walker et al., 2000). When the EEO Index is used, police jurisdictions, such as the New York City Police Department, are forced to confront and explain sustained low levels of racial and ethnic minority representation within them. However, a perfect EEO Index of 1.00 is no guarantee of the absence or minimization of racial and ethnic tension between a community and law enforcement personnel (Walker et al., 2000).

At best, the EEO Index serves as an outcome measure of voluntary or court-mandated efforts to hire racial and ethnic minority law enforcement officers. However, in the context of sustained positive relations between the police and communities of color, such trend data do not account for the political, social, and cultural changes that affect both the macro and micro levels of policing behavior (Walker, 1985). To evaluate any measure of change, the policing profession must be able and willing to examine its own behavior, culture, and organizational history. In this regard, the COP model represents the most drastic paradigm shift in policing and an opportunity for a new kind of research. Contemporary researchers must apply a theoretical and research framework that highlights the changing context of the police subculture (the increase in racial and ethnic minorities and women throughout the ranks) and the response of the police, as an organization, to such changes in personnel.

Law enforcement officers of color, as subjects of scientific inquiry, have received little attention. Although there have been some exceptions (see Alex, 1969, 1976; Chan, 1997; Free, 1996; Georges-Abeyie, 1984; Holdaway, 1997; Polombo & Demarais, 1992; Walker, 1985), for the most part, contemporary research efforts have omitted this group from systematic study. The issue of gender and policing has received more research attention in the past ten years than the social construction of the race and ethnicity of law enforcement officers of color (Feinman, 1994; Martin & Jurik, 1996; Miller, 1998, 1999; Polombo & Demarais, 1992; Worden, 1993). The absence of such a theoretical and research framework seems to suggest that all is going well for these men and women. However, nothing can be further from the truth (see Brooks, 1999; Holdaway, 1997; Lee, 2000; Macey, 1999). Although concerted efforts have been made to hire law enforcement officers of color (see New York Voice, 1999), little empirical research has been conducted on the specific impact, if any, of such hiring and recruitment efforts on the police subculture and public perceptions (see Walker, 1985). Walker (1985) suggested using the following research questions to investigate such new employment patterns:

1. Is it even possible to speak of a police subculture?
2. How does the dominant group respond to the increasing presence of police officers of color?
3. What are the attitudinal and behavioral patterns of police officers of color?
4. How do police officers of color identify themselves in terms of race or gender?
5. Is there a common police outlook? Does it vary according to an officer's gender, race, and ethnicity?
6. How do police officers of color construct a working identity within their own group? Do all Latino police officers adopt the same sociocultural identity?
7. How will a larger Latino population affect recruitment and retention efforts in law enforcement? (pp. 565–566).

In addition to these questions, contemporary policing research must incorporate other research questions that reflect issues and themes specific to a police officer's racial and ethnic personal identity. For example, the African American police officer and the Latino police officer bring to the job qualitatively different political and personal histories with law enforcement. The need to study the social process of race and ethnicity construction as it relates to policing will become even more critical as new police officers are recruited largely from the same communities in which the chasm still exists.

CONCLUSION

It is all too common for policing scholars and practitioners to talk about racial and/or minority issues when there has been some type of public denouncement of police brutality. Before Amadou Diallo, the cases of Abner Louima and Rodney King served as grim reminders that despite modest improvements in the hiring of police officers of color in the past ten years, the police subculture still seems to support such unconscionable behavior. The typical "knee-jerk" reaction of just hiring more people of color as police officers is a limited approach. Policing scholars and practitioners must address the occupational culture of law enforcement and acknowledge and address the obvious dissension among the ranks. For instance, African American and Latino police officers have left the traditional police unions (such as the Police Benevolent Association) to join unions that they believe are representative of their professional needs (such as 100 Black Officers Who Care and the Latino Officers Association). New police recruits, who are hired under the auspices of COP, are more likely to be members of minority groups and, if successful, will be admitted into an organization that has had a tense history with communities of color. The question then is, can COP help repair the strained relationships between law enforcement and communities of color? It may be able to do so if policing scholars and practitioners adopt a theoretical and research framework that begins to address some of the difficult issues facing police officers of color.

DISCUSSION QUESTIONS

1. Discuss how community-oriented policing (COP) represents a "reform strategy" for the law enforcement community.

2. How can COP initiatives be implemented to achieve a true racial and ethnic representation among the rank and file of law enforcement?

3. Describe how recent demographic transformations have affected the law enforcement community.

4. Why is it important to situate the COP model within a racial and/or ethnic context?

5. Do you think there could be inherent differences between officers of color and the profession as a whole? Please explain.

REFERENCES

ALEX, N. (1969). *Black in blue: A study of the Negro policeman.* New York: Appleton-Century-Crofts.

ALEX, N. (1976). *New York cops talk back: A study of a beleaguered minority.* New York: Wiley.

BASTIAN, L., & TAYLOR, B. (1994). Young black male victims. In *Crime data brief: National crime victimization survey.* Washington, DC: U.S. Department of Justice, Office of Justice Programs.

BAYLEY, D. (1994). *Police for the future.* New York: Oxford University Press.

BHATIA, P. (1999, July). New Jersey governor admits police race bias. *India Abroad, 24*(42), 37–40.

BROOKS, C. (1999, December 8). Black and Latino officers fight for free speech: Giuliani gags the police. *New York Amsterdam News,* 1–2.

BUREAU OF JUSTICE STATISTICS. (1999). Sheriffs' departments, 1997. In *Bureau of Justice Statistics executive summary.* Washington, DC: U.S. Department of Justice, Office of Justice Programs.

BURRIS, J., & WHITNEY, C. (1999). *Blue vs. black: Let's end the conflict between cops and minorities.* New York: St. Martin's.

CARNOY, M. (1994). *Faded dreams: The politics and economics of race in America.* New York: Cambridge University Press.

CARTER, D. (1983). Hispanic interaction with the criminal justice system in Texas: Experiences, attitudes, and perceptions. *Journal of Criminal Justice, 11,* 213–228.

CHAN, J. (1997). *Changing police culture: Policing in a multicultural society.* New York: Cambridge University Press.

CHILDREN'S DEFENSE FUND. (1994). *The state of America's children: Yearbook 1994.* Washington, DC: Author.

CORDNER, G. (1997). Community policing: Elements and effects. In R. Dunham & G. Alpert (Eds.), *Critical issues in policing: Contemporary readings.* (3rd ed., pp. 451–468). Prospect Heights, IL: Waveland.

COUNCIL OF ECONOMIC ADVISERS. (1998). *Changing America: Indicators of social and economic well-being by race and Hispanic origin.* Washington, DC: The President's Initiative on Race.

DAVIS, A. (1997). Race, cops, and traffic stops. *University of Miami Law Review, 51,* 425–443.

DEGENESTE, H., & SULLIVAN, J. (1997). Policing a multicultural community. In *Police executive research forum.* Washington, DC: Police Executive Research Forum.

DUFFEE, D., FLUELLEN, R., & ROSCOE, T. (1999). Constituency building and urban community policing. In R. Langworthy (Ed.), *Measuring what matters: Proceedings from the policing research institute meetings* (pp. 91–119). Washington, DC: National Institute of Justice, Office of Community Oriented Policing Services.

DUNHAM, R., AND ALPERT, G. (1997). *Critical issues in policing: Contemporary readings.* (3rd ed., pp. 448–450). Prospect Heights, IL: Waveland.

ESCOBAR, E. (1999). *Race, police, and the making of a political identity: Mexican Americans and the Los Angeles Police Department, 1900–1945.* Berkelely: University of California Press.

FEINMAN, C. (1994). *Women and the criminal justice system* (3rd ed.). Westport, CT: Praeger.

FELKENES, G. (1992). Administration of affirmative action policies. In G. Felkenes & P. Unsinger (Eds.), *Diversity, affirmative action, and law enforcement* (pp. 25–37). Springfield, IL: Charles C. Thomas.

FIELDING, N. (1995). *Community policing.* Oxford, England: Clarendon.

FLOWERS, R.. (1988). *Minorities and criminality.* New York: Greenwood.

FONER, N. (1987). New immigrants and changing patterns. In N. Foner (Ed.), *New immigrants in New York* (pp. 12–32). New York: Columbia University Press.

FREE, M. (1996). *African Americans and the criminal justice system.* New York: Garland.

FRIEDMAN, R. (1992). *Community policing: Comparative perspectives and prospects.* New York: St. Martin's.

GEORGES-ABEYIE, D. (1984). *The criminal justice system and blacks.* New York: Clark Boardman.

HARRIS, D. (1997). Driving while black and all other traffic offenses: The Supreme Court and pretextual traffic stops. *Journal of Criminal Law and Criminology, 87,* 544–582.

HARRIS, F., & WILKINS, R. (1988). *Quiet riots: Race and poverty in the United States,* New York: Pantheon.

HAWKINS, D. (1995). Ethnicity, race, and crime: A review of selected studies. In D. Hawkins (Ed.), *Ethnicity, race, and crime: Perspectives across time and place* (pp. 11–45). Albany: State University of New York Press.

HOLDAWAY, S. (1997). Some recent approaches to the study of race in criminological research: Race as social process. *British Journal of Criminology, 37,* 383–400.

HOOPER, M. (1992). Case study of a departmental response to affirmative action mandates: The Los Angeles Police Department. In G. Felkenes & P. Unsinger (Eds.), *Diversity, affirmative action, and law enforcement* (pp. 115–136). Springfield, IL: Charles C. Thomas.

HOUSE, N. (1999, February). Black police officers' group calls attention to department problems. *Philadelphia Tribune, 115,* 1–6.

JACKSON, P. (1994). Constructions of criminality: Police-community relations in Toronto. *Antipode, 26,* 216–235.

KELLING, G. (1988). Police and communities: The quiet revolution. In *Perspectives on policing, 1.* Washington, DC: National Institute of Justice, U.S. Department of Justice.

KELLING, G, & COLES, C. (1996). *Fixing broken windows: Restoring order and reducing crime in our communities.* New York: Free Press.

KELLING, G., & MOORE, M. (1988). The evolving strategy of policing. In *Perspectives on policing, 4.* Washington, DC: National Institute of Justice, U.S. Department of Justice.

KELLING, G., & WILSON, J.Q. (1982). Broken windows: The police and neighborhood safety. *Atlantic Monthly, 249,* 29–38.

KENNEDY, D., & MOORE, M. (1997). Underwriting the risky investment in community policing: What social science should be doing to evaluate community policing. In R. Dunham & G. Alpert (Eds.), *Critical issues in policing: Contemporary readings.* (pp. 469–488). Prospect Heights, IL: Waveland.

LANGWORTHY, R. (1999). Measuring what matters: A policing research institute. In R. Langworthy (Ed.), *Measuring what matters: Proceedings from the policing research institute meetings,* (pp. 1–4). Washington, DC: National Institute of Justice, Office of Community Oriented Policing Services.

LEE, D. (2000, January 15). Behind the wall of silence: As the numbers of Asian American police officers continue to rise, they find themselves straddling the dual challenges of cultural turmoil within the station houses and mistrust from their communities. *Inside Asian America, 36–42.*

MACEY, P. (1999, November 29). "We're getting there": Senior cop optimistic on eve of black police group's first national conference. *The Voice, 885,* 1–4.

MANGAT, A. (1999, April 6). Police ask citizens of Seattle, "how are we doing": Community policing the subject of all-day forum. *Northwest Asian Weekly, 18,* 1–5.

MANNING, P. (1997). *Police work: The social organization of policing.* Prospect Heights, IL: Waveland.

MARGER, M. (1997). *Race and ethnic relations: American and global perspectives.* Belmont, CA: Wadsworth.

MARTIN, S., & JURIK, N. (1996). *Doing justice, doing gender: Women in law and criminal justice occupations.* Thousand Oaks, CA: Sage.

MASSEY, D., & DENTON, N. (1993). *American apartheid: Segregation and the making of the underclass.* Cambridge, MA: Harvard University Press.

MCKEAN, J. (1996). Race, ethnicity, and criminal justice. In J. Hendricks & B. Byers (Eds.), *Multicultural perspectives in criminal justice and criminology* (pp. 85–134). Springfield, IL: Charles C. Thomas.

MILLER, A. (1999, June 15). Politicians, police, community address D.W.B. in Miami–Dade. *Miami Times, 42,* 1–2.

MILLER, S. (1998). *Crime control and women: Feminist implications of criminal justice policy.* Thousand Oaks, CA: Sage.

MILLER, S. (1999). *Gender and community policing: Walking the talk.* Boston: Northeastern University Press.

MOORE, J., & PACHON, H. (1985). *Hispanics in the United States.* Englewood Cliffs, NJ: Prentice-Hall.

MYERS, L, CINTRON, M., & SCARBOROUGH, K. (1994). Latinos: The conceptualization of race. In J. Hendricks & B. Byers (Eds.), *Multicultural perspectives in criminal justice and criminology* (pp. 185–210). Springfield, IL: Charles C. Thomas.

NEW YORK VOICE. (1999, September 29). Police recruiting drive yields returns. *Harlem U.S.A., 41.* (26), 1–4.

PADILLA, F. (1995). On the nature of Latino ethnicity. In A.S. Lopez (Ed.), *Historical themes and identity: Mestizaje and labels* (pp. 438–452). New York: Garland.

PEAK, K. (1997). African Americans in policing. In R. Dunham & G. Alpert (Eds.), *Critical issues in policing: Contemporary readings* (3rd ed., pp. 356–362). Prospect Heights, IL: Waveland.

PEAK, K, & GLENSOR, R. (1996). *Community policing and problem solving: Strategies and practices.* Upper Saddle River, NJ: Prentice Hall.

PEREZ-MCCLUSKEY, C. (1998). *Policing the Latino community.* East Lansing, MI: Julian Samora Research Institute.

POLOMBO, B., & DEMARAIS, N. (1992). Attitudes, training, performance, and retention of female and minority police officers. In G. Felkenes & P. Unsinger (Eds.), *Diversity, affirmative action, and law enforcement* (pp. 57–90). Springfield, IL: Charles C. Thomas.

PORTES, A. (1995). The rise of ethnicity: Determinants of ethnic perceptions. In A.S. Lopez (Ed.), *Historical themes and identity: Mestizaje and labels* (pp. 423–437). New York: Garland.

PORTES, A., & BACH, R. (1985). *Latin journey: Cuban and Mexican immigrants in the United States.* Berkeley: University of California Press.

RAND, M. (1998, December). Criminal victimization, 1997. In *Bureau of Justice Statistics, National crime victimization survey.* Washington, DC: U.S. Department of Justice, Office of Justice Programs.

REAVES, B., & GOLDBERG, A. (2000, February). Local police departments, 1997. In *Bureau of Justice statistics report,* Washington, DC: U.S. Department of Justice, Office of Justice Programs.

REED, J., & RAMIREZ, R. (1997, March). The Hispanic population in the United States. In *Current population reports: Population characteristics.* Washington, DC: U.S. Department of Commerce, Economics and Statistics Administration, Bureau of the Census.

ROANE, K. (2000, February). Are police going too far? A New York shooting trial weights aggressive policing and civil rights. *U.S. News and World Report,* 25–27.

RODRIGUEZ, O. (1996, May). *The new immigrant Hispanic population: An integrated approach to preventing delinquency and crime.* Washington, DC: National Institute of Justice, U.S. Department of Justice, Office of Justice Programs.

RUSSELL, K. (1998). *The color of crime: Racial hoaxes, white fear, black protectionism, police harassment, and other macroaggressions.* New York: New York University Press.

SCHEINGOLD, S. (1999). Constituent expectations of the police and police expectations of constituents. In R. Langworthy (Ed.), *Measuring what matters: Proceedings from the policing research institute meetings* (pp. 183–192). Washington, DC: National Institute of Justice, Office of Community Oriented Policing Services.

SELLS, W.C., & BLUM, R. (1996). Current trends in adolescent health. In R.J. DiClemente, W.B. Hansen, & L.E. Ponton (Eds.), *Handbook of adolescent health risk behavior* (pp. 5–26). New York: Plenum.

SILVERMAN, E. (1999). *NYPD battles crime: Innovative strategies in policing.* Boston: Northeastern University Press.

SKOGAN, W. (1990). *Disorder and decline: Crime and the spiral of decay in American cities.* New York: Free Press.

SKOGAN, W., & HARTNETT, S. (1997). *Community policing: Chicago style.* New York: Oxford University Press.

SKOLNICK, J. (1994). *Justice without trial: Law enforcement in a democratic society* (3rd ed.). New York: Macmillan.

SPARROW, M. (1988). Implementing community policing. In *Perspectives on policing, 9.* Washington, DC: National Institute of Justice, U.S. Department of Justice,

VARGAS, Z. (1997). *Race matters and so does ethnicity and gender: Ethnic studies for an expanding American community.* East Lansing, MI: Julian Samora Research Institute.

VIVES, L. (1999, March 6). Police shooting of Diallo widens racial divide in New York. *Atlanta Inquirer, 38,* 1–3.

WALKER, S. (1983). Employment of black and Hispanic police officers. *Review of Applied Urban Research, 11,*(6), 1–6.

WALKER, S. (1985). Racial minority and female employment in policing: The implications of "glacial" change. *Crime and Delinquency, 31,* 555–572,

WALKER, S., SPOHN, C., & DELONE, M. (2000). *Race, ethnicity, and crime in America: The color of justice* (2nd ed.). Belmont, CA: Wadsworth.

WALKER, S., & TURNER, K.B. (1992). *A decade of modest progress: Employment of black and Hispanic police officers, 1983–1992.* Omaha: University of Nebraska at Omaha.

WHITE, T. (1999, September). Police discrimination case reopens: Federal funding in jeopardy. *Baltimore Afro-American, 108,* 1–4.

WILLIAMS, H., & MURPHY, P. (1990). The evolving strategy of police: A minority view. In *Perspectives on policing, 13.* Washington, DC: National Institute of Justice, U.S. Department of Justice.

WILSON, W.J. (1996). *When work disappears: The world of the new urban poor.* New York: Vintage.

WORDEN, A. (1993). The attitudes of women and men in policing: Testing conventional and contemporary wisdom. *Criminology, 31,* 203–242.

ZHAO, J., & THURMAN, Q. (1997). Community policing: Where are we now? *Crime and Delinquency, 43,* 345–357.

6

Women in Policing

Helen Taylor Greene

Policewomen can be an invaluable asset to modern law enforcement and their present
role should be broadened. Qualified women should be utilized in such important
staff service units as planning and research, training, intelligence, inspection, public
information, community relations, and as legal advisors. Women could also serve
such units as computer programming and laboratory analysis and communications. . . .
Finally, as more and more well qualified women enter the service, they could assume
administrative responsibilities.

President's Commission on Law Enforcement and
Administration of Justice, 1967, p. 125;
Cited in Miller, 1999, p. 85)

Throughout the history of policing, the number of women employed as either sworn officers or civilians has been low. Martin and Jurik (1996) state that policing is regarded as
men's work because of its association with crime, danger, and coercion. Thus, one of the
most important developments in criminal justice during the 20th century was the entrance
of women (and minorities) into the predominantly white male occupation of policing.
Today, there are more women in policing than ever before, their role has broadened,
and they have assumed administrative responsibilities, thus fulfilling the President's Commission recommendations of more than 30 years ago. Since 1971, the number of sworn
female police officers has increased from less than a dozen (Milton, 1973) to well over

50,000.[1] This progress is tempered by the fact that (1) sworn females have increased their representation by only 3.2 percentage points between 1990 and 1998 (10.6 and 13.8, respectively) and (2) they are underrepresented in top command and supervisory positions (National Center for Women in Policing, 1998). Nevertheless, women advanced during the past three decades in spite of the cultural and organizational barriers that include (1) gender bias pervasive in both a patriarchal society and a male-dominated occupation, (2) exclusion from patrol and investigative duties, (3) unequal pay, (4) sexual harassment, and (5) resistance by male officers.

Women have made their greatest gains in larger municipal agencies, especially in sheriffs' departments (Reaves & Smith, 1995; Bureau of Justice Statistics, 1999). Although the majority of sworn females are white, the number of black and Hispanic females in policing has also increased. Interestingly, as early as 1979, black female officers (BFOs) outnumbered white female officers (WFOs) in Detroit, Michigan, and Washington, D.C. (Townsey, 1982). In 1990, BFOs outnumbered WFOs in 11 cities, including Washington, D.C.; Detroit, Michigan; Baltimore, Maryland; Atlanta, Georgia; Memphis, Tennessee; Cleveland, Ohio; Boston, Massachusetts; New Orleans, Louisiana; Birmingham, Alabama; Miami, Florida; and Columbus, Ohio. In spite of women's' gains, we still know very little about their impact on police administration, operations, and community relations.

WOMEN IN THE HISTORY OF AMERICAN POLICING

Women have performed police duties in the United States since the mid-1800s, although they were not given full police powers until recently. During the 1820s, Quaker and upper-middle-class women, including the Women's Christian Temperance Union, the General Federation of Women's Clubs, and the American Female Moral Reform Society, demanded that prison, jail, and police matrons protect and care for women and children in custody (Van Wormer & Bartollas, 2000). These early reformers were interested in both the morality of incarcerated women (usually) arrested for prostitution, vagrancy, and drunkenness and in protecting them from abuse by males (Feinman, 1994). New York City was among the first to hire police and prison matrons in 1845. These matrons were essentially social workers destined to assist women and children in need of social services and order (Schulz, 1995). In spite of opposition, by 1885 there were police matrons in several other cities (Feinman, 1994). Gradually, their responsibilities extended beyond jails and police lockups and included both preventive and protective work.

Three of the earliest police matrons or policewomen were Marie Owens, the widow of a Chicago police officer, appointed as a "patrolman" by the mayor in 1893; Lola Baldwin, hired as a safety worker in Portland, Oregon, as part of the Lewis and Clark Exposition; and Alice Stebbins Wells, appointed in 1910 as a policewoman in Los Angeles, California. Wells was known both nationally and internationally for her efforts to introduce policewomen in many agencies. She also served as first president of the International Asso-

---

[1]This figure was calculated by multiplying the total number of sworn officers reported by Law Enforcement Management and Administrative Statistics (LEMAS) in 1997 by 13.8%, the figure reported by the National Center for Women in Policing (1998).

ciation of Police Women, an organization she helped found (Horne, 1975). By 1915, 25 cities had appointed female officers (Martin, 1980; Miller, 1999).

According to Dulaney (1996), Georgia A. Robinson, the first black female officer, was also appointed in Los Angeles in 1916, after a campaign by black citizens. Like Wells, Robinson was trained as a social worker and hired to work with black women. Several other urban agencies hired at least one black female before 1920, including Chicago, Illinois; Indianapolis, Indiana; Pittsburgh, Pennsylvania; and New York City, although others did not hire BFOs until the 1930s. The duties of pioneer BFOs mirrored those of the first white female officers (WFOs); in addition to working with women and children, they also were school patrol officers and guardians. They rarely patrolled a beat or enforced the law (Dulaney, 1996).

In spite of limitations placed on most women in policing during the early part of the 20th century, some were granted broad police powers that included patrol duties and detective work. For example, Isabella Goodwin became the first female detective in New York City in 1912 (Feinman, 1994). Dolly Spencer was appointed chief of police for two years in Milford, Ohio, to fight a gambling problem (Horne, 1975). Violet Hill Whyte, appointed in 1937 in Baltimore, was permitted to combine police and social work. She counseled delinquents, collected clothing, prepared holiday baskets, and investigated homicides, robberies, and other cases. A wife and mother, Whyte was known as "Lady Law" in her district. In 1955, she was promoted to sergeant and, shortly before retiring, to lieutenant (Rasmussen, 1997). Nevertheless, after World War I, most women worked in policewomen's bureaus. At the state level, as early as 1930, Massachusetts used women in special situations dealing with women and children. Connecticut followed in 1943 (Feinman,1994).

For most of the 20th century, the role of women in policing remained unchanged. After 1930, their progress slowed considerably as the crime control model of police work was embraced (Martin & Jurik, 1996). The first major breakthrough for women in policing came in 1968, when Indianapolis became the first city to assign women to routine patrol (Martin, 1980; Trostle, 1992). Shortly thereafter, the modern era of women in American policing began. Legislation, Supreme Court decisions, lawsuits, executive orders, and research on female officers contributed to the influx of women during the 1970s (See Table 6.1). At the beginning of the decade, the Supreme Court ruled in *Reed v. Reed* that discrimination on the basis of sex violated the equal protection clause of the Fourteenth Amendment (Feinman, 1994). The 1972 Equal Employment Opportunity Act and the 1973 Crime Control Act were the first two major pieces of federal legislation that required agencies to reconsider their blatant discrimination against women. For the first time, the Crime Control Act prohibited discrimination against women in agencies receiving federal funding. In 1973, Sergeant Fanchon Blake filed a lawsuit against the City of Los Angeles alleging job discrimination after being denied permission to take the examination for promotion to lieutenant in the police department (Palumbo, 1992; Trostle, 1992). Another important development occurred in 1972, when the Pennsylvania State Police became the first state policy agency to hire women for police duties (Horne, 1975).

Even during this so-called modern era, women faced numerous obstacles and barriers. For example, when the first females were assigned to patrol in Indianapolis, only 14 of 74 females did field police work in their agency. Most policewomen worked with juveniles or in secretarial or clerical positions (Horne, 1975; Martin & Jurik, 1996). In police departments across the country, females were subjected to abuse and disrespect that included harassment, discrimination, and isolation. They were forced to wear uniforms designed for

TABLE 6.1   1970s: A Decade of Progress for Women in Policing

Event	Date	Significance
Reed v. Reed	1971	Discrimination based on sex violated the Equal Protection Clause of the Fourteenth Amendment
Gertrude Schimmel	1971	First woman captain (New York City) First woman deputy inspector (New York City)
Equal Rights Amendment	1972	Proposed and submitted to the states
Equal Employment Opportunity Act	1972	Extended Title VII of the Civil Rights Act to state and local governments
First female FBI agents	1972	Two women successfully completed FBI training
New York City	1972	Hired and trained women for patrol duty
Pennsylvania State Police	1972	Females given increased duties
Revenue Sharing Act	1972	Authorized the U.S. Dept. of the Treasury to stop the flow of funds to any jurisdiction engaging in discriminatory practices
Blake v. City of Los Angeles	1973	Sgt. Blake filed a job discrimination lawsuit
Crime Control Act	1973	Prohibited discrimination against women in any agency receiving LEAA (Law Enforcement Alliance of America) aid
Gail Cobb dies of gunshot wounds	1974	First African American female killed in the line of duty in Washington, D.C.
Crime Control Act	1976	Prohibited LEAA from funding any agency on a local, state, or federal level that discriminated against women
Pregnancy Discrimination	1976	Prohibited discrimination on the basis of pregnancy, child birth, or related conditions
Justice System Improvement Act	1979	Authorized the Office of Justice Assistance, Research, and Statistics to withhold funds from any agency that used funds in a discriminatory manner

Source: Palumbo (1992) and Trostle (1992).

males, and they did not have separate facilities. During the 1980s and 1990s, women continued to face resistance and file lawsuits against discriminatory agencies. Today, women in policing still face hostility and harassment, they are underrepresented (especially in comparison to the number of females in the population), and only a few have advanced to command and supervisory positions in local, state, and federal agencies.

Martin and Jurik (1996) attribute the recent progress of women in policing to social, economic, and political conditions (beginning in the 1960s), as well as job and labor queues. Citing Reskin and Roos (1990), Martin and Jurik (1996, pp. 34–35) note how labor queues allow employers to rank waiting workers and job queues permit workers to rank job opportunities. As the barriers against hiring women (and minorities) have been eliminated, more and more women view policing as an attractive occupation. Feinman (1994) believes that women choose policing careers for the tangible rewards, including job security, benefits, and advancement, unlike the first generation of policewomen, who were more interested in helping and protecting women and children. Feinman sees the contemporary female officers as more closely resembling their male counterparts than their female predecessors. These women are more likely to see themselves as generalists (officers) than specialists (social workers). The number of women assigned to routine patrol and investigative functions may or may not lend support to Feinman's position. Female officers still work with women and children either formally in special units (juvenile, community relations, and crime prevention units) or informally in their interactions with female and child victims while on routine patrol.

Today, the majority of women, along with men, hold the rank of police officer, although some have advanced, especially in the larger urban municipal agencies. Women hold 7.5% of top command law enforcement positions and 9.6% of supervisory positions. Yet 30% of the 100 largest police agencies still have no women in top command positions (National Center for Women in Policing, 1998). More important, the progress of women in large municipal agencies cannot be equated to women in smaller agencies.

EMPLOYMENT TRENDS IN LOCAL AND STATE AGENCIES

Martin (1990) reported that females were 4.2% of police in municipal departments in 1978. By 1986, their representation increased to 8.8%. According to the Law Enforcement Management and Administrative Statistics (LEMAS) Program, in 1987 the number of sworn females in local agencies increased to approximately 7.6% (27,000) and to 8.1% (29,000) in 1990 (Reaves, 1989, 1992). By 1993, they represented 9% of sworn officers in municipal departments and 13.7% in large agencies. Women in smaller agencies (cities with populations between 50,000 and 100,000 and less than 50,000, respectively) were only 6.8% and 5.8% of sworn officers (Martin & Jurik, 1996).

Although the majority of sworn females are white, the number of black females, especially in urban agencies, has also increased. In 1987, there were approximately 5,685 (1.6%) black female officers (BFOs) and in 1990, 7,260 (2.0%) (Reaves, 1989, 1992). An analysis of 1987 LEMAS data tapes identified 26 agencies where BFOs outnumbered WFOs in agencies serving large and small populations. At the time, the Richmond, Virginia, City Sheriff's Department employed the highest percentage of BFOs (26%), followed by Fulton County, Georgia (19%), Henrico County, Virginia (15%), Detroit (13.6%), and Montgomery, Alabama (13%). Martin and Jurik (1996, p. 56) reported that black females represented one-third of female officers and 19% of sworn black officers.

Recent published reports by LEMAS describe only the percentage of women in large municipal and state agencies (see Table 6.2). Interestingly, since 1990, sheriffs departments have employed a higher percentage of females. In 1993, sheriffs departments employed 14% of sworn females, and municipal agencies employed 8%. In 1997, sheriffs employed 15% while municipal agencies employed 9% (Bureau of Justice Statistics, 1999). In 1998, Madison, Wisconsin, police had the largest percentage of sworn women officers (29.7%) followed by Cook County, Illinois, Sheriff (26.2%), Pittsburgh, Pennsylvania, Police (24.8%), and Washington, D.C., Metro Police (24.6%). Dayton, Ohio (37.5%), Travis

County, Texas, Sheriff (36.4%), Pittsburgh, Pennsylvania, Police (30.0%) and King County, Washington, Department of Public Safety (28.0%) had the largest percentage of women in top command positions. Washington, D.C., Metro Police (22.5%), Detroit Police (18.2%), Cook County, Illinois, Sheriff (16.9%), and Philadelphia Police (15.6%) had the largest percentage of women officers of color (National Center for Women in Policing, 1998).

Compared with municipal agencies, women have made very little progress in employment in state agencies. In both 1993 and 1997, only 5% of officers in state agencies were women (see Table 6.3). In 1993, female representation in state agencies ranged from 0.6% in North Carolina to 12.4% in Wisconsin. In 1997, there were slight increases in several states, including Louisiana, Wisconsin, North Carolina, Michigan, Florida, and

TABLE 6.2   1993 and 1997 Average Percentage of Sworn Female Officers by Sex

	County		Municipal		Sheriff		State	
Sex	1993	1997	1993	1997	1993	1997	1993	1997
	(33)	(30)	(411)	(454)	(146)	(167)	(49)	(49)
Female	10%	11	8	9	14	15	5	5
Male	90	89	92	91	86	85	95	95

Source: B.A. Reaves and P.Z. Smith, 1995, p. xiii; Bureau of Justice Statistics, 1999, p. xiii.

TABLE 6.3   1993 and 1997 Highest and Lowest Ranked State Agencies by Percentage of Sworn Female Officers

Name	1993	1997
Highest Percentage:		
Wisconsin	12.4%	13%
Michigan	9.7	12
Florida	9.4	11
Massachusetts	8.4	10
Illinois	7.9	—
Lowest Percentage:		
Louisiana	1.1	2
Oklahoma	1.3	1
South Dakota	1.3	1
Wyoming	1.4	1
North Carolina	0.6	1

Source: B.A. Reaves and P.Z. Smith, 1995, p. 48; Bureau of Justice Statistics, 1999, p. 263.

Massachusetts (Reaves & Smith, 1995; Bureau of Justice Statistics, 1999). The low representation in state agencies is worthy of more research.

RESEARCH ON WOMEN IN POLICING

Research on women in policing flourished during the modern era.[2] In addition to historical studies and analyses of employment trends and affirmative action, researchers were interested in (1) determining whether women were capable of performing traditionally male roles (Martin, 1980; Van Wormer & Bartollas, 2000) and (2) identifying the barriers they confront (Remmington, 1983; Dreifus, 1982). Although the research has clearly shown that women can do police work, and bring special skills to the profession, including interpersonal communication and reducing the use of violence, barriers are still an important research topic (see, for example, International Association of Chiefs of Police, 1999; National Center for Women in Policing, 1998). Attitudes of males, females, and citizens (Balkin, 1988; Fry & Greensfield, 1980; Leger, 1997; Weisheit, 1987; Worden, 1993) have also been studied. Recently, job satisfaction (Dantzker, 1994; Dantzker & Kubin, 1998; Fry & Greensfield, 1980; Felkenes, 1991) and stress (Cullen, Lemming, Link, & Wozniak, 1985; Haarr & Morash, 1999; Morash & Haarr, 1995; Wexler & Logan, 1993) have received considerable attention. Other research topics include African American women in policing (Felkenes & Schroede, 1993; Martin, 1994; Townsey, 1982), the gendered police organization (Martin & Jurik, 1996), race and gender issues (Haarr, 1997; Haarr & Morash, 1999), tokenism (Belknap & Shelley, 1993; Zimmer, 1988), and female roles (Martin, 1979).

In spite of past and present barriers, it is surprising that female officers perceptions of job satisfaction are similar to those of males (Dantzker & Kubin, 1998; Felkenes, 1991; Fry & Greensfield, 1980; Morash & Haarr, 1995). Dantzker and Kubin (1998) found that gender by itself was not significant to job satisfaction until they included other demographic variables (age, ethnicity, rank, years of service) in their analysis. Even these factors explained only 6% or less of the variance. Dantzker and Kubin (1998) suggest that when other organizational factors are taken into consideration, along with demographic variables, more of the variance can be explained. However, they do not specify what these other factors might be. Those who study women in policing continue to wonder why females who still confront sexual harassment, discrimination, and other types of differential treatment appear to be as satisfied as their male colleagues. One explanation could be that job satisfaction is not necessarily great for either males or females; methodological problems may also explain the dilemma. These unexpected findings regarding female officer job satisfaction are in line with what Phelan (1994) refers to as the paradox of the contented female officer. Although more research on this issue is certainly needed, we should not lose sight of the fact that women may be content with their careers for reasons that have nothing to do with either barriers they confront or job satisfaction. Instead, women in policing and other occupations usually separate their feelings about their jobs and employers from their attitudes about job satisfaction and the barriers they confront. Additionally, women (and men) in many occupations do not derive much satisfaction from their organization or employer. Rather, they strive to succeed in spite of job-related obstacles. What we need to

[2]Several reviews of the research literature are available elsewhere (see Balkin, 1988).

examine in the future are the similarities and differences in perceptions about job satisfaction of women who work in agencies of different sizes and types. For example, it is important to determine whether there are significant differences in females employed in small, medium-size, and state agencies. It also would be informative to compare attitudes toward job satisfaction among federal agencies, private agencies, and special agencies. Clearly, continued comparisons between men and women are necessary.

As the modern era of women in policing concludes, the need for more substantive research is abundantly clear. Perhaps the next era can be labeled the research era to highlight the importance of increasing our understanding of the role of women in policing. Once researchers accept that what is known about women in policing is extremely limited, they will more willingly embrace the research opportunities that await them in the future. Undoubtedly, females in leadership positions, as well as other sworn females, will have to demand funding support at the federal and state levels. As long as their representation continues to be low, research will not be viewed as a priority without spokeswomen. For example, employment trends of black female officers in urban agencies are practically ignored in spite of the possible implications this trend might have for the future of police administration, operations, and community relations.

Future research must advance the body of knowledge beyond case studies of women in selective agencies to more national and intrajurisdictional analyses. Although case studies will continue to be useful, more comparative research is needed. Immediately, advocates of female police should encourage or mandate that LEMAS report more information on women in policing in their printed publications, with separate publications being made available. Research on women in federal law enforcement agencies should also be recommended.

Two organizations, the National Center for Women in Policing and the International Association of Chiefs of Police (IACP) Ad Hoc Committee on Women in Policing, are playing an important role in setting a research agenda for the 21st century. For instance, IACP (1999, p. 56) recommended further research on the impact of gender discrimination on retention, mentoring programs on officer careers, and determining if perceptions of female officers' skills inhibit assignment opportunities.

Other issues that deserve more research attention are women in state agencies, Hispanic female officers, integration, the experiences of women in supervisory positions, international and comparative studies, and attitudes of women toward male and female partners, supervisors, and colleagues. Perhaps the most important research issues during the next decade are understanding the role of women as police leaders and as community policing officers. An examination of their impact on agency management, personnel, operations, and community relations is long overdue.

DISCUSSION QUESTIONS

1. Describe the cultural and organizational barriers that have tempered the progress of policewomen since 1971.

2. What were the first two major pieces of federal legislation that required agencies to reconsider their blatant discrimination against women?

3. Why is it important for researchers to address the employment trends in local and state agencies? Give examples.

4. Discuss the theoretical application of Phelan's (1994) "paradox of the contented female officer" to the present findings regarding female officers' job satisfaction.

5. What do you envision as future roles of female officers during the 21st century?

REFERENCES

BALKIN J. (1988). Why policewomen don't like policewomen. *Journal of Police Science and Administration, 16*(1), 29–38.

BELKNAP, J., & SHELLEY, J.K. (1993). The new lone ranger: Policewomen on patrol. *American Journal of Police, 12*(2), 47–75.

BUREAU OF JUSTICE STATISTICS. (1999). *Law enforcement management and administrative statistics, 1997 (executive summary).* Washington, DC: Department of Justice.

CULLEN, F.T., LEMMING, T., LINK, B.G., & WOZNIAK, J.F. (1985). The impact of social supports on police stress. *Criminology, 23*(3), 503–522.

DANTZKER, M. (1994). *Understanding today's police.* Upper Saddle River, NJ: Prentice Hall.

DANTZKER, M., & KUBIN, B. (1998). Job satisfaction: The gender perspective among police officers. *American Journal of Criminal Justice, 23*(1), 19–31.

DREIFUS, C. (1982). Why two women cops were convicted of cowardice. In B. Price & N. Sokoloff (Eds.), *The criminal justice system and women,* pp. 427–435. New York: Clark Boardman.

DULANEY, M. (1996). *Black police in America.* Bloomington: Indiana University Press.

FEINMAN, C. (1994). *Women in the criminal justice system.* Westport, CT: Praeger.

FELKENES, G.T. (1991). Affirmative action in the Los Angeles Police Department. *Criminal Justice Research, 6*(4), 1–9.

FELKENES, G.T., & SCHROEDE, J.R. (1993). Case study of minority women in policing. *Women and Criminal Justice, 4*(2), 65–89.

FRY, L., & GREENSFIELD, S. (1980). An examination of attitudinal differences between policewomen and policemen. *Journal of Applied Psychology, 65,* 123–126.

HAARR, R. (1997). Patterns of interaction in a police patrol bureau: Race and gender barriers to integration. *Justice Quarterly, 14*(1), 53–85.

HAARR, R., & MORASH, M. (1999). Gender, race, and strategies of coping with occupational stress in policing. *Justice Quarterly, 16*(2), 303–336.

HORNE, P. (1975). *Women in law enforcement.* Springfield, IL: Charles C. Thomas.

INTERNATIONAL ASSOCIATION OF CHIEFS OF POLICE. (1999). The future of women in policing: Mandates for action. *Police Chief, 66*(3), 53–56.

LEGER, K. (1997). Public perceptions of female police officers on patrol. *American Journal of Criminal Justice, 21*(2), 231–249.

MARTIN, S.E. (1979). Policewomen and policewomen: Occupation role dilemmas and choices of female officers. *Journal of Police Sicence and Administration, 7,* 314–323.

MARTIN, S.E. (1980). *Breaking and entering: Policewomen on patrol.* Berkeley and Los Angeles: University of California Press.

MARTIN, S.E. (1990). *On the move: The status of women in policing.* Washington, DC: Police Foundation.

MARTIN, S.E. (1991). The effectiveness of affirmative action: The case of women in policing. *Justice Quarterly, 8,* 489–504.

MARTIN, S.E. (1994). "Outsider within" the station house: The impact of race and gender on black women police. *Social Problems, 4*(3), 383–400.

MARTIN, S.E., & JURIK, N.C. (1996). *Doing justice doing gender.* Thousand Oaks, CA: Sage.

MILLER, S. (1999). *Gender and community policing.* Boston, MA: Northeastern University Press.

MILTON, C. (1973). *Women in policing.* Washington, DC: Police Foundation.

MORASH, M., & HAARR, R.N. (1995). Gender, workplace problems, and stress in policing. *Justice Quarterly, 12*(1), 113–136.

NATIONAL CENTER FOR WOMEN IN POLICING. (1998). *Equality denied: The status of women in policing: 1998.* Washington DC: National Center for Women in Policing.

PALUMBO, B.J. (1992). "Affirmative Action and the law." In G.T. Felkenes & P.C. Unsinger (Eds.), *Diversity, affirmative action and law enforcement* (pp. 38–56). Springfield, IL: Charles C. Thomas.

PHELAN, J. (1994). The paradox of the contented female worker: An alternative explanation. *Social Psychology Quarterly, 57*(2), 95–107

PRESIDENT'S COMMISSION ON LAW ENFORCEMENT AND THE ADMINISTRATION OF JUSTICE. (1967). *Task force report on the police.* Washington, DC: U.S. Government Printing Office.

RASMUSSEN, F. (1997, February 2). Lady law did more than just her duty. *Baltimore Sun,* p. 6K.

REAVES, B.A., & SMITH, P.Z. (1995). Law enforcement management statistics, 1993: Data for individual and local agencies with 100 or more officers. Washington, DC: U.S. Department of Justice, Bureau of Justice Statistics.

REAVES, B.A. (1989). *Profiles of state and local law enforcement agencies, 1987.* Washington, DC: U.S. Department of Justice.

REAVES, B.A. (1992). *Law enforcement management and administrative statistics, 1990: Data for individual state and local agencies with 100 or more officers.* Washington, DC: U.S. Department of Justice.

REMMINGTON, P.W. (1983). Women in the police: Integration or separation? *Qualitative Sociology, 6*(2), 118–135.

RESKIN, B., & ROOS, P. (1990). *Job queues, gender queues: Exploring women's inroads into male occupations.* Philadelphia: Temple University Press.

SCHULZ, D.M. (1995). *From social worker to crimefighter: Women in United States municipal policing.* New York: Praeger.

SULTON, C., & TOWNSEY, R.D. (1981). *A progress report on women in policing.* Washington, DC: Police Foundation.

TOWNSEY, R.D. (1982). Black women in American policing: An advancement display. *Journal of Criminal Justice, 10,* 455–468.

TROSTLE, L.C. (1992). Recruitment, hiring, and promotion of women and racial minorities in law enforcement. In G.T. Felkenes and P.C. Unsinger (Eds.), *Diversity, affirmative action and law enforcement,* pp. 91–114. Springfield, IL: Charles C. Thomas.

VAN WORMER, K., & BARTOLLAS, C. (2000). *Women and the criminal justice system.* Boston: Allyn and Bacon.

WEISHEIT, R.A. (1987). Women in the state police: Concerns of male and female officers. *Journal of Police Science and Administration, 15*(2), 137–144.

WEXLER, J., & LOGAN, D. (1993). Sources of stress among women police officers. *Journal of Police Science and Administration, 13*(2), 98–105.

WORDEN, A.P. (1993). The attitudes of women and men in policing: Testing conventional and contemporary wisdom. *Criminology, 31*(2), 203–241.

ZIMMER, L. (1988). Tokenism and women in the workplace. *Social Problems, 33,* 64–77.

7

U.S. Policing in Black and White

A Cross-Racial Comparison of How Black and White Youth Experience Policing

Delores Jones-Brown

❖

Using both qualitative and quantitative descriptive methods, this chapter examines the existence and manifestations of differences in how black and white youth perceive of and have contact with the police. The findings suggest a uniform negative perception of police among black youth regardless of their socioeconomic status or level of delinquency involvement. Although the black youth in the sample report having had some direct negative encounters with the police, the primary source of negative police feelings within the group appears to be vicarious (indirect) negative contact involving relatives, a consequence of which may be a reduced willingness to cooperate with the police.

An ever-growing body of research has documented that perceptions of justice and injustice with regard to American legal institutions vary across race and/or ethnic group (Kolodziejski, Stilwell, Torchiana, & Markowitz, 2000; Russell, 1998; Jesilow, Meyer, & Namazzi, 1995; Webb & Marshall, 1995; Browning, Cullen, Cao, Kopache, & Stevenson, 1994; Lasley, 1994; Bessent & Tayler, 1991; Tyler, 1990; Hagan & Albonetti, 1982; Davis, 1974; Feagin & Hahn, 1973). Although the courts and correctional system have had their share of problems, policing is still perhaps the single formal legal mechanism over which the greatest divide in perceptions of justice and injustice has centered.

The fairness and effectiveness of law enforcement in the United States is the area of criminal justice administration that, over the years, has proven to be the most volatile when examined against a racial backdrop. Criminologists and criminal justice practitioners argue over the actual existence of overt discrimination within the American system of justice (see Wilbanks, 1987; Mann, 1993; MacLean & Milovanovic, 1990), but contemporary events serve as continuous reminders that race matters in how justice is perceived in America.

Specifically, events involving police action or inaction serve as the primary source of disagreement when issues of race, crime, and the perception of justice converge. In this chapter, both quantitative and qualitative methods are used to examine the existence and manifestation of differences in how a matched sample of black and white youth perceive of and have contact with the police.

SIGNIFICANCE

Why should society be concerned with how different segments of the population feel about the police? Many may feel that the two entities—police and citizens—have prescribed finite roles: the former to enforce the law, the latter to obey it. Individuals who hold such views fail to recognize the complexity of human interaction and the role that *experience,* both historical and contemporary, plays in influencing attitudes and behaviors among social beings.

Why focus on how youth feel about the police? The answer is at least twofold. On the one hand, Rusinko, Johnson, and Hornung (1978) note that "citizen cooperation is essential for effective law enforcement" (p. 54) and that "attitudes toward police are strongly related to cooperation with police" (citing Holman, 1967; Kenney & Pursuit, 1965; Robison, 1963 at p. 54). In addition, they note that "the adolescent years are crucial in the development of these attitudes" (p. 54), which generally persist into adulthood (Bouma, 1969; Kobetz, 1971; Portune, 1971). They note further that, even within the adolescent years, successful police efforts at preventing and controlling youth crime require a level of cooperation from youthful citizens. Such cooperation may be difficult to come by when youth hold negative attitudes toward the police.

In addition to affecting levels of cooperation, theoretically, youth attitudes toward the police and formal legal mechanisms may have implications for the direct production or prevention of delinquency. In 1969, Hirschi put forth a theory of social control that suggested that to the extent youth are bonded to conventional social institutions they are less likely to become delinquent. Although Hirschi's work focused primarily on the young person's bond to family, school, and peers, he also suggested that the police are a part of the conventional institutions with which youth may bond or fail to bond, with consequent implications for delinquency.

Under Hirschi's formulation, "lack of respect [for police] precedes delinquent acts and does not simply follow from contact with the police" (p. 201). However, he does note that the strong relation between his "respect for police" item and his official delinquency measure suggested that actual contact with the police might, in fact, have an influence on both youth attitudes and behavior.

Despite the "chicken or egg" quality of the discussion of whether negative attitudes toward the police precede or are caused by police encounters (Jones-Brown, 2000a; Leiber, Nalla, & Franworth, 1998), it is generally expected that nondelinquent (or minimally delinquent) youth will have more positive attitudes toward the police, as will youth of middle-class socioeconomic status (SES) (Leiber, Nalla, & Franworth, 1998, Rusinko, Johnson, & Hornung, 1978; Hirschi, 1969; Cloward & Ohlin, 1960; Cohen, 1955). Findings from the current research suggest that when delinquency status and SES are controlled for, race exerts a significant influence on police encounters and how the police are perceived among adolescent males.

THE STUDY

Between the fall of 1993 and 1994, the author interviewed 199 males, ages 15 through 18, with a modified version of the Internalization of Legal Values Inventory (ILVI) (Finckenauer, 1995). The 21-page instrument was designed to tap into various aspects of the interviewees' legal socialization, which was defined as the development of attitudes, values, and behaviors toward law and legal mechanisms (Tapp, 1987; Finckenauer, 1995). In its modified version, the instrument consists of 183 substantive items and 14 demographic items. The items include both open-ended and closed-end questions. Twenty-one items pertain directly to the police. Eleven of those 21, adopted from Finckenauer's (1970) police satisfaction survey, make up a "Police Experience" section, the results of which will be reported here.

Items regarding respondents' attitudes toward the police and their willingness to cooperate were adopted from other research instruments with established reliability and validity (Hess & Tapp, 1969; Law-Related Education Evaluation Project, 1983; Rafky & Sealey, 1975; Tapp & Levine, 1974). Not reported here were items pertaining to the subjects' knowledge of substantive law and items gauging their level of legal reasoning, legal self-perceptions, and values. The instrument also contained 29 items measuring self-reported delinquency.

The interviews took place within a suburban county in New Jersey where community-oriented policing techniques were reportedly being utilized. The research sites were located in five towns within the county. Participants were recruited from three high schools, a boys' and girls' club, a summer basketball league, and a housing authority summer work program. Each site was within a 20-mile radius of the others.

Printed flyers were used at each site to advertise the study. There were also verbal reminders issued by the site staff and the researcher. The study was advertised as open to all males age 16 or 17. However, if they were within three months of the target ages, 15- and 18-year-olds were interviewed as well. All subjects under age 18 were required to provide a signed parental consent form before being interviewed. Subjects self-selected to participate in the study by returning the parental form and/or voluntarily signing a subject assent form. To reduce the possibility of selection bias on the part of staff, at four of the sites all age-eligible participants were identified through computer-generated lists and notified of their eligibility to volunteer for the study.

The instrument was administered verbally to each participant. Each interview took place on-site in a closed setting with only the researcher and the participant present. Interviews lasted for 45 minutes to an hour, and each person completing the interview was paid a $10 participation fee.

The target population for the study was 125 African American males who were defined as persons of black racial identity, at least the second generation born in the United States. Responses from this target group were to be compared with the responses of an equal number of interviewees who identified themselves as European American or white. After a full year of interviewing, the author was able to secure only 25 European American participants, and the responses of 49 interviewees were excluded from the analysis because their self-identities did not fall into either of the two categories of interest.

The study, as originally conceived, focused on African American and European American samples, taking into account the country's racialized legal history (Jones-Brown, 2000b; Kennedy, 1997; Mann, 1993; McIntyre, 1993). Given that history, the study proceeded from three main assumptions:

1. As a group, African Americans have stood in a different position vis-à-vis the law than have other Americans.
2. Because of this and other environmental factors, African Americans (regardless of SES) may tend to develop negative attitudes and values toward law and legal institutions.
3. These negative attitudes and values, influenced by various *environmental* factors, may relate to an individual's propensity to obey or violate the law.

There were two main research questions:

1. How do African-American adolescent males experience the law?
2. Does their experience differ significantly from European American/white counterparts?

To attempt to answer these two questions, given the low number of responses from white youth, a comparative subsample of African American youth ($n = 25$) was drawn from the target population of 125 and matched to the available European American/white sample, using SES and living arrangements and family structure as two primary factors.

In addition to SES and living arrangements, consistent with the cognitive developmental theory of legal socialization (see Tapp & Kohlberg, 1971; Tapp & Levine, 1970, 1974, 1977; Tapp, 1987; Cohn & White, 1986, 1990), age and grade were chosen as the secondary matching factors. Based on the notion that individuals' social participation contributes to or retards their cognitive development (Tapp, 1987), subjects' work status was the final factor considered in making a match.

For purposes of presenting the comparative results, in this chapter the subsample of the African American youth are referred to as black(s) and the non–African American youth are referred to as white(s). Given the small sample sizes ($n = 25$ each), descriptive tables involve the calculation of mean scores from each sample who responded within a particular category on individual items.

At the conclusion of data collection and analysis of the data from the individual interviews, a focus group discussion was held to gather more detailed information about the aggregate results. The focus group was held at one of the three high school sites with a previously formed group—seven African American males, one African American female, one European American female, and a teacher who facilitates the group—called the Peer Group Connection. All but one of the males had participated in the study. The discussion lasted approximately one hour and 45 minutes. Although the schedule of questions for the focus group was designed to gather information about four different topics—courts, police, law, and parents—the discussion continued to drift back to treatment by the police.

FINDINGS

Description of Sample

With regard to the family structure and SES variables, the matched groups came from predominantly two-parent households (80% for both groups; 20 of 25), and there were slightly more middle-SES than low-SES subjects in each group (subjects' SES was determined using the Rating Scale of Parental Occupations). T-tests were performed to confirm that the two groups did not differ significantly on the SES variable (t value $= -1.31$ $p = .195$).

The results on the policing items for the full sample ($N = 125$) of black males are reported elsewhere (see Jones-Brown, 2000a). The data from these matched samples indicated that, in aggregate, the delinquency index scores for each group were similar. Collectively, the members of each group are minimally involved in delinquency, despite, as discussed later, the negative feelings about police that were expressed by some group members. The target populations, the black subsample and the white sample, each average roughly a 12 on a delinquency index score that ranges from 0 to 87. Given the predominance of middle-SES respondents and this low level of delinquency, one would expect relatively positive attitudes toward the police.

With regard to expressions of feelings toward or about the police, the results indicate that despite their demographic similarities, the black youth in the subsample responded to policing questions in a way that was similar to the larger sample from which they were drawn and dissimilar to the white group with which they were being compared. Specifically, as a group, in comparison to their white counterparts, the black youth reported:

- significantly less likelihood of having respect for the police (see Table 7.1)
- fewer feelings of guilt for disobeying police orders (see Table 7.1)
- a greater belief in the punitiveness of the police (see Table 7.1)

Bonding Variables

Three items were used to measure the extent to which each group saw the police as legitimate mechanisms of social control: "I have a lot of respect for the police in my town." "Police always have a good reason when they stop somebody." "Police try to give all young people an even break." The responses to these items were coded on a Likert scale from one to five, with the lowest number representing strongly disagree and the highest number representing strongly agree. On each of the items, the mean score for the black subsample was lower than that of the white sample, indicating that black respondents tended to disagree with each of the statements. The mean scores for each group are presented in Table 7.1. The difference in means on the "respect for police" item was statistically significant ($p = .01$).

When asked, "If you broke a police officer's orders and no one knew, would you feel bad?" on a five-point Likert scale (1 is never; 5 is always), the mean score for the black youth was equivalent to "almost never" and the white youth averaged a response of "sometimes." The difference in means was statistically significant at the .05 level. Only teachers fared slightly worse than the police for engendering feelings of guilt among the black youth. Although teachers scored below the police for white youth as well, in both authority

TABLE 7.1   Responses to Selected Items

	Mean Score		
	Black	White	*t*-ratio
Perceived Legitimacy of the Police across Race			
Items			
Respect for police	3.20	4.00	−2.72**
Police have good reason to stop	2.08	2.36	−1.04
Police give an even break	2.60	2.84	−0.75
Feeling Bad for Breaking Rules, Laws, or Orders across Race			
Authority Figure			
Parents	3.64	3.80	−0.44
U.S. Law	2.56	3.16	−1.50
Police	2.12	3.00	−2.01*
Teachers	1.96	2.72	−1.94*
Friends	2.24	3.48	−3.19**
Power to Punish Items across Race			
Authority Figure			
Parents	4.60	4.20	—
Judges	4.40	4.16	—
Police	3.76	3.56	—
Teachers	3.64	3.52	—
Friends	1.80	2.24	−1.24*

Scale of 1 to 5 with 1 being never and 5 being always

 *Significant at .05 level.
**Significant at .01 level.

figure categories (police and teachers), the white mean exceeded the black mean by almost an entire score (see Table 7.1).

By contrast, when both groups were asked, "Can police officers punish you if you do something wrong?" the mean score for the black group was closer to a response of "almost always" and the white mean was closer to "sometimes." Taken together, these results indicate that the police are viewed substantially differently by the two groups, both with regard to the legitimacy of their role (as mechanisms of social control) and as to the extent and operation of their power (i.e., internalized versus externalized) (see Table 7.1).

Cooperation

Given the results presented thus far, it may not be surprising to find that the two groups differed on the extent to which they might be willing to cooperate with the police when it came to providing information about a friend. When asked, "If your friend got into trouble with the police, would you be willing to lie to protect them?" a third more black than white youth (47% versus 30%) responded that they would be willing to lie to the police to protect their friend. Although a greater percentage of whites responded that they would not lie to the police to protect their friend, they were less certain about lying to others for that same purpose.

Police Contact

The relationship between the police and the community has been noted to have both physical and emotional components (Jones-Brown, 2000a). As noted earlier, attempts to specify the direction of the relationship between the two components has proved problematic. Hence, rather than attempt to specify any direction here, the author will merely report the responses of the comparative groups and later provide additional explanatory comments based on information gleaned from the focus group discussion.

The formation of attitudes toward the police may be much more complex than previously considered (Jones-Brown, 2000a). The results from the small samples here *suggest* that attempts to link direct positive or negative encounters with the police to the formation of singularly positive or negative attitudes toward or perceptions of them may be terribly misleading. The Police Experience section of the modified ILVI was designed to gather data about both direct and indirect (vicarious) contact with the police. It asks the interviewee to report not only his own police experiences but also such experiences as they may have been relayed to him by friends or relatives. Although the attitudes of the current subjects in some cases vary greatly across the two groups, as self-reported, their direct police contacts proved to be surprisingly similar (see Table 7.2).

Subjects from both groups responded exactly the same on whether they had *ever* been stopped (a direct contact or encounter) by the police (88% for each group). For both groups, the stops were usually while they were with friends. However, significantly more black youths than white youths reported primarily having been stopped within the last year preceding the interview. Among those reporting having been stopped at least twice, both groups believed that the officer "acted the way s/he-they should have acted." Only once subjects are questioned about indirect police contact do differences begin to emerge.

When asked, "Have any of your friends or relatives had any experiences with the police that made a particular impression on you?" almost twice as many whites as blacks noted that their indirect impressions of the police from friends were unfavorable (i.e., had involved situations in which the police did not behave as the respondent thought they should have). When the indirect impression involved a relative, however, nearly four times as many blacks as whites reported unfavorable impressions about police coming from relatives (significant at .01).

By contrast, when asked, "Have the police ever helped your friends or relatives in any way?" nearly twice as many black respondents as white respondents reported that they

TABLE 7.2   Police Contact across Race

| | Mean Score | | |
Item	Black	White	*t*-value
Stopped by police	1.12	1.12	0.00
When stopped	2.00	1.81	2.11*
With whom	2.73	2.59	0.54
Exptype 1	2.41	2.26	0.95
Number of contacts	1.44	1.32	0.86
Exptype 2	2.20	2.28	0.56
Indirect impression from friends	1.40	1.72	−1.25
Indirect impression from relatives	2.20	1.44	3.01**
Direct police help	1.54	1.52	0.13
Indirect police help	1.75	1.43	2.27*

*Significant at .05 level.
**Significant at .01 level.

TABLE 7.3   Difference in Police Experience Items across Race

Item	*t*-ratio
Frequency of contact	0.86
Exptype 1	0.68
Exptype 2	0.26
Indirect impression relative	3.01**
Indirect police help	−2.27*

*Significant at .05 level.
**Significant at .01 level.

could not recall a situation in which a friend or relative had been helped, even though each group was roughly equally divided in its members' reporting having received direct (personal) assistance from the police. In response to the indirect "help" question, this time significantly more black youth than white youth reported that they had no information from relatives.

T-tests reveal that there were no significant differences in the responses across the two groups with regard to the reported frequency of contact with police and whether their direct contacts with police were favorable or unfavorable (measured by responses to the question, "Was there anything that you did not like about the way s/he-they [the police] acted?"; if the response was yes, subjects were asked to explain their response in detail). However, there were highly significant differences by race with regard to the "indirect impression" and "indirect help" questions (see Table 7.3).

DISCUSSION

What is to be made of these findings? Some appear to be consistent with previous findings (see Browning et al., 1994), but others appear to be "all over the place." However, subjects' detailed descriptions of what they found wrong with their direct police encounters and their responses during a focus group discussion highlighted the role of race within the subjects' police experiences (both direct and indirect). Subjects' qualitative statements reveal racial influences even where quantitative results appear to indicate no real difference. For example, subjects from both groups expressed an awareness that so-called community policing efforts can create "community" conflicts or infringe the Constitutional rights of certain individuals. Examples of such conflicts included reports that:

- Black youth were stopped for "being in" white neighborhoods.
- White youth were stopped for "being in" black neighborhoods.
- Both black and white youth were stopped for "being together" in various neighborhoods.

According to McElroy, Casgrove, and Sadd (1993), community policing efforts are based on the assumption that "the effectiveness of current police strategies in controlling crime can be improved if the police increase the quantity and quality of citizen contacts and collaborations" (pp. 655–656). The current comparison across race based on matched samples indicates that an increased *quantity* of police contacts occurred for black youth and their families with little, if any, increase in the *quality* of such contacts. Specifically, despite their middle-class status and low level of self-reported delinquency, more black youth and their relatives than their white counterparts were contacted by the police for law enforcement purposes rather than for rendering assistance.

The white youth who had black friends or who had themselves had unfavorable encounters with the police, based on (in their perceptions) their association with black youth, reported unfavorable impressions of the police. Such youth also responded similarly to their black counterparts regarding whether: "The police always have a good reason to stop someone" and "Police try to give all young people an even break." These associations may account, in part, for the closeness of the aggregate means for the two groups in response to these two items (see Table 7.3). Conversely, because as a group white youth had fewer direct contacts with the police and more indirect contacts that were viewed as favorable and involving assistance to their relatives, this difference may explain, in part, the significantly more positive response to the "respect for police" item.

As noted in Jones-Brown (2000a), among the target population ($N = 125$), black youth expressed several recurrent themes regarding their direct contacts with the police: (1) "They stopped us because we were black"; (2) "They stopped us because we were black in a white neighborhood"; (3) "They stopped us because we were in a car, so it must be stolen"; (4) "They stopped us because we were a group of black kids together"; (5) "They stopped us because we were black in a 'drug neighborhood' so we must have been selling drugs"; and (6) "They stopped us because we were black, so we looked suspicious." Thus, the black youths' middle-class status did not protect them from multiple negative police encounters, both directly and indirectly.

As one low-SES white youth who scored a 57 on the delinquency index noted, "Yes, I get stopped by the police. They ask me what I am doing and where I am going. I could have just burglarized a house, but they believe whatever I tell them and let me go on my way. My black friends, who aren't doing anything, get taken to the police station before they are released." Several of the black interviewees confirmed this statement, adding, "The police never believe what we say."

Particularly tragic in this study's findings is that although a majority of the two samples are from two-parent, middle-SES households, factors that empirically place them at a reduced risk for involvement in delinquency, for the black youth, these factors do not necessarily reduce their risk of police contact, especially via indirect means. It also does not reduce the likelihood that such indirect contacts (and the impressions created from them) will be viewed as unfavorable. The reports of such contacts included arrests and assaults (verbal and physical) by the police on their friends and relatives, as well as reports that the police failed to render assistance when needed.

Perhaps not coincidentally, in response to a series of questions relating to whether they would be bothered by legal "problems," members of the black sample indicated being less bothered by the possibility of such problems than did their white counterparts. This finding may be due to a feeling among the black youth that contact with formal legal mechanisms, especially the police, is inevitable and that this inevitability is correlated more with race than with actual wrongdoing. The following quotes were gleaned from the focus group discussion:

- "They [the police] look at black people almost like we're animals."
- "The first thing they [the police] think is that 'black people' are going to try to do something bad or fight them back or something."
- ". . . it is like they [the police] go crazy when they see a black person."

Along similar lines, one black subject described driving a "nice" car and being stopped by the police "for nothing" and then let go. He went on to talk about how "people with nice clothes and nice cars" in his neighborhood are assumed by the police to be drug dealers. He also expressed his dissatisfaction with a situation in which the police stopped him and three friends, one white and two black. He indicated that he and his two black friends automatically put their hands up, but their white friend did not. This subject stated that he believed that "the police were afraid [of us] and about fifteen cop cars came." He thought that it was particularly significant that his white friend did not feel any immediate need to raise his hands when all three black members of the group did.

CONCLUSIONS

While the country is engaged in debate over the existence (or not) of racial profiling in law enforcement activities, and, if it does exist, how best to curtail it, the research results presented in this chapter indicate that, to a degree, both black and white youth perceive that race plays a role in how people are policed. As perceived by these youth, the influence of race cuts across social class and affects the life of both blacks and whites. Even the white female who participated in the focus group reported having been stopped by the police on a suspicion that she was buying drugs because she was in a "black neighborhood."

From this and other research, young black males appear to bear the brunt of racial influences in policing. Even if its impact is not experienced directly, disturbing ripples emanate from the experiences of others (friends but primarily relatives) and are absorbed and transformed into attitudes that may be counterproductive to efforts at preventing and controlling crime.

Despite its small sample size, this study has some merit because the findings are consistent with the findings of larger studies in the literature. The findings also undeniably parallel the qualitative complaints currently being raised against the police by minority groups across the country. Given the history and consistency of complaints of discrimination and abuse lodged by blacks against police officers in this country, and the sometimes violent reactions to the government's failure to address them, the current findings suggest that credible changes in police policy and practice are necessary first steps toward creating the collective sense of equal justice expected in a democratic society.

DISCUSSION QUESTIONS

1. Describe Hirschi's theory of social control.

2. What is the "chicken or egg" argument?

3. What is the Internalization of Legal Value Inventory?

4. What is a target population?

5. What are the main assumptions of the study?

REFERENCES

BESSENT, A., & TAYLER, L. (1991, June 2). Police brutality: It is no problem? *Newsday,* p. 5.

BOUMA, D. (1969). *Kids and cops: A study of mutual hostility.* Grand Rapids, MI: Eerdmans.

BROWNING, S., CULLEN, F., CAO, L., KOPACHE, R., & STEVENSON, T. (1994). Race and getting hassled by the police: A research note. *Police Studies, 17*(1), 1–11.

CLOWARD, R., & OHLIN, L. (1960). *Delinquency and opportunity: A theory of delinquent gangs.* New York: Free Press.

COHEN, A. (1955). *Delinquent boys.* New York: Free Press.

COHN, E., & WHITE, S. (1986). Cognitive development versus social learning approaches to studying legal socialization. *Basic and Applied Social Psychology, 7*(3), 195–209.

COHN, E., & WHITE, S. (1990). *Legal socialization: A study of norms and rules.* New York: Springer–Verlag.

DAVIS, J. (1974). Justification for no obligation: Views of black males toward crime and the criminal law. *Issues in Criminology, 9,* 69–87.

FEAGIN, J., & HAHN, J. (1973). *Ghetto revolts: The politics of violence in American cities.* New York: MacMillan.

FINCKENAUER, J. (1970). *Police community contact: The stereotypical view of a police department.* Unpublished doctoral dissertation, New York University.

FINCKENAUER, J. (1995). *Russian youth.* New Brunswick, NJ: Transaction.

HAGAN, H., & ALBONETTI, C. (1982). Race, class and the perception of criminal injustice in America. *American Journal of Sociology, 88*(2), 329–355.

HESS, R., & TAPP, J. (1969). *Authority, rules, and aggression: A cross-national study of the socialization of children into compliance systems, Part I.* Washington, DC: U.S. Office of Education.

HIRSCHI, T. (1969). *Causes of delinquency.* Berkeley: University of California Press.

HOLMAN, M. (1967). *The police officer and the child.* Springfield, IL: Charles C. Thomas.

JESILOW, P., MEYER, J., & NAMAZZI, N. (1995). Public attitudes toward the police. *American Journal of Police, 16*(2), 67–88.

JONES–BROWN, D. (2000a). Debunking the myth of officer friendly: How African American males experience community policing, *Journal of Contemporary Criminal Justice, 16*(2), 209–229.

JONES–BROWN, D. (2000b). *Race, crime and punishment.* Philadelphia: Chelsea House.

KENNEDY, R. (1997). *Race, crime and the law.* New York: Pantheon.

KENNEY, J., & PURSUIT, D. (1965). *Police work with juveniles.* Springfield, IL: Charles C. Thomas.

KOBETZ, R. (1971). *The police role and juvenile delinquency.* Gaithersburg, MD: International Association of Chiefs of Police.

KOLODZIEJSKI, D., STILWELL, J., TORCHIANA, K., & MARKOWITZ, M. (2000). Black and white perceptions of the appropriateness of police conduct. In M. Markowitz & D. Jones-Brown (Eds.), *The system in black and white: Exploring the connections between race, crime and justice* (pp. 125–134). Westport, CT: Praeger.

LASLEY, J. (1994). The impact of the Rodney King incident on citizen attitudes toward police. *Policing and Society, 3,* 245–255.

LAW-RELATED EDUCATION EVALUATION PROJECT. (1983). *Social science education consortium.* Boulder, CO: Center for Action Research.

LEIBER, M., NALLA, M., & FRANWORTH, M. (1998). Explaining juveniles' attitudes toward the police. *Justice Quarterly, 15*(1), 151–173.

MACLEAN, B., & MILOVANOVIC, D. (Eds.) (1990). *Racism, empiricism and criminal justice.* Vancouver, British Columbia, Canada: Collective Press.

MANN, C. (1993). *Unequal justice: A question of color.* Bloomington, IN: Indiana University Press.

MCELROY, J., CASGROVE, C., & SADD, S. (1993). *Community policing: The CPOP in New York.* Newbury Park, CA: Sage.

MCINTYRE, C. (1993). *Criminalizing a race: Free blacks during slavery.* Queens, NY: Kayode.

PORTUNE, R. (1971). *Changing adolescent attitudes toward police.* Cincinnati, OH: W. H. Anderson.

RAFKY, D., & SEALEY, R. (1975, April). The adolescent and the law: A survey. *Journal of Crime and Delinquency, 21*(2), 131–137.

ROBISON, S. (1963). *Juvenile delinquency.* New York: Holt, Rinehart & Winston.

RUSINKO, W., JOHNSON, K., & HORNUNG, C. (1978). The importance of police contact in the formulation of youths' attitudes toward the police. *Journal of Criminal Justice, 6,* 53–67.

RUSSELL, K. (1998). *The color of crime.* New York: New York University Press.

TAPP, J. (1987, September). *Legal socialization across age, culture, and context: Psychological considerations for children and adults.* Paper presented at Rutgers University, Newark, NJ.

TAPP, J., & KOHLBERG, L. (1971). Developing senses of law and legal justice. *Journal of Social Issues, 27*(2), 65–91.

TAPP, J., & LEVINE, F. (1970). Persuasion to virtue: A preliminary statement. *Law and Society Review, 4,* 566–582.

TAPP, J. & LEVINE, F. (1974). Legal socialization: Strategies for an ethical legality. *Stanford Law Review, 27,* 1–72.

TAPP, J., & LEVINE, F. (Eds.). (1977). *Law, justice and the individual in society.* New York: Holt, Rinehart & Winston.

TYLER, T. (1990). *Why people obey the law.* New Haven, CT: Yale University Press.

WEBB, V., & MARSHALL, C. (1995). The relative importance of race and ethnicity on citizens' attitudes toward the police. *American Journal of Police, 16*(2), 45–66.

WILBANKS, W. (1987). *The myth of a racist criminal justice system.* Monterey, CA: Brooks/Cole.

SECTION III
Corrections

8

Get Tough Policies and the Incarceration of African Americans

Janice Joseph, Zelma Weston Henriques, and Kaylene Richards Ekeh

Although the crime rate has been decreasing in recent years, the U.S. criminal justice system has responded to the public's fear of crime by getting tough on criminals. In particular, it has been sentencing offenders to longer periods in prison. This "get-tough" approach has created several problems for the African American community. This chapter examines several get-tough laws—specifically, mandatory laws, drug laws, and "three-strikes-and-you're-out" legislation—and their impact on the incarceration of African Americans. Policy implications are also discussed.

GET TOUGH LEGISLATION

State and federal governments have responded to the public's fear of crime by enacting punitive laws. Such measures include mandatory sentences, antidrug laws, and three-strikes-and-you're-out legislation.

Mandatory Sentences

Mandatory sentences require judges to impose a specified length of sentence for certain offenses or for certain categories of offenders. These laws deny judges discretion, and there is no option for probation or suspension of the sentence. All 50 states and the federal government have established some form of mandatory laws. Thirty-four states also have "habitual offender" laws that require enhanced mandatory prison terms for repeat offenders, in some cases regardless of the seriousness of the crime. Thirty-two states have mandatory laws for certain drug offenses, and 42 for some weapons offenses (Bureau of Justice Assistance, 1996).

Studies at the federal and state levels indicate that African Americans and Hispanics are more likely than whites to be given mandatory sentences or receive enhanced sentences under habitual offender laws. This disparity occurs despite the fact that the offenses and criminal histories of whites and minority groups are similar (Mauer, 1994a). A study by Irwin and Austin (1993) found that African Americans were twice as likely as whites to receive habitual offender sentences even after controlling for the offender's offense and criminal record. According to U.S. District Judge Terry Hatter of Los Angeles, the toughest sentences are now imposed basically against one group of people: poor minority people (Reiman, 1998).

ANTIDRUG LEGISLATION

One political response to drug abuse and drug-related offenses has been tougher laws and longer sentences. In 1986, the federal government passed the Federal Antidrug Abuse Act, which required prison sentences for low-level drug carriers and dealers, and in 1987 Congress imposed stiff mandatory minimum sentences for federal drug law violations (Anti-Drug Abuse Act, 1986). In 1988, this legislation was amended to mandate life sentences without parole for offenders with two or more prior drug felony convictions of selling or conspiring to sell more than five kilograms of cocaine or one kilogram of heroin (Anti-Drug Abuse Act, 1988). The Violent Crime Control and Law Enforcement Act of 1994 tripled the penalties for using children to deal drugs near schools and playgrounds. It also established "drug-free zones" by increasing penalties for drug dealing near schools, schoolyards, video arcades, youth centers, and housing projects (Violent Crime Control and Law Enforcement Act, 1994).

For the most part, state laws mirror federal statutes, and states have undertaken a number of initiatives to make the prosecution and conviction of drug offenders a top priority. States have created special prosecutors to focus on drug-related crimes, and, if convicted, drug offenders receive long sentences. For example, New York's penalties for the sale or distribution of dangerous substances can be as long as 25 years in prison (Siegel, 1995).

The implementation of the antidrug laws has been unfair to African Americans and other minorities. Nationally, blacks[1] are four times more likely than whites to be arrested for drug offenses. Furthermore, in 30 major cities, blacks are at least ten times more likely than whites to be arrested for drugs. Blacks are eight times more likely than whites to be arrested for drug violations in the Midwest, four times more likely in the Northeast and the West, and five times more likely in the South (Meddis, 1993a).

The most blatant disparity in sentencing is for powder cocaine and crack cocaine. Federal law stipulated that the possession or the distribution of five grams of crack cocaine or 500 grams of powder cocaine results in a mandatory five-year sentence without parole. This means that, gram for gram, possession of crack cocaine is punishable at a much higher rate than powder cocaine, a ratio of 100:1. This legislation treats crack cocaine as 100 times worse than powder cocaine.

Federal judges, defense attorneys, and civil rights leaders, such as Reverend Jesse Jackson, have strongly criticized this legislation. Other critics argue that this policy, while racially neutral in its language, discriminates against African American drug users who frequently use crack (Stuart, 1996). The U.S. Sentencing Commission in 1995 recommended that the 100:1 ratio for crack versus powder cocaine be changed to a 1:1 ratio. Representative Charles Rangel of New York sponsored the Crack Cocaine Equitable Sentencing Act of 1995 to erase the inequity in the sentencing for possession of crack and cocaine, but when the legislation reached the floor of the House, it was defeated (Stuart, 1996). In April 1997, the Supreme Court refused to hear the argument that legal distinction between powder cocaine and crack cocaine discriminates against African Americans (*Edwards v. U.S.,* 1997; Biskupic, 1997).

The federal Drug Enforcement Agency has waged its war against crack almost exclusively in African American communities, even though three times as many whites as blacks use crack cocaine (Weikel, 1995). Given the racial differences in the use of crack cocaine and powder cocaine, it was inevitable that the federal legislation would increase the number of African Americans incarcerated in prison.

Drug violations constitute the single most significant factor contributing to the rise in prison population of young African Americans, who represent 12% of the U.S. population, 11% of the nation's illicit drug users, almost 37% of those arrested for drug violations, and more than 42% of those in federal prisons for drug violations (Substance Abuse and Mental Health Services Administration, 1997; U.S. Department of Justice, 1997a). About 90% of those convicted of crack cocaine in federal courts are black, 4% are white, and 6% are of other races. As a result, the average prison sentence served by black federal prisoners is 40% longer than the average for whites (Reiman, 1998). In 1995, the U.S. Sentencing Commission reported that 88% of offenders sentenced for crack offenses in federal court were African Americans and 4% were white (Mauer & Huling, 1995). Between 1990 and 1996, 82% of blacks in federal prison were incarcerated for drug violations (Gilliard & Beck, 1998). Likewise, under the 1988 Anti-Drug Abuse Act, 88% of all those convicted for crack cocaine in 1993 were blacks, although 52% of crack cocaine users and 75% of powder cocaine users are whites (Stuart, 1996). McDonald and Carlson (199e) reported that after the full implementation of minimum mandatory guidelines for illegal drugs, African Americans were given sentences 41% longer than those given whites.

The situation in state prisons is similar to that in the federal penal system. Fifty-six percent of drug offenders in state prison nationwide are black. The proportion of sentenced drug offenders among all black offenders sent to state prison ranged among states from a high of 61% in New Hampshire to a low of 16% in Oregon, with 30% to 40% in a majority of the states. In contrast, drug offenders constituted 24% of all whites sent to state prison nationwide. More blacks were sent to state prison nationwide on drug charges than for crimes of violence. Only 27% of black admissions to prison were for crimes of violence, whereas 38% were for drug offenses in 1998 (U.S. Department of Justice, 1999). Human Rights Watch (2000) examined the drug incarceration rates in 37 states. The study, which used census data and prison admission records collected by the Justice Department, found that the ten states with the greatest racial disparities are Illinois, Wisconsin, Minnesota,

Maine, Iowa, Maryland, Ohio, New Jersey, North Carolina, and West Virginia. In these states, black men are sent to prison on drug charges at 27 to 57 times the rate of white men. The Human Rights Watch's study reported that in Maryland and Illinois 90% of inmates serving time on drug charges are black, although blacks account for only 27% of the population in Maryland and 13% in Illinois. The study also found that although five times as many whites use drugs, black offenders are far more likely to go to prison, and that in one-third of the states, blacks are more than 75% of all drug admissions. In all the states, the proportion of drug offenders admitted to state prison who are black greatly exceeds the proportions of the state population that is black (Fellner, 2000).

Since the Rockefeller Drug Laws were passed in 1973, New York has experienced a tremendous increase in the number of blacks entering its prison system. Between 1980 and 1997, there has been an astonishing 1,615% increase of blacks in New York incarcerated for drug violations in comparison to a 283% increase for whites (Gangi, Schiraldi, & Ziedenberg 1998). In North Carolina, the rate of white prisoners stayed the same (at under 200 per 100,000) while the African American rate rose from about 500 to 960 per 100,000 between 1980 and 1990. The black admissions rate almost doubled between those years, while that of whites remained the same (Tonry, 1995).

The disparity in the rates of incarceration for drug violations between blacks and whites is greatest among males over the age of 18. The drug offender admissions rate for black men over age 18 ranges from 60 to 1,146 per 100,000 black men, whereas that for white men ranges from 6 to 139 per 100,000 white men. On average, black men are sent to prison on drug charges at 13 times the rate of white men (Fellner, 2000).

According to Tonry (1995), "the recent blackening of America's prison population is the product of malign neglect of the drug war's effects on black Americans" (p. 115). Tonry contends that the government knew full well that, by implementing a war on drugs aimed at street level users and dealers, it would be arresting and imprisoning mainly young minority males. He suggests that the rising rates of African Americans in prison "are the foreseeable effects of deliberate policies spearheaded by Reagan and Bush administrations and implemented by many states" (p. 4). Miller (1996) characterized the war on drugs as a case of "search and destroy" directed at young African Americans. Overall, two of five blacks sent to prison are convicted of drug offenses, compared with one in four whites (Fellner, 2000).

Although the incarceration rates of minority men are rapidly increasing because of the "war on drugs," the greatest impact of these laws has been on minority women. These ultrarepressive antidrug policies have succeeded in criminalizing minority women who have been victimized by society. Nationwide, 42.2% of all black women and 36.1% of white women admitted to prison were convicted of drug offenses. Even in the states with the lowest percentages of female drug offender admissions, the figure is more than one in five. Black women are 6.3% of the national adult population and 7% of prison drug admissions; white women are 43.2% of the national adult population but only 5.4% of drug admissions. Black female drug offenders constituted a greater percentage of total admissions than white female drug offenders in half the states (Fellner, 2000). In 1995, the incarceration rate for white and Latin American women combined was 68 per 100,000. For black women, it was 456 per 100,000 (Bureau of Justice Statistics, 1997). Regardless of similar or equal levels of illicit drug use during pregnancy, black women are ten times more likely than white women to be reported to child welfare agencies for prenatal drug use

(Neuspiel, 1996; Chasnoff, Landress, & Barrett, 1990). Consequently, they are charged with child abuse more often than white women. The drug-related provisions of the Violent Crime Control and Law Enforcement Act of 1994 will further increase the number of young African American females in prison.

The racial double standard with regard to drugs can be illustrated by the fact that judges have a tendency to recommend medical and rehabilitation services for white drug users and prison for African American drug users. This double standard holds particularly strongly when affluent white drug users are compared with poor black drug users (Meddis, 1993b). The Human Rights Watch has found that the disproportionate incarceration of African Americans, largely due to drug offenses, violates international human rights (Fellner, 2000).

Three-Strikes-and-You're-Out Laws

Public concern about violent crimes has led to the passage of three-strikes-and-you're-out legislation that is designed to incarcerate dangerous felons who habitually commit crimes. By 1995, 37 states and the federal government had proposed some form of three-strikes legislation. These laws require that three-time felons be sentenced to life imprisonment without parole. Although these laws are referred to as three-strikes laws, there is some variation in how many "chances" offenders receive. Alaska, Massachusetts, and Pennsylvania allow one strike; Georgia, Arkansas, and Tennessee allow only two strikes; and Maryland allows four strikes (Turner, Sundt, Applegate, & Cullen, 1995). In addition to the variation in the number of strikes allowed, states also differ on the crimes for which these laws can be used. Texas, for example, has used the legislation for sex offenders who prey on children, and in California it is imposed for any felony conviction (Levinson, 1995).

The three-strikes legislation already has had an effect on the incarceration rate of African Americans. Washington was the first state to pass such legislation. In four years, 113 offenders were sentenced in Washington under this legislation. Of these, 58% are white and 34% are black, even though blacks make up only 4% of Washington's population. Washington's three-strikes legislation has been criticized for discriminating against African Americans, but public defenders argue that, because black defendants historically have been more willing than white defendants to plead guilty in return for lower sentences, those pleas cost them "strikes" even before the law went into effect (Seven, 1997). Whatever the reason, the Washington three-strike legislation has disproportionately affected African Americans.

The three-strikes legislation has been used widely in California. Discretion in the implementation of the law raises questions of fairness for African Americans, who were charged with a third-strike crime at 13 times the rate of whites. African Americans are 7% of California's population, but they represent 43% of all three-strike defendants sent to state prisons (Davis, Estes, & Schiraldi, 1996). Shiraldi and Godfrey (1994) reported that blacks in Los Angeles County are 10% of the population but 57% of those charged with three-strike felonies. Mauer (1994b) warns that African Americans face an increased risk of being sentenced under three strikes in California, thus expanding the disparity in sentencing. As a consequence, California's three-strikes law has been criticized as racist. According to Schiraldi (1994), racism is the only explanation for this disparity. He argues that the law has led to white prosecutors filing second and third strikes against African American and Latino defendants. Davis, Estes, and Schiraldi (1996) refer to the implementation of three-strikes law in California as the new apartheid.

The three-strikes legislation will drastically increase the number of African Americans in prison because in some states a drug violation can be a third strike. For the most part, drug violations do not constitute a prior strike, but they can be used to enhance a sentence. Under the terms of the three-strikes laws, a drug violation with two prior convictions for other crimes can result in a life sentence. Given the fact that one of the most common offenses for which African Americans are arrested is a drug violation, they will continue to be three-strikes casualties. According to Haney and Zimbardo (1998), because of harsh new sentencing guidelines such as three-strikes laws,

> A disproportionate number of young Black and Hispanic men are likely to be imprisoned for life under scenarios in which they are guilty of little more than a history of untreated addiction and several prior drug-related offenses. . . . States will absorb the staggering cost of not only constructing additional prisons to accommodate increasing numbers of prisoners who will never be released but also warehousing them into old age. (p. 178)

IMPACT OF INCARCERATION ON THE AFRICAN AMERICAN COMMUNITY

Because of these get-tough measures and repressive policies, the overall incarceration rate of African Americans in the United States is extremely high. The United States incarcerates African American men at a rate that is approximately four times the rate of incarceration of black men in South Africa (Haney & Zimbardo, 1998). All major Western European nations' incarceration rates are about or below 100 per 100,000. In the United States, in 1995, the incarceration rate for African American women was 456 per 100,000 and for African American men 6,926 per 100,000 (Currie, 1998; Bureau of Justice Statistics, 1997). Black males were seven times more likely than white males to be incarcerated in prison. In some cities more than half of young black males are under correctional supervision (Duster, 1995; Mauer & Huling, 1995). In the nation as a whole, one in four black males between the ages of 20 and 29 is under the control of the nation's prison system (Mauer & Huling, 1995). The rate of imprisonment for black women is more than eight times the rate of imprisonment of white women; the rate of imprisonment of Hispanic women is nearly four times the rate of imprisonment of white women (Amnesty International, 1999). In ten states and the District of Columbia, blacks are incarcerated at a rate of more than ten times that at which whites are incarcerated. Nationally, in 1997, blacks were incarcerated at a rate of 8.14 times that of whites (Gilliard & Beck, 1998). Miller predicts that by the year 2010, the majority of black men ages 18 to 39 will live behind bars. According to Miller, few people will come in daily contact with black men ages 18 to 39 years (National Association for the Advancement of White People, 1999). If current rates of incarceration remain unchanged for black men, 28.5% of black men will be confined in prison at least once in their lifetimes, a figure six times greater than that for white men (U.S. Department of Justice, 1997a). In fact, at current levels of incarceration, newborn black males in this country have a greater than 25% chance of going to prison during their lifetimes, whereas Latin American males have a 1 in 6 chance, and white males have a 1 in 23 chance of serving time.

The high incarceration of so many African Americans under the get-tough legislation has undoubtedly contributed to the social deterioration of African American communities. Given the high number of African Americans, especially males, incarcerated in prison, the social and financial impact on the black community is tremendous. Donzier (1996) argues that "we are on the verge of a social catastrophe because of the sheer number of African Americans behind bars" (p. 99). According to Haney and Zimbardo (1998), crime control policies are a major contributor to the disruption of the family, the prevalence of single-parent families and children raised without a father, and the "inability of people to get the jobs still available" (p. 716). Blacks in prison do not exist in a vacuum. Every black man in prison is a person without a regular job to support his family. Moreover, long-term imprisonment for African Americans makes it difficult, if not impossible, for them to return to society for a productive, conventional life.

According to King (1993), the financial impact of an incarcerated black male is six to eight times greater on the African American community than on the white community when a white man is incarcerated. King argues that the cost starts with the loss of the imprisoned individual's income. The responsibility for supporting the family is often left to mothers who may be unemployed or employed in low-paying jobs. King also identified other financial costs, including bail, lawyers' fees (if a private attorney is used), collect calls from incarcerated males, lost wages of those incarcerated, travel expenses to prisons, and providing financial support to those who are incarcerated.

One of the long-term impacts of get-tough measures and the high incarceration rate of African Americans is the massive disenfranchisement of large numbers of African Americans and their exclusion from the political process. Because of the high incarceration rate of black men, three in ten adult African American males will be temporarily or permanently deprived of the right to vote. In fact, because of felony conviction and imprisonment, 1.4 million black men—13% of all blacks in the United States—have had their right to vote taken away. In states with the most restrictive voting laws, 40% of the next generation of black men is likely to be *permanently* disenfranchised. The rate of black voter disenfranchisement is seven times the national average. Given current rates of incarceration, three in ten of the next generation of black men will be disenfranchised at some point in their lives (Mauer & Fellner, 1998). To date, there are no estimates of the number of black women who will be disenfranchised because of felony convictions. However, given the fact that black women are incarcerated at a rate eight times that of white women, their disenfranchisement rate would undoubtedly be extremely high in relation to white females. The large number of African Americans who are now disenfranchised and will be disenfranchised in the future will have a devastating effect on the African American community, especially at a time when more blacks have been getting involved in the political process.

The high incarceration rate of African Americans also has an impact on the number of African Americans enrolled in college. At the start of the 1990s, the United States had more black men (between the ages of 20 and 29) under the control of the nation's criminal justice system than in college (Haney & Zimbardo, 1998). This situation is particularly acute in such states as New York and California. In New York, more blacks have entered prison than have graduated from the State University of New York (SUNY) system every year since 1989. Since 1989, there have been more blacks entering the prison system for drug offenses each year than there were graduating from SUNY system with undergraduate, masters, and doctoral degrees combined. In fact, for white youth in New York, "going upstate" means attending one of the dozen SUNY schools in the state. For the black youth in New York, "going upstate" means a trip to one of the state's new prisons (Gangi, Schiraldi, & Ziedenberg, 1998). There is a similar pattern in California and Maryland. In California, five times more black men are in California's prisons than in its public universities (Macallair, Taqi–Eddin, & Schiraldi, 1998; McDermid, Connolly, Macallair, & Schiraldi, 1996). Likewise, in Maryland, African Americans are 25% of college students but 78% of state prisoners. What this means is that in the past ten years or so, these states increased their use of prisons for African Americans faster than they increased their use of public colleges for African Americans (Schiraldi, 1998). It costs state and federal governments $11.6 billion annually to incarcerate African American males (Mauer, 1994a). In fact, New York, California, Maryland, and the District of Columbia are spending more money on prison construction while funding for secondary and post-secondary education has dropped (Schiraldi, 1998; Associated Press, 1998). Traditionally, education has been an investment in the future of society. The fact that more African American men are in prison than in college represents a disinvestment in the future of African American males that will continue to erode the social fabric of the African American communities.

When African Americans are imprisoned, the impact on their children is tremendous. Black children who lose their fathers to the penal system are at risk for involvement themselves in the juvenile justice system. When African American mothers are imprisoned, their children are the ones who suffer the most from the incarceration. Many of these children sometimes suffer a variety of debilitating problems that are later expressed in the form of crime and delinquency. Furthermore, the loss of their mothers can be traumatic for children. The multiple effects of the incarceration of black parents on children should not be underestimated.

GET-TOUGH MEASURES AND REDUCTION OF CRIME

The basic question is whether get-tough legislation effectively reduces crime in the African American community. The idea of punishing the few to deter the many is counterproductive because potential criminals either think that they are not going to get caught or are so emotionally desperate or psychologically distressed that they do not care about the consequences of their actions. Incarceration has a role in public safety, but it is not the cure-all. Its value is limited, and its use should be limited.

Many criminologists question whether long prison terms imposed by three-strikes laws will reduce crime much at all. The argument is that criminal behavior peaks between the ages of 14 and 24. The middle-aged and the elderly serving life terms would commit few crimes, if any, if they were released. Therefore, those serving long sentences are the least likely to commit crimes if released (Walker, 1998).

A 1996 report on sentencing in a variety of states found no correlation between incarceration rates and crime rates (Bureau of Justice Assistance, 1996). Benekos and Merlo (1993) report no discernible effect on crime rates despite the institution of get-tough measures in some states. Zimring and Hawkins (1995) conducted a multistage comparison of incarceration and found no clear correlation between incarceration rates and crime rates. Tonry (1992) remarked that "mandatory penalties do not work" (p. 243).

The Rand Commission of California reports that three-strikes laws would reduce serious crime by only 28%. It points out that the greatest reductions would be in assaults and burglaries but not in murders, rapes, and robberies. The Rand report also indicated that the cost to implement the three-strikes legislation could completely wipe out the state's budget for higher education in exchange for a mere 28% reduction in crimes (Greenwood, Rydell, Albrahmse, Caukins, Model, & Klein, 1994).

Tough sentences for those convicted of drug violations have not been effective in reducing crime. The lack of legitimate opportunities in the black community creates a pool of potential new drug offenders, and those imprisoned for drug violations can easily be replaced by others who are willing to sell drugs for the financial rewards. Some criminologists refer to this as the "replacement phenomenon" (Walker, 1998). Drug use and crimes associated with drugs have remained high among the underclass, especially African Americans, the primary targets of the war on drugs (Walker, 1998). It is, therefore, obvious that the arrest and imprisonment of African Americans have no deterrent effects on crimes.

DEALING WITH THE OVERREPRESENTATION OF MINORITIES IN PRISON

The reasons why African Americans enter the penal system are complex and need to be addressed in a comprehensive way. The following are some recommendations:

Legislative Reform

- The federal government should reform the legislation that creates a sentencing disparity between use of crack cocaine and powder cocaine. The legal distinction between crack cocaine and powder cocaine should be dropped, and the penalties for each type of drug should be equal. In other words, 100 grams of crack or powder cocaine should result in the same amount of time in prison.

- Mandatory sentences should be abolished because of their ineffectiveness. They create prison overcrowding, a high cost of imprisonment, and a growing number of (black) elderly and geriatric inmates in prison. Mandatory sentencing laws need to be repealed. The Human Rights Watch has made similar suggestions (Fellner, 2000).

- Governments should examine all sentencing policies and practices, with the goal of reducing the use of incarceration for African Americans. Governments should develop effective alternatives to incarceration.

Criminal Justice Reform

- Law enforcement should redirect antidrug efforts toward catching higher level dealers while providing alternatives for nonviolent offenders (Fellner, 2000). The focus on low-level drug dealers results in high incarceration rates, especially of blacks.

- Prisons and prison programs should be designed to rehabilitate African American prisoners and reduce the likelihood that they will return to the system. Prison programs should provide prisoners with the necessary skills to succeed after incarceration.

- States need to use more front-end strategies for African Americans, such as probation, fines, and community service, electronic monitoring, shock incarceration, and diversion. Incarceration is appropriate for offenders who endanger the community, but other sanctions could be used more often for nonviolent, low-risk African American offenders. These sanctions promote rehabilitation and reintegration of the offenders..

- Judges should refer more African Americans convicted for drug violations to community-based corrections. States should expand the treatment programs for African Americans with drug problems. Drug addiction is a medical disease, not a criminal offense, and should be treated as such. It should be seen as a public health problem rather than a criminal justice problem (Fellner, 2000).

- States and the federal government should spend more money on diversion and rehabilitation programs for African Americans instead of on incarceration. Incarceration should be used as a last resort for offenders who cannot be diverted or rehabilitated.

- States and the federal government should eliminate the sentencing disparity that exists in the criminal justice system. Today, race and ethnicity matter in criminal justice. Those who are white and poor are processed differently in the criminal justice system than those who are African American and poor. Poor whites may receive probation while poor African Americans may receive imprisonment for the same crime. There is a need for social justice. This form of discrimination should be eliminated.

Crime Prevention

Given the fact that get-tough legislation appears to have little or no deterrent effect on crime rates among African Americans and the fact that the high rate of incarceration of African Americans has social and financial consequences for the community, the question is, How can the number of African Americans in prison be reduced? The answer lies in crime prevention and treatment strategies and the elimination of discrimination in the criminal justice system.

Punitive measures to combat crimes are after-the-fact solutions to the crime problem in the African American community; that is, these measures attack crime and criminals rather than the social factors that are linked to the criminal behavior of African Americans. Instead of after-the-fact efforts, governments need to provide before-the-fact comprehensive social programs to prevent criminal behavior among African Americans.

Solutions to the crime problem must focus on factors that predispose African Americans to criminal behavior. Although a high percentage of African Americans have more contact with the criminal justice system than many whites do, race or ethnicity is not related to criminal behavior. Instead, social class is a more important factor than either race or ethnicity. Many African Americans reside in inner city areas that are socially disorganized, physically decayed, and economically deprived. Much of the African American population is perennially unemployed, uneducated, and improvised. In 1996, the poverty (less than $15,569 for a family of four) rates for blacks were double of whites (Hale, 1997). Half the children born to African American parents are born in poverty. The life expectancy for a black man in Harlem is less than that for a man in Bangladesh (Olsen, 1996). These personal circumstances are conducive to high rates of crime. The social environment of African Americans is, therefore, primarily responsible for crime rate differences (Duster, 1987).

The most effective way to curb crime among African Americans is to prevent African Americans from committing the acts in the first place. Governments, therefore, need to refocus their crime-control measures from incarceration to increased employment policies and educational programs. Specifically, they should:

- Focus on poverty and the lack of economic opportunities in the African American community by providing more jobs and job training programs. Given the role of poverty and economic inequities in fostering crime among African Americans, it is plausible that reducing poverty and the economic disparity between blacks and the rest of society would help to reduce their criminal behavior.

- Provide African Americans with early childhood developmental programs, parent-training programs, educational and recreational programs, drug treatment programs, and counseling programs. Criminal behavior among African Americans would be more effectively reduced by education and treatment, with prison as a last resort.

- Provide preventive measures that are more effective and significant than punitive reactions. Punishment may be necessary, but punishment often fails to teach new, alternative means to achieve desired goals.

These recommendations are both short and long term. The tendency is for governments to focus on short-term policies and ignore long-term strategies. The problem of crime cannot be solved entirely with legislative and criminal justice policies and strategies because they are reactive in nature. What is also necessary is prevention, which requires long-term policies and strategies. Governments have to focus more on prevention if they are to deal with crimes among African Americans.

SUMMARY

Criminal justice policies are often short-sighted and formulated in response to emotional appeals. The media sensationalism of particular crimes and criminals and the political power of the crime issue usually prompt new policies—policies that often lack proper planning and thorough examination of their long-term impact. Getting tough has always been a quick fix for crimes that society fears. State and federal governments have passed get-tough policies that have had very little impact on crime but instead seem to victimize and penalize the black community. If the current penal policies are left unchallenged and unchanged, the number of blacks incarcerated will increase and the so-called get-tough measures will continue to be detrimental to the black community. To break this cycle and reduce the number of imprisoned blacks, states and the federal government need to reexamine their get-tough legislation. In addition, there needs to be much more discussion about drug policies and a reexamination of their effectiveness. States and the federal government should provide social programs for African Americans to break the cycle of poverty, unemployment, and crime. Criminal behavior can be reduced in the African American community if governments provide education and jobs. The choice is clear; schools and jobs should be available to African Americans instead of imprisonment. When states choose to build prisons instead of providing better schools and job opportunities for African Americans, then these policies are criminal. Ironically, the public seems eager to build more prisons but is reluctant to spend money on social reform and social justice.

DISCUSSION QUESTIONS

1. What are mandatory sentences?

2. Describe the sentencing disparity between powder cocaine and crack cocaine.

3. Describe three-strikes-and-you're-out legislation.

4. Explain what is meant by the "massive disenfranchisement of large numbers of African Americans."

5. Why are "get-tough" measures rarely effective?

N O T E

1. The term "blacks" and not "African Americans" is used in many statistical reports. The term "blacks" is used to refer to not only African Americans but also people from the Caribbean and Africa. Because the majority of blacks in the United States are African Americans, the terms will be used interchangeably.

R E F E R E N C E S

AMNESTY INTERNATIONAL. (1999). *Not part of my sentence: Violations of the human rights of women in custody.* Washington, DC: Author.

ANTI-DRUG ABUSE ACT, PUBLIC LAW, 99–570, U.S.C. 1501 841 (1986).

ANTI-DRUG ABUSE ACT, PUBLIC LAW, 100–690; 21 U.S.C. 1501; Section 7001, Amending the Controlled Substances Abuse Act, 21 U.S. 848 (1988).

ASSOCIATED PRESS. (1998, October 9). High school students in California protest spending on prisons, *New York Times,* p, 28.

BENEKOS, P. J., & MERLO, A.V. (1993). Three strikes and you're out! The political sentencing game. *Federal Probation, 59,* 3–9.

BISKUPIC, J. (1997). Supreme Court rejects claims that crack laws target blacks. *The Washington Post,* p. 3.

BONCZAR, T.P., & BECK, A.J. (1997). *Lifetime likelihood of going to state or federal prison.* Washington DC: U.S. Government Printing Office.

Bowman, L. (1998, September 10). Value of drug treatment shows on the streets. *Boston Herald,* p. 34.

Bureau of Justice Assistance, (1996), *National assessment of structured sentencing.* Washington, DC: Government Printing Office.

Bureau of Justice Statistics. (1997). *Sourcebook of criminal justice statistics 1996.* Washington DC: U.S. Government Printing Office.

Butterfield, F. (1996, February 13). Study finds a disparity in justice for blacks. *New York Times,* p. A8.

Chasnoff, I.J., Landress, H.J., & Barrett, M.E. (1990). The prevalence of illicit-drug or alcohol use during pregnancy and discrepancies in mandatory reporting in Pinellas County, Florida. *New England Journal of Medicine, 322,* 1202–1206.

Currie, E. (1998). *Crime and punishment in America.* New York: Metropolitan Books, Henry Holt.

Davis, C., Estes, R., & Schiraldi, R. (1996). *Three strikes: The new apartheid.* San Francisco,CA: Center on Juvenile and Criminal Justice.

Donzier, S.R. (1996). *The real war on crime: The report of the National Criminal Justice Commission.* New York: Harper Perennial.

Duster, T. (1987). Crime, youth unemployment, and the black urban underclass. *Crime and Delinquency, 33*(2), 300–316.

Duster, T. (1995). The new crisis of legitimacy controls, prisons, and legal structures. *American Sociologist, 26,* 20–29.

Edwards v. U.S., No. 96–1492, 61CrL3015. U.S. Sup Ct 1997.

Fellner, J. (2000, May). United States: Punishment and prejudice: Racial disparities in the war on drugs. *Human Rights Watch, 12*(2). Accessed April 10, 2000, at: http://www.hrw.org/reports/2000/usa/.

Gangi, R., Schiraldi, V., & Ziedenberg, J. (1998). *New York's state of mind: Higher education vs. prison funding in the Empire State, 1988–1998.* Washington, DC: Justice Policy Institute.

Gilliard, D., & Beck, A.J. (1998). *Prisoners in 1997.* Washington DC.: Bureau of Justice Statistics, U.S. Department of Justice.

Greenwood, P., Rydell, C.P., Albrahmse, A.F., Caukins, J.C., Model, K.E., & Klein, S.P. (1994). *Three strikes and you're out: Estimated benefits and costs of California's new mandatory law.* Santa Monica, CA: Rand.

Hale, T. (1997). *A profile of the working poor.* Washington, DC: U.S. Department of Labor.

Haney, C., & Zimbardo, P. (1998). The past and future of U.S. prison policy: Twenty-five years after the Stanford prison experiment. *American Psychologist, 53*(7), 709–727.

Human Rights Watch. (2000, June 8). Stark race disparities in drug incarceration found across U.S. New York: Human Rights Watch.

Irwin, J., & Austin, J. (1993). *It's about time: America's imprisonment binge.* Belmont, CA: Wadsworth.

King, O.A.E. (1993). The impact of incarceration on African American families: Implications for practice. *Family in Society, 74,* 145–153.

Levinson, A. (1995, September 24). "Three strikes" laws not used. *Denver Post,* pp. 31A–32A.

Macallair, D., Taqi–Eddin, K., & Schiraldi, V. (1998). *Class dismissed: Higher education vs. corrections during the Wilson years.* Washington, DC: Justice Policy Institute.

Mauer, M. (1994a). *Americans behind bars: The international use of incarceration, 1992–1993.* Report 1–27. Washington, DC: The Sentencing Project.

Mauer, M. (1994b). *Testimony before the U.S. Congress House Judiciary on three strikes and you're out.* Washington, DC: The Sentencing Project.

Mauer, M., & Fellner, J. (1998, October). Losing the vote: The impact of felony disenfranchisement laws in the United States. *Human Rights Watch and the Sentencing Project,* p. 13.

MAUER, M., & HULING, T. (1995). *Young black Americans and the criminal justice system: Five years later.* Washington, DC: The Sentencing Project.

McDERMID, L., CONNOLLY, K., MACALLAIR, D., & SCHIRALDI, V. (1996). *From classrooms to cell blocks: How prison building affects higher education and African American enrollment.* Washington, DC: Justice Policy Institute

McDONALD, D.C., & CARLSON, K.E. (1993). *Sentencing in federal courts: Does race matter? The transition of sentencing guidelines, 1980–1990.* Washington, DC: Bureau of Justice Statistics.

MEDDIS, S.V. (1993a, July 23). Is the drug war racist: Disparities suggest the answer is "yes." *USA Today,* pp. 1A–2A.

MEDDIS, S.V. (1993b, July 26). In twin cities: A tale of two standards. *USA Today,* p. 6A.

MILLER, J.G. (1996). *Search and destroy: African American males in the criminal justice system.* New York: Cambridge University Press.

NATIONAL ASSOCIATION FOR THE ADVANCEMENT OF WHITE PEOPLE. (1999). More black men headed to prison: According to the Department of Justice. Accessed April 11, 2000, at: http://www.naawpcom/more_black_men_in_prison.htm

NEUSPIEL, D.R. (1996). Racism and perinatal addiction. *Ethnicity and Disease, 6,* 47–55.

OLSEN, J. (1996). Gardens of the law. In E. Rosenblatt (Ed.), *Criminal injustice, confronting the prison crisis.* Boston, MA: South End Press.

RAND CORPORATION. (1997, May 12). *Study finds current sentencing laws undermine drug control goals.* Santa Monica, CA: Rand Corporation.

REIMAN, J. (1998). *The rich get richer and the poor get prison.* Boston, MA: Allyn and Bacon.

REUTERS. (1998, September 10). Report says drug rehab works, urges more funding. *Boston Globe,* p. A26.

SCHIRALDI, V. (1994). *The undue influence of California's prison guard union: California's correctional-industrial complex. In brief.* San Francisco, CA: Center for Juvenile and Criminal Justice.

SCHIRALDI, V. (1998). *Is Maryland's system of higher education suffering because of prison expenditures?* Washington, DC: The Justice Policy Institute.

SCHIRALDI, V., & GODFREY, M. (1994). *Racial disparities in the charging of Los Angeles County's "third strike" cases. In brief.* San Francisco, CA: California Center on Juvenile and Criminal Justice.

SEVEN, R. (1997, November 7). Three-strikes law casting a wide net. *Seattle Times,* p. A2.

SIEGEL, L. (1995). *Criminology, patterns, and typologies.* St. Paul, MN: West.

STUART, R. (1996, May). The sentencing game. *Emerge, 7,* 51–53.

SUBSTANCE ABUSE AND MENTAL HEALTH SERVICES ADMINISTRATION. (1997). *National household survey on drug abuse: Population estimates 1996.* Rockville, MD: Substance Abuse and Mental Health Services Administration, Bureau of Justice Statistics.

TONRY, M. (1993). Mandatory penalties. In M. Tonry (Ed.), *Crime and justice: A review of research,* Vol. 16 (pp. 243–273). Chicago: University of Chicago Press.

TONRY, M. (1995). *Malign neglect: Race, crime, and punishment.* New York: Oxford University Press.

TURNER, M.G., SUNDT, J., APPLEGATE, B.K., & CULLEN, F.T. (1995). Three strikes and you're out legislation. A national assessment. *Federal Probation, 59*(3), 16–35.

U.S. DEPARTMENT OF JUSTICE. (1997a, March). *Lifetime likelihood of going to state or federal prison.* Washington, DC.: U.S. Government Printing Office.

U.S. DEPARTMENT OF JUSTICE. (1997b). *Prisoners in 1996.* Washington, DC.: U.S. Government Printing Office.

U.S. DEPARTMENT OF JUSTICE. (1999). *Prisoners in 1998.* Washington, DC.: U.S. Government Printing Office.

VIOLENT CRIME CONTROL AND LAW ENFORCEMENT ACT, Public Law 103–322, 1994.

WALKER, S. (1998). *Sense and nonsense about crime and drugs: A policy guide.* Belmont, CA: West/Wadsworth.

WEIKEL, D. (1995, May 21). Crack war raged by race. *Denver Post,* pp. 1A, 7A.

ZIMRING, F., & HAWKINS, G. (1995). *Incapacitation: Penal confinement and the restraint of crime.* New York: Oxford University Press.

9

Children of Imprisoned Mothers

What Does the Future Hold?

Lanette P. Dalley

> Children begin by loving their parents; as they grow older they judge them;
> sometimes they forgive them.
>
> *Oscar Wilde*

Women prisoners have always represented a small number of the prison population in the United States. Between 1990 and 1999, however, the female prison population grew 106% compared with only a 75% increase in the male inmate prison population (Beck, 2000, p. 5). Criminologists and sociologists suggest a variety of reasons for this dramatic increase, including the effect of mandatory sentencing guidelines and gender-neutral sentencing. Not surprisingly, these sentencing policies result in the further deterioration of the mother–child relationship, as well as increasing the social, emotional, and behavioral problems of the children. Currently, it is estimated that 1.3 million children have mothers who are under correctional supervision, and of these 1.3 million children, more than 400,000 children are separated from their mothers, who are in either prison or jail (Greenfield & Snell, 1999, p. 5).[1]

Children of imprisoned mothers are often referred to as the "silent" victims of enforced separation for several reasons (Gable & Johnston, 1995; Henriques, 1982). First, the empirical data on this population are mostly limited to maternal perceptions only; few studies have actually interviewed or surveyed the children because of the inherent problems of accessing the children. Second, the criminal justice system typically ignores the children, from the time their mothers are arrested to their imprisonment. The children have

121

no advocates to represent their best interests until they have been labeled abused, neglected, dependent, or delinquent. However, in many cases these children do not fit neatly into these legal categories and go without essential services and resources.

Most researchers focusing on imprisoned mothers and their children have studied maternal perceptions in exploring the concerns and needs (Henriques, 1982; Baunach, 1985; Bloom & Steinhart, 1993; Gable & Johnston, 1995). The studies have made significant contributions of uncovering many problems and characteristics associated with this population. Yet, numerous questions remain relatively unanswered. For instance, we know that children experience problems during maternal imprisonment. Not surprisingly, many assume that the children's problems are directly associated with the imprisonment of the mother. What has not been examined is whether the children's problems were present *before* incarceration and were merely exacerbated during the enforced separation.

Recent research has shown that the children's problems are also related to the intergenerational cycle of incarceration. These studies suggest that children whose family members have been imprisoned are at a higher risk to be imprisoned than other children (Johnston, 1991, 1992; Gable & Johnston, 1995; Pollock, 1998). Other studies have also revealed that specific events beginning in early childhood (i.e., parent–child separation, abuse, witnessing violence, and parental substance abuse) increase the likelihood of arrest and imprisonment in adolescence or young adulthood (Widom, 1989, 1995, 1996; Earls & Reiss, 1994; Gable & Johnston, 1995). Thus, it is essential to study the present *and* prior characteristics of the inmate mother's children because they are likely to be the second and in some cases the third generation of prisoners.

This chapter presents a portion of the findings from a study of female prisoners in Montana. The findings reveal that the women have deep-seated, cyclical problems that often make the women and their problems resistant to viable intervention. Sadly, these problems are often passed on to their children, thus beginning or continuing the cycle of incarceration. This chapter begins with a brief overview of the data collection process, including a demographic description of the inmate mothers, the study's findings in relation to the children's problems, and recommendations to address the emerging intergenerational cycle of imprisonment.

OVERVIEW OF STUDY

Similar to other states that have experienced a substantial increase in female offenders, the female correctional population (i.e., prison, prerelease, and community correctional facilities) in Montana has also sharply increased, by almost 180% between 1994 and 1998.[2] Seventy percent of female prisoners in Montana are mothers of minor children.[3] Data presented relating to the first phase of the study are from three correctional facilities: the prison, the prerelease center, and the community correctional facility.[4] Phase I involved administering a survey to the women. The survey was adopted from Bloom and Steinhart's (1993) *Why Punish the Children?*[5] Once the women were administered the survey, they were divided into focus groups of 5 to 9 women.[6] This research process was repeated until all the women who volunteered completed the process. In addition, to validate the data collected, a variety of ancillary methods were also used, including reviewing inmate correctional files, conducting informal interviews with correctional staff, and documenting field observations.

Forty-four inmate mothers who had a total of 89 children participated in the study ($N = 62$).[7] The average age of the women was 32, and the average age of the children was 8. Seventy-three percent of the women were white, 27% were Native American, and one woman was pregnant and gave birth during the study. Almost two-thirds (65%) were single mothers. The majority were unemployed at the time of their arrest (70.5%) and had an annual income of less than $10,000. Most of the women committed nonviolent offenses (43.2%) or drug-related offenses (27%), and it was not uncommon for them to be incarcerated for probation violations as well (40%).[8] Only one-quarter of the women were expected to be separated from their children for a short period of time (two years or less). In sharp contrast, 32% were sentenced to spend 11 to 20 years or more behind bars.

In addition, as discussed throughout the chapter, drugs and alcohol were persistent problems for the majority of the women, which affected every facet of their lives but particularly the relationship with their children. In fact, nearly 80% of the women reported being regular users (weekly or daily) at some point in their lives.[9] The women also reported having long family histories of criminality (i.e., imprisonment). More than half had family members in prison, either currently or in the past (59.1%). On a more personal level, an overwhelming number of inmate mothers reported being physically abused as children, adults, or both (84%). It was also not uncommon for the women to have been abused by their parents. As a result, one-quarter of the women reported being placed in foster homes during childhood. Sadly, the findings show almost half of the women who were abused as children later became the victims of abuse in their adult relationships. This pattern correlates with the cyclical nature of abuse that has been noted by a number of experts and is also addressed in this chapter (Wallace, 1996; Widom, 1995, 1996; Wolfe, 1999).

Data clearly illustrate that the majority of the children suffered either emotional or physical problems for a variety of reasons. Unfortunately, the maternal image that emerges from these data is far from the traditional image of women as mothers. In fact, by their own accounts their relationships with their children were often very disturbing. A sincere effort has been made to present an accurate portrayal of this population, as well as a realistic assessment of their lives and their often desperate situations.

CHILDREN'S PROBLEMS

Overall, 82 of the 89 children were experiencing at least one problem (92%). In the majority of the cases, though, many of the children were experiencing a combination of problems. It is also likely that their problems greatly surpassed what was reported by the inmate mothers for several reasons. First, the inmate mothers often did not know what was happening with their children during or prior to their imprisonment; many of the women either had lost custody or their children were staying with another relative or with friends before their imprisonment. Also for a variety of reasons, several of the mothers had very little contact, if any, with their children during imprisonment; therefore, it was difficult for them to provide details of their children's characteristics or situations.

Second, many inmate mothers lacked knowledge about particular childhood problems such as developmental delays, fetal alcohol syndrome, learning disabilities, and other emotional and health problems. Third, even if they were aware of the problems, they did not identify the problems until the focus group interview. In some cases, it seemed that hearing other women talk about their children's problems made something "click," and the women were then able to describe their children's problems. The women were not attempting to be deceptive; they were having a difficult time either comprehending the questions or remembering or even acknowledging their children had "handicaps."

The majority of the mothers who did report problems knew about them because an agency (school, Division of Family Services, psychiatric hospital, etc.) had identified the problem.[10] These problems were also confirmed through the inmate records and discussions with correctional staff who knew these women and their children extremely well.

Problems Prior to Imprisonment

As previously mentioned, many studies either made the assumption that these children experienced these problems during and after their mother's incarceration or simply did not address *when* these problems initially began. One is left with the impression that the children's problems were a result of their mother's incarceration. In this study, however, the inmate mothers reported that 72% of the children were experiencing their problems as described next *before* their mother's incarceration. The severity of the children's problems during maternal imprisonment increased by only 14%.[11]

The data presented next also reflect a relationship between the children's ages and problems. The older children (seven and older) were reported as having a higher rate of problems than the younger children (younger than seven). This was not unexpected. In contrast with younger children, older children are more easily identified as having problems because this age group is in school and comes into more frequent contact with professionals who are trained in identifying emotional and health problems, developmental delays, or learning disabilities. The average age of the 89 children was eight.

Mental Health.   Difficulties associated with the children's mental health were the most commonly reported problem area with 68 of the 89 children having emotional problems (76.4%). Five categories of mental health problems were identified: General anxiety disorders, the first and most frequently reported category, includes children experiencing separation anxiety, nightmares, bedwetting, and encopresis (28%). The most prevalent problem mentioned in this category was separation anxiety. Children with this type of anxiety exhibit behaviors such as unusual crying spells, hysteria, and clinging, either when visiting their mothers or while living with their caregivers. During one focus group interview, a mother recalled visiting her children while they were in foster care shortly before her imprisonment:

> I remember putting them in the car 'cause they were in foster care and my daughter is six. She would say, "Mommy no, no please don't let me go back, I don't want to go back!" I kept telling her it's O.K. and she did come home. (Gr.1, Gm. 1)[12]

Another woman during a focus group interview described her child's separation anxiety after a visit at the prison and her concerns regarding her parents as caretakers and her daughter's developmental regression:

> When they [maternal parents] first took her away from me, she reverted. She had been potty trained, and when they came and got her she went back to using diapers again. And she won't go outside. She doesn't like to be away from people. Somebody always has to be with her,

and I'm sure she's got a lot of anger because she's trying to deal with what they told her and me not being there. (Gr. 7, Gm. 38)

A common theme that was repeatedly mentioned was the mothers' concern that their children's anxiety resulted primarily from the impact of family violence (either witnessing or directly experiencing it) or from being sexually or physically abused.

Aggressive behaviors, the second category associated with the children's emotional problems, included children abusing animals, exhibiting violent outbursts, and sexually offending other children (11.2%). Violent outbursts were the most common behavior problem. For example, one woman described her eight-year-old son's behavior:

> You know they're [psychiatric facility] telling me there must have been a lot of violence in the home. Did you show him a lot of violence because he wants to hurt kids. I mean right down to animals. Choked this one dog right out. He was a malamute dog and he [son] was really small when he [son] did it, and he almost choked the dog. . . . He might have learned that from seeing me get beat up. But, he was pretty little when he was with me. But he did see some bad stuff. (Gr.7, Gm. 38)

Depression, the third category of the children's emotional problems, was reported as children displaying behaviors such as withdrawal, poor self-esteem, suicidal gestures, and pronounced sadness (10%). In several of the cases, the mothers reported again that their children were experiencing depression as a result of being physically abused by someone other than themselves or because of growing up in violent families. Withdrawal and sadness were most commonly reported. During a focus group interview, one woman described her four-year-old acting out her depression aggressively:

> My little girl is going through a lot of depression. She's really depressed, you know, and I asked my mom to get her into counseling. . . . And I've talked to a mental health counselor and she told me that, "Well, you know this could be because she's seen some of your behaviors and she might be missing you." And I don't know; it's just really weird. She chews her dolls' heads off, and they say that's part of a kid being angry and depressed. It's really weird. (Gr. 7, Gm. 39)

One woman discussed her seventeen-year-old daughter's depression, leading to her daughter attempting suicide because of the woman's abusive relationships:

> I carry a lot of guilt around because all my relationships have been abusive except for one. And this last relationship I had I got out of before I met my boyfriend. It was really awful and sometimes you think your kids are strong, but my daughter almost committed suicide because of this man. (Gr. 1, Gm. 2)

Another woman was a heroin addict and, as a result, had been imprisoned six times and lost custody of all five of her children (three of whom were born addicted). She discussed her children's depression, particularly her oldest daughter's, in relation to feeling abandoned by her mother throughout her childhood and still having the need to "protect" and care for her mother:

> I don't think they feel real secure and they seem depressed. They have depressions like I do. I think that's from some of the things that they had to deal with when they were growing up. My daughter has a real hard time to this day with anybody leaving her that she loves, no

matter who it is. She still has a hard time with me leaving and it's real hard for her. But she has a boyfriend and she's afraid that he is going to leave her. And I feel like that's because she lost me at such a young age. You know she just has a real fear, and when I'm there she doesn't want me to leave, she wants to protect me, she wants to stay with me, and she feels responsible for me, so I think that has to do with it, too. With my son, I think he's real detached in relationships. He's having a real hard time with his marriage and I feel like some of that is due to his anger towards me. (Gr. 2, Gm.13)

This is an example of not only depression but also role reversal. Essentially, in role reversal the child assumes the role of the parent and takes on the parenting responsibilities (i.e., providing nurturance and emotional support to the parent and raising their siblings). Recent research has found that role reversal (often referred to as "parentification") frequently has long developmental consequences for children (Chase, 1999). Children who perform the role of parent at the expense of their own developmentally appropriate needs can acquire profound emotional disabilities such as depression, anxiety, low self-esteem, and an inability to establish a stable relationship in their adult lives. Perhaps more important, research suggests that parentified children are likely to grow up and repeat these behaviors with their own children (Jacobvitz, Riggs & Johnson, 1999).

In this study, 9% of the 89 children were reported as taking on the role of the parent. While some women recognized this behavior as a problem, the majority did not and discussed it as a common, *normal* relationship. In fact, the vast majority of the women and their children experienced role reversal in their daily lives. Many of the women described their children's primary role as meeting their mothers' physical and emotional needs, particularly in relation to their addictions. Therefore, the number of children reported to be experiencing role reversal may not accurately reflect the actual number.

An example of failure to recognize role reversal as a problem is a Native American woman's description during a focus group interview of her dependence on her nine-year-old son's protective, enabling behavior. His parenting went to the extreme of controlling the family finances:

When I had a hangover, I'd be laying on the couch and I'd tell my son that I was sick . . . and then all of it would come back up and I'd have to make a beeline towards the bathroom. My son would be standing there with his hand on my back patting me on my back, "Poor mommy." My older son, he was my little man. I had him hide the stuff for me. I didn't do drugs but I like my booze. I'd have him hide it so his dad wouldn't see it. . . . I don't know where he hid it because I went looking for it once and I couldn't find it. So I asked him and he said, "Wait!" I was gonna follow him and he said, "No, you wait!" So he'd take off and he'd come back with my pint. So that kid had a hiding place in that house that I never knew of. . . . It's like you're the kid, you sit still, and I'm the big person. . . . He was my little lifesaver. . . . That kid went so far as taking my money away from me and putting it in his pocket. He was gonna take care of the money. (Gr. 5, Gm. 26)

This woman's presentence investigation report indicated that this Native American boy and his younger brother had been recently diagnosed with fetal alcohol syndrome and with diabetes.

One of the few inmate mothers who did show insight into the negative consequences of role reversal recalled during a focus group interview how her older children parented her younger children and the negative effects it had on them:

And they . . . my older girls, were more so the caretakers of the younger kids, you know. When they were babies, when they were toddlers, they'd go to school. They couldn't concentrate on school because they were too worried about what was going on at home. (Gr. 2, Gm. 12)

This woman's correctional file reported that she was also abandoned, neglected, and physically abused as a child. By age two, this woman's biological mother died as a result of her "natural, alcoholic father beating her [mother] to death." The biological father was sentenced to prison and later died of cirrhosis of the liver. The woman and her sister were placed in foster care, where they were both physically and sexually abused by the foster parents. The abusive situation was discovered only after the foster parent poured boiling water on the woman's sister, badly scalding her.

After that, the woman and her sister were in numerous foster homes and eventually were separated by the welfare department. By the time the woman was nine years old, she became "hooked on hallucinogenic" drugs. When she was 14, she ran away from her foster placement and became involved in prostitution. By the time she was 15, she had her first child, and in the next five years she had four more children.

The fifth and last mental health problem reported was fetal alcohol syndrome (7.9%). The percentage of the women who reported this particular problem is obviously much lower than the other identified problem areas; however, the number may be significantly higher. For instance, at least two women did not disclose that their children had been diagnosed with fetal alcohol syndrome. Their children's conditions were discovered through their prison records and during interviews with the program directors. One director explained that the women were willing to discuss their children's problems that were not directly attributed to them but that the women often failed to acknowledge or discuss the problem of fetal alcohol syndrome because they would then need to admit to harming their children. This attitude is not unusual in that many parents in general typically have difficulty taking responsibility for harming their children.

Fetal alcohol syndrome is a completely preventable condition in children because the sole cause is the mother's consumption of alcohol during pregnancy. It is a "grave and disabling condition with lifelong consequences to children" (Streissguth, Ladue, & Randels, 1988, p. 23). The condition usually involves growth deficiencies, central nervous system disorders, and various facial and bodily abnormalities. Child development experts agree that children with this condition typically have below-average IQs and do not typically outgrow their early intellectual handicaps (Streissguth et al., 1988; Crosson-Tower, 1999).

Additionally, these children's behavior is difficult for caretakers to manage because they often have difficulty in learning, remembering, problem solving, and understanding cause and effect (relating discipline to the unwanted behavior) (Crosson-Tower; 1999; Kelley, 1992; Kropenske et al., 1994). They often exhibit speech problems, impulsiveness, lack of appropriate judgment, and aggressive behaviors (Streissguth et al., 1988).

Children who are exposed to smaller doses of alcohol during gestation may be more difficult to diagnose because they typically do not have pronounced physical abnormalities, yet they still suffer from neurological and cognitive impairment. These children are referred to as having fetal alcohol effects (Fishbein & Pease, 1996). Thus, another possible explanation for mothers' lack of response to this category may be that the inmate mothers may not actually know about this condition.

Health Problems.   The next most frequently reported problem area was health. Forty-two of the 89 children were reported as having serious and often chronic health problems (47%). The inmate mothers described these problems as their children having diabetes, kidney malfunction, defective hearts, asthma, brain tumors, epilepsy, underdeveloped teeth, migraines, and underdeveloped bronchial tubes. Asthma was the most frequently mentioned health problem. Of the 42 children, 24 suffered permanent health problems (27%).

Health problems resulting from the mother's use of drugs or alcohol during pregnancy (7.9% of the 47%) include cases of children who experienced tremors from fetal alcohol syndrome and infants who were addicted to heroine, methamphetemine, or cocaine or who were failing to thrive. One child was born blind. Failure to thrive and drug-addicted infants were the most frequently mentioned problems. Failure to thrive is defined as follows:

> [The] infants are usually small and emaciated. They look sick and are unable to digest food properly. Sometimes they start eating as soon as they arrive at the hospital; at other times they are listless and withdrawn, almost immobile. These infants often avoid eye contact. . . . By definition, failure-to-thrive infants weigh in the [bottom] 3% for their age group. (Craig, 1996, p. 228)

One woman candidly discussed her daughter's having failed to thrive as result of her drug use and her daughter's abusive foster home:

> When my daughter was just a baby, the drugs probably affected her the most because the first foster home she was in was abusive. And I put her in there, in the foster care. I didn't put her there but my behavior led up to that. . . . She had that failure-to-thrive problem. She was slow for her first year of life. I think my drugs affected her because I wasn't no good to her. I didn't care for her, you know. When you have a little baby, they need attention, and I couldn't do that because I was out doing drugs. (Gr. 1, Gm. 8)

A review of the same woman's correctional file indicated that her presentence investigation reported that her daughter was a drug-addicted infant. She was in foster care, and Division of Family Services had temporary custody of her daughter.

Health problems associated with abuse and neglect from someone other than the inmate mother (i.e., relative or foster parents) included failure to thrive, hearing loss, back injury, and broken legs and arms (4.5%). Failure to thrive was again the most frequently mentioned problem.

Behavioral Problems.   The third most frequently reported problem area was behavioral. Of the 89 children, 38 children were characterized as having behavioral problems (43%). Aggressive behaviors, such as fire setting, violent outbursts, rebelliousness, and fighting with peers, were the most frequently reported (22.5%). Violent outbursts were the most common problem of all the aggressive behaviors.

Inconsolable children were also reported. They are described by the inmate mothers as irritable, constantly crying, having severe temper tantrums, and needing incessant attention (11.2%). Other behaviors mentioned were withdrawal, lack of social skills, and hyperactivity (6.7%).

A Native American woman during the focus group interview described her son's aggressive behaviors and how he learned these behaviors from her:

I couldn't talk to him because it didn't matter. What I showed him and what I told him was two different things. I'd say, "Well you know you can't do that, that's not right to hit some-body, you know. It's not right to put them in a head lock and ram their heads against the door because you can't have your own way." And he'd say, "Well you do it!" (Gr. l, Gm. 3)

The woman's correctional file revealed that her 17-year-old son had an extensive juvenile court record and was residing in a secure youth group home. However, shortly before the study was completed, her son ran from his placement. The woman indicated that once her son was found he would be placed in a juvenile correctional facility until he reached his eighteenth birthday.

School Problems.   Of the 89 children, 30 children were described as having problems in school (33.7%). Children were characterized as having learning disabilities, difficulty in staying on task and concentrating, or a diagnosis of attention deficit disorder (23.6%). Chil-dren experiencing problems with concentrating and staying on task were the most fre-quently mentioned. For example, a Native American woman discussed during the focus group interview her sons' problems in school shortly before her imprisonment:

> Well, my 9-year-old and 15-year-old was kind of hard because I was taking them to the psy-chiatrist at the clinic that the school sent them to . . . because they were very disruptive at school so that's why they sent them to the psychiatrist. It was about a week before I was to go to court to get my sentence, and I know they was worried that I was to get my sentence, and I know they was worried that I was going to leave them. They wouldn't do nothin' and stuff . . . and I was going to court but they [children] wouldn't listen. But now they're doing all right in school and stuff. (Gr. 4, Gm. l9)

This woman reported having eight children ranging in age from 1 to 15. Five of the children had been adopted by her relatives on the reservation. Both of the boys she dis-cussed were diagnosed with fetal alcohol syndrome and were in special education. The oldest child was described as functioning "like a nine-year-old." He also had a speech ther-apist, was on medication to control his tremors that were caused by the fetal alcohol syn-drome, and was also on juvenile probation. Her correctional file also included a reference to the fact that during her sentencing hearing she requested leniency because she was needed at home to care for her two brothers, who also had fetal alcohol syndrome.

Teasing by their peers at school because their mothers were in prison was another school problem (5.6%). One inmate mother during the focus group interview described her son being teased:

> You know it was really hard for him. He was teased and taunted, you know. "Hey John, we need some money, write us a hot check!" He's learned how to deal with his anger now, he's gotten over the teasing. (Gr. 5, Gr.25)

This 17-year-old adolescent was later home-schooled by his mother because of his violent outbursts. His behavior problems escalated to the point where he put his fist through a glass door at school when the teasing became severe.

Developmental Delays.   The majority of the inmate mothers did not know what this concept meant. Developmental delay was defined for the women as "children who had difficulty walking, running, talking, or as infants they had problems rolling over and hold-ing their heads up," thus providing the women with specific examples that helped clarify the question. Of the 89 children, 25 were then characterized with either motor skills or speech delays (28.1%).

Speech problems were the most frequently reported delay (l4.6%). These chil-dren were described as having problems with stuttering, speaking too slowly, or failing to speak well beyond the appropriate age.[13] Normal speech development was defined under the following criteria: children who are two years old should be able to string two or more words together; by age three they should be able to use two-word and longer phrases; and at age four, children should be expected to at least speak in short sentences (McCormick & Schiefelbusch, l990; Harryman, & Krescheck, l989). Children in grade school should use longer sentences and also demonstrate an increase in their vocabu-lary skills.

One woman provided an excellent example during a focus group interview of her inability to identify her daughter's speech delays because she was a "child herself":

> My daughter wasn't quite a year old when I had my second one. My mom would come over
> later and she wouldn't even talk. I fed her; I took care of her needs; there was no reason for
> her to talk. When my mother took her, she kept her for three months; she brought her back
> and she chattered about everything. She drove me nuts (chuckles). You know I didn't know
> her not talking wasn't normal. I was a child myself. (Gr. 1, Gm. 7)

Motor difficulties, another category of developmental delays, was described as not walking until well after their first birthday, not attempting to crawl until after the age of one, and difficulty in lifting their heads or turning over as infants (6.7%). It was not uncom-mon for many of these children to also be diagnosed by physicians with "failure to thrive" and fetal alcohol syndrome.

The remainder of the children's problems consisted of drug and alcohol abuse, and teen pregnancy. The extremely low rates described by the inmate mothers could partially be due to the fact that the average age of the children was eight. However, as to the older chil-dren, once again this number may not reflect the problems associated with the adolescents because of the women's own denial or simply not knowing.

Agency intervention.   One of the few positive findings of this study was that 52% of the children were receiving some kind of intervention from social or criminal justice agen-cies, including Division of Family Services, speech and occupational therapists through the school or a specialized program, juvenile court, or a psychiatric facility. Because the chil-dren had multiple problems, some were receiving services from more than one agency. However, the remaining children were not receiving intervention, which clearly leaves unanswered questions regarding these children's welfare.

Separation was another problem that the children often endured. Separation was not only due to their mother's current imprisonment but also because of other separations that took place before maternal imprisonment. Examining the issue of separation provides insight into the quality of the mother–child relationship before imprisonment. Additionally, it may also explain why separation anxiety was the most common mental health problem reported.

Quality of Mother–Child Relationship before Incarceration.

Separation. The psychological theory of attachment was used as the basis for exploring the mother–child relationship. The fundamental principle of attachment theory holds that for children to become emotionally healthy adults they must form a strong and *uninterrupted* attachment to a *consistent* and nurturing caregiver (Gaudin, 1984). The consequences of interrupting the attachment can seriously affect children forever. As Ainsworth and Bowlby (1991) suggest, "The quality of attachment indicates the character of a parent-child relationship and is a good predictor of a child's future behavior" (p. 307). Thus, it is important to examine separation *before* imprisonment and the reasons associated with these separations, particularly in that many past studies have not addressed this issue (McGowan & Blumenthal, 1978; Henriques, 1982; Baunach, 1985; Bloom & Steinhart, 1993).

The findings from this study strongly indicate that the children's attachment process had been interrupted *prior* to their mother's current imprisonment. The vast majority of the children (88%) had been separated at least once before their mother's current imprisonment. Furthermore, of the 88%, 39% had separated from their mothers more than twice. The number of times the children had been separated from their mothers ranged from 0 to 14 times.

The mothers reported various reasons for these separations. The most frequently mentioned was losing custody (17.4%) to Division of Family Services, typically for either neglect or drug and alcohol abuse. Incarcerated in jail (15.7%) and other imprisonment (7.9%) were the next most frequently given reasons. A few of the women who entered drug and alcohol treatment also lost custody of their children for failing to maintain their sobriety (6.7%). Other reasons included children living with relatives or friends, children admitted into psychiatric juvenile detention facilities, or their mothers being hospitalized.

Coupled with these separations, the children experienced changes in their caregivers, legal custody, and living situations. In essence, most of the women reported being separated because of their addictions. In fact, 77% of the women had problems with drugs or alcohol. In relation to such problems, a woman reflected on the numerous times she had been separated from her children and the different caregivers her children had:

> When I decided to go out partying and drinking, I would make plans to do it and make the plans for my kids to be away from me for a couple of days so I could go out and drink, come home and sober up, and then the next day I would feel O.K. to take care of them so there would be three days boom! They'd be gone and they knew when they went to the sitters . . . they'd be gone for three days away from me. . . . They knew what I was doing and my alcohol. (Gr. 7, Gm 42)

This woman reported being separated from her children because of her alcoholism and later losing custody of her children to her ex-husband, also because of her alcoholism.

A Native American woman also described her frequent separations from her eight children and their different caretakers, and, in particular, how the separations affected her relationship with her oldest son:

> Every time I drank I'd take them to a baby-sitter. I wasn't around for them and stuff. They'd stay at a baby-sitter. I wasn't around for them. They'd stay at a baby-sitter a couple of days or so, then I would go after them. And my drinking, with my oldest son, my mom raised him mostly because I was always drunk. Once in a while he calls me Mom, but I always had them at baby-sitters, I wasn't around them. (Gr. 4, Gm. 19)

This Native American reported being separated from her oldest son because of previous imprisonments, drug and alcohol treatment, or giving birth to her other children. Her three youngest children and two biological brothers had been diagnosed with fetal alcohol syndrome.

As these two cases indicate, parental neglect was often associated with separation. In fact, the findings from this study clearly suggest that in most cases when separation did occur, parental neglect also occurred. Clearly, this further compounds the children's problems.

Neglect. Neglected children can experience two types of neglect from their caregivers: (1) lack of emotional need fulfillment (i.e., nurturance and support) and (2) lack of physical need fulfillment (i.e., food, clothing, shelter, or medical care). The second category of neglect often includes not being provided or taught essential life skills (daily hygiene rituals).

A Native American woman aptly described neglect during a focus group interview:

> To neglect, you're not doing your housework like you're supposed to . . . you're not feeding your kids the right way. I mean if you're drunk, you're lucky you don't burn the house down if you try to cook. You neglect their education because you're not up to get them up. (Gr. 4, Gm. 21)

Only in the last decade have experts begun examining whether neglect had detrimental effects on children, similar to physical abuse. In a well-known study, Widom (1995) conducted a series of longitudinal studies that examined the lives of adults who were victims of abuse and neglect in their childhoods. Widom found that 49% of the experimental group had been arrested, compared with only 38% of the control group. A significant finding was that neglect appeared to be just as damaging as physical abuse and that the rate of arrest for violent crimes among adults who were neglected as children was almost as high as the rate for those adults who had been abused as children.

Many child abuse experts have noted the residual effects of neglect in later life, including difficulty in trusting others, low self-esteem, anger, impaired intelligence, impaired parenting abilities, and abuse of drugs and alcohol (Helfer, 1978; Briere, 1992; Crosson-Tower, 1999). The extent of the psychological effects largely depends on the type and severity of neglect (Dworetzky, 1996).

One woman candidly summarized what parental neglect and numerous separations from children can result in:

> I was incapable of giving them emotionally what they needed because of drugs, you know. The drugs made me real cold, and when I first started them (heroin) I thought as long as they were fed and they were clean and taken care of, that is what was necessary, but they weren't given the love or any emotional things that they needed from me. Towards the end I couldn't even take care of the other parts. The house was dirty, they didn't get to school on time. I left them with people I really didn't know that well and my kids were abused, sexually abused, and I feel like if I had been more together and I was responsible . . . not using drugs and alcohol, maybe I could have checked out people more. It didn't matter as long as they were with somebody. You know they went through a lot with abuse from their father, and my son had a lot of nightmares. One time he woke up and said that he dreamed that daddy killed mommy, and I'm sure that that affected him a lot. A lot of that was due to the alcohol and drugs. I had people with guns around them. Dangerous people. I had people break into my house to rob me. The kids weren't there, but they could have been. And because of the drugs and alcohol, basically, I've never been able to raise them. They had to be raised without their mom and dad. (Gr. 2, Gm. 13)

SUMMARY

Findings from this study present a dismal picture of these children's characteristics and demonstrate that the majority of their problems were not directly caused by their mothers' imprisonment. Rather, their problems existed *before* their mothers' imprisonment. Mental health and health problems, the most frequently reported problems, prevent many children from progressing emotionally, developmentally, and socially. Without early intervention, these problems also have the potential for handicapping the children forever. Compounding their problems, many of the children were neglected and separated from their mothers before imprisonment, largely because of their mothers' addictions. By the women's own accounts, the quality of their relationship with their children before their incarceration was marginal at best.

According to the basic premise of the intergenerational cycle of incarceration, children who experience traumatic childhood events (abuse, neglect, parental addiction) in addition to parental incarceration are more likely than other children to be imprisoned (Gable & Johnston, 1995; Widom, 1995; Earls & Reiss, 1994; American Correctional Association, 1993). Clearly, most of these children have experienced most if not all the variables associated with the intergenerational cycle of incarceration and are at risk for becoming the second or third generation of inmates.

The implications for policy changes and future research agendas are significant. The data clearly suggest that intervention must take place long before the mother's imprisonment. Legislatures must be educated on the needs and concerns of this population and the economic cost to society of not addressing the intergenerational cycle of incarceration. The necessary policy changes, along with implementing the interventions, will obviously take time, planning, and coordination of agencies. In the meantime, we must continue to study this population and use data as evidence for policy change. Future research should directly involve the children because many of the inmate mothers simply did not know a great deal about their children. Larger samples must also be taken to target the adolescent population. Empirical and descriptive data could provide a clearer direction for future interventions with these children and the generations of children yet to be born. Exploring the children's lives *before* imprisonment will provide data on a relatively obscure area of the children's lives and provide a clearer direction for interventions.

Only by a thorough evaluation of the true causation of these children's problems will we be able to appropriately address those problems. And only through empirical research will we be able to determine the true cause for the burgeoning intergenerational cycle of incarceration.

DISCUSSION QUESTIONS

1. Discuss the intergenerational cycle of incarceration.

2. What is role reversal?

3. What is fetal alcohol syndrome?

4. What are developmental delays?

5. Discuss the fundamental principle of attachment theory.

N O T E S

1. See Gable & Johnston, 1995; Bloom & Steinhart, 1993. There are no exact numbers on how many children are affected by their mothers' imprisonment. Most state correctional facilities do not gather data on these children, and inmate mothers are also reluctant to disclose information regarding their children, fearing state agencies will intervene and sever their parental rights.

2. In 1994 there were 85 female offenders and in 1998 there were 245 female offenders. (Telephone interview with Steve Hall and Steve Griffin, Montana Department of Corrections in Helena and Billings, MT, respectively, May 26, 1999).

3. According to Montana correctional officials, it appears that the percentage of female prisoners who are mothers of minor children remains approximately the same as when this study was conducted, although there are no specific numbers available to confirm this assessment since the Department of Corrections data do not differentiate between inmate mothers who have adult children and inmate mothers who have minor children. (Telephone interview with Steve Hall and Steve Griffin, Montana Department of Corrections in Helena and Billings, MT, respectively, May 26, 1999).

4. The original site was scheduled to be at the women's prison; however, shortly before the study began, fifty percent of the women were transferred to either the pre-release center or the community correctional facility. The major shift in population resulted from an ACLU lawsuit concerning overcrowding conditions of the prison. Thus, even though the women were housed in different facilities, their characteristics remained virtually the same. Each woman volunteered and signed a consent form to participate and to review her correctional file.

5. See Bloom and Steinhart (1993). The questionnaire was modified to meet the characteristics of the population (e.g., urban versus rural, Native American, children's legal custody and rights, and so on). The survey was read to each woman to address illiteracy problems. The interviews (lasting from one and one-half hours to two hours) and the focus group interviews (lasting two hours) were conducted in the parenting room, conference room, or staff offices. The interviews occurred during various times of the day or evening, depending on the women's programming and the correctional facility's schedules.

6. A total of seven focus group interviews were conducted. The focus group interview schedule had five broad questions with corresponding probing questions. The purpose of the focus group interview was to expand on survey data. The variability of the number of women participating in the group interviews was due to the availability of the women at the time. In some instances, women were working, became ill, or were placed in maximum security or jail. To accommodate schedule changes, the women participated in different groups than those originally assigned.

7. Of the remaining 18 inmate mothers who did not participate, only 9 women refused (14.5%). The other 9 women were either inappropriate (former client of the researcher or had killed their children) or were unavailable (in jail, maximum security, or ill). Phase II involved interviewing six guardians ad litem, attorneys for the inmate mother's children. For data from Phase II, see Dalley, 2000.

8. Nonviolent offenses include burglary, larcency/theft, fraud, stolen property. The remainder of the offenses included violent crimes (29.5%) defined as any act that caused bodily harm or threat to commit bodily harm.

9. History of drug and alcohol use as reported by the women: more than 10 years, 34.1%; 6 to 10 years, 18.2%; 5 years or less, 25%; None, 22.7%.

10. Division of Family Services is the Montana state agency that is legally responsible for investigating child abuse and neglect and for providing services and resources to children and their families.

11. The seemingly small percentage of exacerbating problems among the children during maternal imprisonment may be due to the mothers' having little contact with their children during their imprisonment and accordingly lack knowledge of this.

12. *Gr.* represents the number assigned to each focus group; *Gm.* represents the inmate mother 's assigned number.

13. The causes of the speech delays as reported by the inmate mothers were (1) a hearing problem resulting from abuse by another relative; (2) their own use of drugs during pregnancy; and (3) malformed tongue.

REFERENCES

AINSWORTH, M. (1973). The development of infant-mother attachment. In B.M. Calwell & H.N. Riccuti (Eds.), *Review of child development of research,* Vol. 1. (pp. 60–75). Chicago: University of Chicago Press.

AINSWORTH, M.D., & BOWLBY, J. (1991). An ethnological approach to personality development. *New American Psychologist, 46*(4), 333–341.

AMERICAN CORRECTIONAL ASSOCIATION. (1993). *Female offenders: Meeting the needs of a neglected population.* Baltimore, MD: United Book Press.

BAGLEY, K., & MERLO, A.V. (1995). Controlling women's bodies. In A. Merlo & J.M. Pollock (Eds.), *Women, law and social control,* pp. 135–154. Boston: Allyn and Bacon.

BAUNACH, P. (1985). *Mothers in prison.* New Brunswick, NJ: Transaction Books.

BECK, A.J. (2000). *Prisoners in 1999.* (Rep. No. 183476). Washington, DC: Bureau of Justice Statistics, U.S. Department of Justice.

BLOOM, B., & STEINHART, D. (1993). *Why punish the children?* San Francisco: National Council on Crime and Delinquency.

BRAZELTON, B.T. (1987). *What every baby knows.* Reading, MA: Addison-Wesley.

BRAZELTON, B.T. (1992). *Touchpoints: Your child's emotional and behavioral development.* Reading, MA: Addison-Wesley.

BRIERE, J.N. (1992). *Child abuse trauma.* Newbury Park, CA: Sage.

CARP, S., & SCHADE, L. (1992). Tailoring facility programming to suit female offenders' needs. *Corrections Today, 54*(6), 152–159.

CHASE, N.D. (Ed.). (1999). *Burdened children: Theory, research, and treatment of parentification.* Thousand Oaks, CA: Sage.

CHESNEY-LIND, M., & POLLOCK, J.M. (1995). Women's prisons: Equality with a vengeance. In A. Merlo & J. M. Pollock (Eds.), *Women, law and social control,* (pp. 155–176). Boston: Allyn and Bacon.

CRAIG, G. (1996). *Human development.* (7th ed.). New York: Prentice-Hall.

CROSSON-TOWER, C. (1999). *Understanding child abuse and neglect* (4th ed.). Boston: Allyn and Bacon.

DALLEY, L. (Fall, 2000). Imprisoned mothers and their children: Their often conflicting legal rights. *Hamline Journal of Public Law and Policy, 22*(1), pp. 1–44.

DROPENSKE, V., HOWARD, J., BREITENBACH, C., DEMBO, R., EDELSTEIN, S.B., & WEISZ, V. (1994). *Protecting children in substance abuse families.* Washington, DC: U.S. Department of Health and Human Services.

DWORETZKY, J.P. (1996). *Child development.* (6th ed.). St. Paul, MN: West.

EARLS, J.E., & REISS, A.J. (1994). *Breaking the cycle: Predicting and preventing crime.* Washington, DC: U.S. Department of Justice.

FISHBEIN, D.H., & PEASE, S.E. (1996). *The dynamics of drug abuse.* Boston: Allyn and Bacon.

GABLE, K., & JOHNSTON, D. (EDS.). (1995). *Children of incarcerated parents.* New York: Lexington.

GAUDIN, J.M. (1984). Social work roles and tasks with incarcerated mothers. *Social Casework, 65,* pp. 279–286.

GREENFIELD, L., & SNELL, T. (1999). *Women Offenders.* (Rep. No. 176588). Washington, DC: Bureau of Justice Statistics, U.S. Department of Justice.

HARRYMAN, N.E., & KRESCHECK, J. (1989). *Terminology of communication disorders: Speech-language-hearing* (3rd ed.). Baltimore: Williams & Wilkins.

HART, S.N., GERMAIN, R.B., & BRASSARD, M.R. (1987). The challenges to better understanding and combating psychological maltreatment of children and youth. In M.R. Brassard, R. Germain, & S.N. Hart (Eds.), *Psychological maltreatment of children and youth* (pp. 3–24). New York: Pergamon.

HELFER, R.E. (1978). *Childhood comes first: A crash course in childhood for adults.* East Lansing, MI: Ray E. Helfer.

HENRIQUES, Z.W. (1982). *Imprisoned mothers and their children: A descriptive and analytical study.* New York: University Press of America.

JACOBVITZ, D., RIGGS, S., & JOHNSON, E. (1999) Cross-sex and same-sex family alliances: Immediate and long-term effects on sons and daughters. In N.D. Chase (Ed.), *Burdened children: Theory, research, and treatment of parentification.* Thousand Oaks, CA: Sage.

JOHNSTON, D. (1991). *Jailed mothers.* Pacific Oaks, CA: Pacific Oaks Center for Incarcerated Parents.

JOHNSTON, D. (1992). *Children of offenders.* Pacific Oaks, CA: Pacific Oaks Center for Incarcerated Parents.

KELLEY, S.J. (1999). Parenting stress and child maltreatment in drug-exposed children. *Child Abuse and Neglect, 16*(3), 317–328.

KROPENSKE, V., HOWARD, J., FREITENBACH, C., DEMBOO, R., EDELSTEIN, S.B., MCTAGGERT, K., MOORE, A., SORENSON, M.B., & WEISZ, V. (1994). *Protecting children in substance-abusing families.* Washington, DC: U.S. Department of Health and Human Services.

MCCORMICK, L., & SCHIEFELBUSCH, R.L. (1990). *Early language intervention: An introduction.* New York: Macmillan.

MCGOWAN, B., & BLUMENTHAL, K. (1978). *Why punish the children?* Hackensack, NJ: National Council on Crime and Juvenile Delinquency.

MERLO, A., & POLLOCK, J.A. (EDS.) (1995). *Women, law and social control.* Boston: Allyn and Bacon.

POLANSKY, N., CHALMERS, M.A., BUTTENWIESER, E., & WILLIAMS, D. (1981) *Damaged parents: An anatomy of child neglect.* Chicago: University of Chicago Press.

POLLOCK, J. (1998). *Counseling female offenders.* Thousand Oaks, CA: Brooks/Cole.

STREISSGUTH, A.P., LADUE, R.A., & RANDELLS, S.P. (1988). *A manual on adolescent and adults with fetal alcohol syndrome with special reference to American Indians.* Washington, DC: U.S. Department of Health and Human Services.

WALLACE, H. (1996). *Family violence.* Boston: Allyn and Bacon.

WIDOM, C.S. (1989). The cycle of violence. *Science, 244,* 160–165.

WIDOM, C.S. (1995). *Victims of childhood sexual abuse—later criminal consequences.* (Rep. No.151525). Washington, DC: U.S. Department of Justice.

WIDOM, C.S. (1996). *The cycle of violence revisited.* (Rep. No. 153272). Washington, DC: U.S. Department of Justice.

WOLFE, D.A. (1999). *Child abuse implications for child development and psychopathology* (2nd ed.). Thousand Oaks, CA: Sage.

10

Disparate Treatment in Correctional Facilities: Looking Back

Roslyn Muraskin

As of the year 2000, there were known to be an annual average of about 2.1 million violent female offenders. Three of four violent female offenders commit simple assault. An estimated 28% of violent female offenders are juveniles. An estimated 4 in 10 women who commit violent crimes are perceived as being under the influence of alcohol and/or drugs at the time the crime was committed. In 1998 alone, there were an estimated 3.2 million arrests of women. And since 1990, the number of female defendants convicted of felonies in state courts has grown at more than twice the rate of increase of male defendants (U.S. Dept. of Justice, 2000).

The providing of services and programs is all part of good correctional practice. It ensures that inmates returned to society can be reintegrated into society. With the number of women incarcerated, there exists the need for proper treatment within correctional facilities. This chapter reviews the problems and cases of the past, demonstrating that services legally mandated have not been fully delivered.

CURRENT HISTORY: OVERVIEW

In the latter part of the 20th century, an estimated 950,000 women were under the care, custody, or control of correctional agencies, a rate of about one of every 109 U.S. adult women. In examining the racial and ethnic composition of the general population, we find

This chapter was reprinted from *It's a Crime: Women and Justice* (3rd ed.). (2002). Prentice Hall.

that "Non-Hispanic black females outnumber non-Hispanic black males by nearly 1.9 million, accounting for more than a quarter of the total difference in the number of males and females in the general population" (Bureau of Justice Statistics, 1999). The average age of females in the general population is about 2½ years older than that of males. See Table 10.1 for a comparison of violent crimes committed by females and males.

Black and white offenders accounted for nearly equal proportions of women committing robbery and aggravated assault; however, simple assault offenders were more likely to be described as white.

With regard to women who murder:

> Since 1993 both male and female rates of committing murder have declined. Rates of committing murder in 1998 were the lowest since statistics were first collected in 1976. The estimated rate for murder offending by women in 1998 was 1.3 per 100,000—about 1 murderer for every 77,000 women. The male rate of murder offending in 1998 was 11.5 per 100,000, about 1 murderer for every 8,700 males. (Bureau of Justice Statistics, 1999, p. 10).

> In 1998 there were an estimated 3.2 million arrests of women, accounting for about a fifth of all arrests by law enforcement agencies. Women were about 17% of those arrested for the Part I violent crimes (murder, rape, robbery, and aggravated assault) and 29% of those arrested for Part I property crimes (burglary, larceny, and motor-vehicle theft). Women accounted for about 16% of all felons convicted in State Courts in 1996. Women were 8% of convicted violent felons, 23% of property felons, and 17% of drug felons. Women defendants accounted for 41% of all felons convicted of forgery, fraud, and embezzlement. (Bureau of Justice Statistics, 1999, p. 11)

According to the National Institute of Justice, there exists the common observation that the criminal behaviors of women are not to be deemed important problems. Over these many years, it has been believed that women, if they were to commit any crimes, would commit only minor crimes, and, therefore, they have always constituted a small fraction of

TABLE 10.1   Violent Crimes Committed by Females and Males

Offense	Average annual number of offenders reported by victims, 1993–97		Women as a percent of violent offenders (%)
	Female	Male	
All	2,135,000	13,098,000	14
Sexual assault	10,000	442,000	2
Robbery	157,000	2,051,000	7
Aggravated assault	435,000	3,419,000	11
Simple assault	1,533,000	7,187,000	18

About 1 of 7 violent offenders described by victims was a female. Women accounted for 1 in 50 offenders committing a violent sex offense including rape and sexual assault, 1 in 14 robberies, 1 in 9 offenders committing aggravated assault, and more than 1 in 6 offenders described as having committed a simple assault.

TABLE 10.2   Characteristics of Violent Female Offenders

Offense	Race of Female Offenders		
	White (%)	Black (%)	Other (%)
Violent offenses	55	35	11
Robbery	43	43	14
Aggravated assault	45	46	10
Simple assault	58	31	10

the correctional population. But these facts have veiled a trend that has attracted everyone's attention. Although crime rates are down, there is a growing population within the correctional facilities on account of tougher and longer sentences. For women, however, the ranks of inmates who are female is growing at a rate higher that than of men. There has been a call among academics to redefine justice. According to Samuels:

> Whether justice should promote unalloyed equality, be blind to the circumstances in which crime is committed, and consider only the gravity of offense and prior record, is still a matter of debate. In the current sentencing environment, the view of those who favor equity above all other considerations has won the day. There is another perspective—the belief that sanctions ought to be tailored to the specific characteristics and circumstances of individual offenders. (p. 2)

LOOKING BACK INTO HISTORY

In the United States, no Constitutional obligation exists for all persons to be treated alike. The government frequently, and in fact, does treat disparate groups differently. However, this does not excuse invidious discrimination among potential recipients (Gobert & Cohen, 1981, pp. 294–295). What is required is that where unequal treatment exists, the inequalities must be rational and related to a legitimate interest of the state (Pollack & Smith, 1978, p. 206). Laws have created categories in which some people may be treated unequally. These categories have always included women incarcerated in the correctional facilities. The question that still arises is "whether the inequalities by the law are justifiable—in legal terms whether the person upon whom the law's burden has been denied equal protection of the law" (Pollack & Smith, 1978, p. 206–207).

Since the decision in *Holt v. Sarver* (1970), in which the court declared an entire prison to be in violation of the Eighth Amendment and imposed detailed remedial plans, the judiciary has taken an active role in the administration of correctional facilities. Many of the landmark cases challenged the inequity of treatment between male and female prisoners.

Ostensibly, the needs of male and female prisoners would appear to be the same. They are not. Although some inmate interests are similar, others are separate and distinct. In many institutions, criteria developed for men were applied automatically to women, with no consideration given for gender differences. Research has shown that female offenders have always experienced more medical and health problems than male inmates. Classification officials have noted that female offenders have needed help in parenting skills, child welfare, pregnancy and prenatal care, and home stability, as well as an understanding of the circumstances of their crime. But typically, assignments to programs and treatment resources within the correctional facilities have always been based on what is available rather that what should be available.

A review of the literature and of the cases and issues that have dealt with disparate treatment has revealed that each takes note of the fact that women historically have represented a small minority in both the prisons and jails. Yet the effects of incarceration have been in many but not all respects similar for men and women. Each has suffered the trauma of being separated from family and friends. When either a man or a woman becomes imprisoned, he or she experiences a loss of identity as well as a devaluation of his or her status. Regardless of the inmate's sex, prison life has coerced conformity to an environment alien to the individual, where one's every movement is dictated each and every minute (Muraskin, 1989).

Most challenges to prison conditions have neglected the special needs of female prisoners, especially in the jails, where both males and females are located together. Traditionally, correctional facilities for women have not received funding comparable to that of correctional facilities for men. Education and vocational training programs for women have been historically and seriously underfunded. "Benign neglect [has] . . . created a situation of unequal treatment in many states" (Hunter, 1984, p. 133). Correctional administrators have insisted that "the small number of female offenders [has] made it too expensive to fund such programs." The courts, however, have ruled "that cost is not an acceptable defense for denying equal treatment" (Hunter, 1984, pp. 133–134). Historically, females have been subject to policies designed for the male offender. "Women have deferred to males in the economic, social, political spheres of life. In the legal realm, more specifically in the imprisonment of the female, women have been forced into the status of being less than equal" (Sargent, 1984, p. 83).

REVIEW OF CASES: WOMEN AND EQUALITY/PARITY

When inmates similarly situated find themselves being treated differently, there may exist a violation of equal protection. A review of the cases discussed here demonstrates for us what established the discrimination against incarcerated women.

Constitutionally, no obligation exists for the government to provide any benefits beyond basic requirements. However, this principle should not be an excuse for invidious discrimination among potential recipients (Gobert & Cohen, 1981, pp. 294–295). Case law has held that benefits afforded some cannot be denied solely on the basis of race or sex.

In any equal protection challenge, the central question that has been raised is the "degree of state interest which can justify disparate treatment among offenders" (*Reed v. Reed,* 1971). As established, the "classification must be reasonable, not arbitrary and must bear a fair and substantial relation to the object of the legislation or practice" (*Reed v. Reed*). Courts, for example, have found sex classifications to be irrational because they appear to be enacted solely for the convenience of correctional administrators (see *Craig v.*

Boren, 1976[1]; *Weinberger v. Wisenfeld,* 1975[2]; *Eslinger v. Thomas,* 1973[3]. Existing differences in conditions, rules, and treatment among inmates have proven fertile ground for equal protection challenges. Administrative convenience is not an acceptable justification for disparity of treatment (*Cooper v. Morin,* 1979, 1980), nor is lack of funds an acceptable justification for disparate treatment (*State ex rel Olson v. Maxwell,* 1977).

Legal uprisings against intolerable conditions in correctional facilities and prisoners' rights litigation were initiated by male attorneys and male prisoners. In the early stages of this litigation, female inmates did not turn to the courts, nor did officials at female institutions fear lawsuits, condemnation by the public, or inmate riots. With so few women incarcerated, there was little the women felt they could do. This situation has changed. Female prisoners sued and demanded parity with male prisoners. The Fourteenth Amendment has been the source for issues of violation of privacy, and the Eighth Amendment is used for cases involving cruel and unusual punishment.

Differential sentencing of similarly situated men and women convicted of identical offenses has been found to violate the equal protection clause. A review of the cases dealing generally with sentencing in correctional institutions include prior rulings in the case of *United States ex rel Robinson v. York* (1968), which held that it was a violation of the equal protection clause for women who were sentenced to indeterminate terms under a Connecticut statute to serve longer maximum sentences than men serving indeterminate terms for the same offenses. In *Liberti v. York* (1968), the Court held that female plaintiffs' indeterminate sentences of up to three years violated the equal protection clause because the maximum term for men convicted of the same crime was one year. In *Commonwealth v. Stauffer* (1969), a Pennsylvania court held then that the practice of sentencing women to state prison on charges for which men were held in county jail to be a violation of a woman's right to equal protection.

In *Williams v. Levi* (1976), dealing with disparate treatment in the issue of parole, male prisoners in the District of Columbia were placed under the authority of the D.C. Board of Parole, whereas women prisoners were placed under the authority of the U.S. Board of Parole's stricter parole standards of violence. In *Dawson v. Carberry* (1973), it was held that there must be substantial equivalence in male and female prisoners' opportunities to participate in work-furlough programs.

In *Barefield v. Leach* (1974), women at the Women's Division of the Penitentiary of New Mexico claimed that conditions there violated their rights to an uncensored press, to have their persons free from unreasonable searches, to be free from cruel and unusual punishment, and to be allowed due process and equal protection of the law regarding disciplinary procedures and rehabilitative opportunities, respectively. The court held that "[w]hat the equal protection clause requires in a prison setting is parity of treatment as contrasted with identity of treatment, between male and female inmates with respect to the conditions of their confinement and access to rehabilitative opportunities." *Barefield* is especially important as the first case to enunciate the standard against which disparity of treatment of men and women in prison was to be measured.

Still further, in *McMurray v. Phelps* (1982), there was a challenge to conditions for both men and women at the Quachita County Jail, where the jail ordered an end to the disparate treatment of female detainees. And in *Mary Beth G. v. City of Chicago* (1983), a strip-search policy under which female arrestees underwent a full strip search without reason to believe that a weapon or contraband was present was ruled to be a violation of the equal protection clauses as well as the Fourteenth Amendment.

In *Bounds v. Smith* (1977), the court held that access to the courts by prisoners was a fundamental constitutional right. The court noted that there existed an affirmative obligation on the part of state officials to ensure court access by providing adequate law libraries or some alternative involving a legal assistance program. It was further noted in the court's decision that females had less access to library facilities than did male inmates. This situation was ordered remedied. In *Cody v. Hillard* (1986), the court held that inmates at the state women's correctional facility, which had neither a law library nor law-trained assistants, were denied their constitutional right of meaningful access to the courts.

In a case dealing with the transfer of female inmates out of state because of a lack of facilities (*State ex rel Olson v. Maxwell,* 1977), female inmates filed a petition for a supervisory writ challenging the North Dakota practice of routinely transferring them to other states to be incarcerated, alleging a denial of equal protection and due process. It was held that North Dakota must not imprison women prisoners outside the state unless and until a due process waiver hearing was held or waived and the state admitted that it could not provide women prisoners facilities equal to those of male prisoners.

"From a policy perspective, discriminatory distribution of prison privileges . . . will appear counter-rehabilitative, fueling inmate administration animosity and generating inmate peer jealousies" (Gobert & Cohen, 1981, p. 295). In *Canterino v. Wilson* (1982, 1983), it was indicated that "restrictions imposed solely because of gender with the objective of controlling lives of women inmates in a way deemed unnecessary for male prisoners" would not be tolerated. The Court concluded that "males and females must be treated equally unless there is a substantial reason which requires a distinction be made" (1982). Case law has established that discriminatory selection for work release that is based on race, religion, gender, or even mental impairment is not an acceptable practice. Any arbitrary or capricious selection for participation in work programs has been prohibited by the courts.

Because of the small numbers of women in men's correctional facilities, services and treatment programs appear to have been reduced. Such reduced services included medical services. Generally, there has always been a wider range of medical services provided for male inmates than for female inmates. Thus, in both *Todaro v. Ward* (1977) and *Estelle v. Gamble* (1976), the issues were medical. In the former case, the medical system in the Bedford Hills Correctional Facility was found to be unconstitutionally defective; in the latter, there was found to be deliberate indifference to the medical needs of the females. This was a violation of the Eighth Amendment.

In *Bukhari v. Huto* (1980), it was held that no justification existed for disparate treatment based on the fact that women's prisons serviced a smaller population and the cost would be greater to provide programs equivalent to the men's institutions. Cost could not be claimed as an excuse for paucity of services.

The landmark case on women's prison issues was *Glover v. Johnson* (1979). This was a comprehensive case challenging a disputed system of educational, vocational, work, and minimum security programs in the Michigan prison system based on due process and equal protection. The Court ruled that female prisoners must be provided program opportunities on a parity with male prisoners. The case resulted in an order requiring the state to provide postsecondary education, counseling, vocational programs, and a legal education program (in a companion case, *Cornish v. Johnson* 1979), as well as other relief. "Institutional size is frankly not a justification but an excuse for the kind of treatment afforded women prisoners" (*Glover v. Johnson*, 1979)

In a facility in Nassau County, New York, in the case of *Thompson et al. v. Varelas* (1985), the plaintiffs asked for:

> Declaratory and injunctive relief regarding the discriminatory, oppressive, degrading and dangerous conditions of . . . their confinement within the Nassau County Correctional Center . . . alleged in their action was the existence of inadequate health care, lack of private attorney visiting facilities, inadequate and unequal access to employment, recreation and training; unequal access to library facilities and newspapers, and excessive confinement; unsanitary food preparation and service; and, inadequate and unequal access to religious services. . . .

They claimed that lack of these facilities and services violated their rights as guaranteed by the First, Fifth, Sixth, Eighth, Ninth, and Fourteenth Amendments to the Constitution of the United States, but not until September 1985 was a consent judgment entered in the *Thompson* case. *Thompson* makes a further argument for the need of checklist standards against which to assess what constitutes disparate treatment in correctional facilities.

Prior to these cases, the female prisoner was the "forgotten offender." Testimony by a teacher in the *Glover* case indicated that whereas men were allowed to take shop courses, women were taught at a junior high level because the motto of those in charge was "keep it simple, these are only women."

Although litigation has provided the opportunity for inmates to have a role in altering their conditions of confinement, a judicial opinion does not necessarily bring about change, then or now. Viewed from a nonlegal perspective, litigation is simply a catalyst for change rather than an automatic mechanism for ending wrongs found. All the cases held that invidious discrimination cannot exist.

REVIEW OF THE LITERATURE

The first penal institution for women opened in Indiana in 1873. By the beginning of the 20th century, women's correctional facilities had opened in Framingham, Massachusetts; Bedford Hills, New York; and Clinton, New Jersey. The Federal Institution for Women in Alderson, West Virginia, opened in 1927, and the House of Detention for Women (the first separate jail for women) opened in New York City in 1931. These institutions all shared one thing in common: "traditional values, theories and practices concerning a woman's role and place in society. . . . The staffs, architectural design and programs reflected the culturally valued norms for women's behavior" (Feinman, 1986, p. 38).

Historically, disparate treatment of male and female inmates started when state penitentiaries first opened. "Female prisoners . . . were confined together in a single attic room above the institution's kitchen. [They] were supervised by the head of the kitchen below. Food was sent up to them once a day, and once a day the slop was removed. No provision was made for privacy or exercise and although the women were assigned some sewing work, for the most part they were left to their own devices in the 'tainted and sickly atmosphere' " (Rafter, 1983, p. 135). Female convicts were morally degraded to a greater extent than male convicts. The reformatories built for female prisoners "established and legitimated a tradition of deliberately providing for female prisoners treatment very different from that of males" (Rafter, 1983, p. 148).

"From Lombroso to the present, criminological thought has been wrought with the sexism inherent in assuming that there exists only two distinct classes of women—those on pedestals and those in the gutter" (Lown & Snow, 1980, p. 195). The differential law enforcement handling seems to be built into our basic attitudes toward woman. The operation of such attention can be called euphemistically the chivalry factor (Reckless, 1967).

This chivalry factor meant that women should be treated more leniently than men. The nature of treatment and programs for female inmates appears to indicate the assumption of such a theory. Theories have always abounded concerning the causes of criminality by female offenders. The chivalry factor once accepted does not appear to be held in favor today. Once the female enters the correctional facility, she has not necessarily benefited from the benevolence of the criminal justice system. The theories of female crime have always emphasized the natural differences between men and women but have failed to explain why women commit the crimes they do. It is clear that female prisoners have historically been treated differently and sometimes worse than male prisoners. Often, as an alternative to differential treatment, the model followed has been than of the male prisons, a model that has frequently ignored the obvious physical differences of female inmates. An almost total lack of enforcement of standards exist for the confinement of women.

In addition to the historically poor quality and minimal services that have been made available to female inmates, they have continued to suffer the same miserable conditions of incarceration as male inmates. Women have suffered even more in the jails because of the failure to classify them according to the seriousness of their crime. Women have always lived in crowded facilities, often finding themselves under squalid conditions, lacking privacy, and faced with insensitive visiting rules, callous treatment, and the threat of, or actual, sexual abuse. Two other stresses on the female inmate continue to stem from her separation from her family and children.

Much of the neglect in assessing disparate treatment has been attributed by writers believing that the experiences in prison for both men and women are the same and are not areas calling for special investigation. As Rafter indicated in 1983, not until the 1970s did literature dealing with women's prisons begin to take notice of their specialized problems (p. 130). Feinman (1982) indicated that, for the most part, programs in correctional facilities for women continued to be based on the belief that "the only acceptable role for women is that of wife/mother" (p. 12). The female offender continues to be described as poor, African American, Hispanic, or other, undereducated, and lacking in both skills and self-confidence. Although nearly two-thirds of the women under probation supervision are white, nearly two-thirds of those confined in local jails and state and federal prisons are minority—black, Hispanic, and other. The majority of the women who are incarcerated have graduated from high school. About 70% of women in correctional facilities have minor children. These women are reported to have an average of 2.11 children. These estimates convert into more than 1.3 million children who are the offspring of incarcerated women. Female prisoners demonstrate more difficult economic circumstances than their male counterparts: About 40% of women in state prisons reported that they were employed full-time prior to being arrested, whereas nearly 60% of men had been working full-time. The up-to-date figures show that about 44% of women who are incarcerated had been physically or sexually assaulted. About half of the women used alcohol or drugs at the time they were caught. "About 6 in 10 women in State prisons described themselves as using drugs in the month before the offense, 5 in 10 described themselves as a daily user of drugs, and 4 in 10 were under the influence of drugs at the time of the offense" (Bureau of Justice Statistics, 2001, p. 19). In 1998, the highest per capita rate of women who were confined was in the state of Oklahoma (1,222), and the lowest was in both Maine and Vermont (9 in each) (Bureau of Justice Statistics, 2000, p. 21). There are currently about 138,000 women confined in correctional facilities, which represents a "tripling of the number of incarcerated women between the years 1985–1997" (latest available figures) (Bureau of Justice Statistics, 2000, p. 8).

In the 21st century, indications are that more women will be involved in committing crimes than ever before. And yet when women are released back into the community, studies continue to show that men still represent a disproportionate majority in community programs. The way these community programs continue to be structured continues to provide evidence of the lack of sensitivity and the differential treatment afforded women.

Historically, the women's correctional system was not to replicate that of the men's but rather was to differ somewhat radically along a "number of key dimensions, including its historical development, administrative structures, some of its disciplinary techniques and the experience of inmates" (Rafter, 1983, p.132). Today's women's facilities have changed little from the beginning of the 20th century. Today, women's prisons appear to be smaller and fewer in number (Pollock-Byrne, 1990, p. 97). Characteristically, women's prisons are located further from friends and families, with the "relatively small number of women in prison and jail [being] used to 'justify' *low levels of specialization* in treatment and failure to segregate the more serious and mentally ill offenders from the less serious offenders (as is done in male prisons and jails)" (Pollock-Byrne, 1990, p. 7).

The attitude that has persisted throughout the literature over these many years illustrates that women have been regarded as moral offenders and men have continued to *assert* their masculinity. "[I]nstitutional incarceration needs to become more reflective of the ongoing changing social climate" (Sargent, 1984, p. 42). Most states continue to have one (in some cases, two) facilities for women, which of necessity must be of maximum security; local jails house both men and women. Population size has become a justification for ignoring the plight of women prisoners. However, as pointed out in the decision in *Glover*, size is but "an excuse for the kind of treatment afforded women prisoners" (p. 1,078). The disparate treatment of female and male prisoners "is the result of habitual and stereotypic thinking rather than the following of a different set of goals for incarceration" (Lown and Snow, 1980, p. 210).

If administrators in corrections continue to assign women's corrections low priority in budget allocation, staff development, and program development, continued conflict can be expected between the needs of the correctional facilities and such treatment afforded women in this century. Because of overcrowding in both types of facilities, men's and women's equality may well become less of an issue, thereby producing equality—undesirable conditions for both. Regardless, disparate treatment continues to permeate the correctional institutions of today. Adequate care and continuity in the delivery of services to all inmates are important. Standards must be applied equally. Such standards as were developed over the years are meant to serve efficiency, provide greater cost-effectiveness, and establish better planning than we have at present.

According to Richie, Tsenin, and Widom (National Institute of Justice, 2000), "there is a common perception that the criminal behavior of women and girls are not serious problems. Women are more likely to commit minor offenses and have historically constituted a very small proportion of the offender population. But these facts mask a trend that is beginning to attract attention. The dramatic rise in the number of prison and jail inmates is fairly well known; less so is that the ranks of women inmates are increasing much faster than those of their male counterparts. The pace at which women are being convicted of serious offenses is picking up faster than the pace at which women are convicted" (National Institute of Justice, p. 2). These researchers have asked for a redefining of justice. "Whether justice should promote unalloyed equity, be blind to the circumstances in which crime is committed, and consider only gravity of offense and prior record, is still a matter of debate. In the current sentencing environment , the view of those who favor equity above all other considerations has won the day. . . . [w]omen and girls who are caught up in the justice system enter it as a result of circumstances distinctly different from those of men, and so find themselves at a distinct disadvantage" (National Institute of Justice, 2000, p. 3).

If the cases are the catalyst for change, change must occur. Words have little meaning if actions do not follow (Muraskin, 1989, p. 126).

DISCUSSION QUESTIONS

1. Discuss why those concerned with disparate treatment in correctional facilities cannot ignore the plight of the violent female offender.

2. How did the decision in *Holt v. Sarver* (1970) affect the inequality of treatment between male and female prisoners?

3. Differentiate between the sentencing disparity issues of dealing with similarly situated men and women convicted of identical offenses. Cite cases.

4. Why was *Glover v. Johnson* (1979) considered the landmark case on women's prison issues?

5. Describe current problems that demonstrate that services legally mandated for inmates' reintegration into society have not been fully delivered.

NOTES

1. In *Craig v. Boren* (1976), it was held to "withstand [a] constitutional challenge under the equal protection clause of the Fourteenth Amendment, classification by gender must serve important governmental objectives and must be substantially related to achievement of those objectives."

2. *Weinberger v. Wisenfeld* (1975) was a case in which a widower was denied benefits for himself on the ground that survivors' benefits were allowable only to women under 42 USCS sec. 4029(g): "a provision, heard, 'Mother's insurance benefits,' authorizing the payment of benefits based upon the earnings of a deceased husband and father covered by the Social Security Act, to a widow who has a minor child in her care." The Court held that "(1) the sex-based distinction

of 42 USCS sec. 402(g) , resulting in the efforts of women workers required to make social security contributions producing less protection for their families than was produced by the efforts of men, violated the rights to equal protection under the due process clause of the Fifth, and (2) the distinction could not be justified on the basis of the "non-contractual character of social security benefits, or on the ground that the sex-based classification was one really designed to compensate women beneficiaries as a group for the economic difficulties confronting women who sought to support themselves and their families."

3. *Eslinger v. Thomas* (1973) was an action brought by a female law student who alleged that she was denied employment as a page because of her gender. Citing *Reed,* the Court indicated that the "Equal Protection Clause (denies) to States the power to legislate that different treatment be accorded to persons placed by a statute into different classes on the basis of criteria wholly unrelated to the objective of that statute."

The Court quoted from an article by Johnson and Knapp that "on the one hand, the female is viewed as a pure delicate and vulnerable citizen who must be protected from exposure to criminal influences; and on the other, as a brazen temptress, from whose seductive blandishments the innocent must be protected. Every woman is either Eve or Little Eve—and either way she loses" (1971).

The decision of the lower court was reversed, there being no "fair and substantial 'relation between the object of the resolution' which was to combat the appearance of impropriety, and the ground of difference, which was sex. . . ."

CASES

Barefield v. Leach, Civ. Action No. 10282 (1974).

Bounds v. Smith, 430 U.S. 817 (1977).

Bukhari v. Huto, 487 F.Supp. 1162 (E.D. Va., 1980).

Canterino v. Wilson, 546 F.Supp. 174 (W.D. Ky., 1982) and 562 F.Supp. 106 (W.D. Ky., 1983).

Cody v. Hillard, 799 F.2d 447 (1986).

Commonwealth v. Stauffer, 214 Pa.Supp. 113 (1969).

Cooper v. Morin, 49 N.Y.2d 69 (1979), *cert. denied,* 446 U.S. 984 (1980).

Cornish v. Johnson, No. 77–72557 (E.D. Mich., 1979).

Craig v. Boren, 429 U.S. 190 (1976).

Dawson v. Carberry, No. C-71–1916 (N.D. Cal., 1973).

Eslinger v. Thomas, 476 F.2d. (4th Cir., 1973).

Estelle v. Gamble, 429 U.S. 97 (1976).

Glover v. Johnson, 478 F.Supp. 1075, 1078 (1979).

Holt v. Sarver, 309 U.S. F.Supp. 362 (E.D. Ark., 1970).

Liberti v. York, 28 Conn.Supp. 9, 246 A.2d. 106 (S.Ct., 1968).

Mary Beth G. v. City of Chicago, 723 F.2d 1263 (7th Cir., 1983).

McMurray v. Phelps, 535 F.Supp. 742 (W.D.L.A., 1982).

Molar v. Gates, 159 Ca.Rptr. 239 (4th Dist., 1979).

Reed v. Reed, 404 U.S. 71 (1971).

State ex rel Olson v. Maxwell, 259 N.W.2d 621 (Sup.Ct. N.D., 1977).

Thompson et al. v. Varelas, Sheriff, Nassau County et al., 81 Civ.0184 (JM) September 11 (1985).

Todaro v. Ward, 431 F.Supp. 1129 (S.D. N.Y., 1977).

United States ex rel Robinson v. York, 281 F.Supp. 8 (D.Conn., 1968).

Weinberger v. Wisenfeld, 420 U.S. 636, 43 L.Ed. 2d 514 (1975).

Williams v. Levi, Civ. Action No. Sp. 792–796 (Superior Court of D.C., 1976).

REFERENCES

ALLEN, H.E., & SIMONSEN, C.E. (1978). *Corrections in America: An introduction.* Encino, CA: Glencoe.

AMERICAN CORRECTIONAL ASSOCATION. (1985, April). *Standards for adult local detention facilities* (2nd ed.). In cooperation with the Commission on Accreditation for Corrections.

ARDITI, R.R., GOLDBERG, F., JR., PETERS, J., & PHELPS, W.R. (1973). The sexual segregation of American prisons. *Yale Law Journal, 6*(82), 1229–1273.

ARON, N. (1981). Legal issues pertaining to female offenders. In N. Aron (Ed.), *Representing prisoners.* New York: Practicing Law Institute.

BELKNAP, J. (1996). *The invisible woman.* Belmont, CA: Wadsworth.

BUREAU OF JUSTICE STATISTICS. L.A. Greenfeld & T.L. Snell, December 1999 and Revised 10/03/2000. Available at: http://www.ojp.usdoj.gov/bjs/pub/ascii/wopris.txt.

FABIAN, S.L. (1980). Women prisoners: Challenge of the future. In N. Aron (Ed.), *Legal rights of prisoners.* Beverly Hills, CA: Sage.

FEINMAN, C. (1982). Sex role stereotypes and justice for women. In B.R. Price & N.J. Sokoloff (Eds.), *The criminal justice system and women* (pp. 131–139). New York: Clark Boardman.

FEINMAN, C. (1986). *Women in the criminal justice system.* New York: Praeger.

GIBSON, H. (1973). Women's prisons: Laboratories for penal reform. *Wisconsin Law Review.*

GOBERT J.J., & COHEN, N.P. (1981). *Rights of prisoners.* New York: McGraw Hill.

HUNTER, S. (1984). Issues and challenges facing women's prisons in the 1980's. *Prison Journal, 64*(1).

JOHNSON, J., & KNAPP, J. (1971). Sex discrimination by law: A study in judicial perspective. *New York University Law Review, 75,* 704–705.

INCIARDI, J.A. (1984). *Criminal justice.* Orlando, FL: Academic Press.

LEWIS, D.K. (1982). Female ex-offenders and community programs. *Crime and Delinquency, Rights of Prisoners, 28,* 40–52.

LOWN, R.D., & SNOW, C. (1980). Women, the forgotten prisoners: *Glover v. Johnson.* In N. Aron (Ed.), *Legal rights of prisoners.* Beverly Hills, CA: Sage.

MURASKIN, R. (1989). *Disparity of correctional treatment: Development of a measurement instrument.* Doctoral dissertation 9000053, City University of New York. Dissertation Abstracts International.

MURASKIN, R. (2000). *It's a crime: Women and justice.* Upper Saddle River, NJ: Prentice Hall.

NATIONAL INSTITUTE OF JUSTICE. B.E. Richie, K. Tsenin, & C.S. Widom, "Research on Women and Girls in the Justice System," (September 2000).

POLLACK, H., & SMITH, A.B. (1978). *Civil liberties and civil rights in the United States.* St. Paul, MN: West.

POLLOCK, J.M., & BYRNE, J.M. (1999). *Criminal woman.* Cincinnati, OH: Anderson.

RAFTER, N. (1983). Prisons for women, 1790–1980. In M. Tonry & N. Morries (Eds.), *Crime and justice: An annual review of research,* vol. 5. Chicago: University of Chicago Press.

RECKLESS, W. (1967). *The crime problem.* New York: Appleton-Century-Crofts.

SARGENT, J.P. (1984). The evolution of a stereotype: Paternalism and the female inmate. *Prison Journal, 64*(1), 37–45.

SARRI, R. (1979). Crime and the female offender. In E.S. Gomberg &. V. Frank (Eds.), *Gender and disordered behavior: Sex differences in psychopathology.* New York: Brunner/Mazel.

SINGER, L. (1979). Women and the correctional process. In F. Adler & R. Simon (Eds.), *The criminality of deviant women.* Boston: Houghton Mifflin.

WILLIAMS, V.L., FORMBY, W.A., & WATKINS, J.C. (1982). *Introduction to criminal justice.* Albany, NY: Delmar.

WOOD, D. (1982). *Women in jail.* Milwaukee, WI: Benedict Center for Criminals.

11

Native Americans and the Criminal Justice System

David Lester

Although the crime rate has been decreasing nationally, the crime rate for minorities has been increasing. In addition, racial minorities are disproportionately arrested, prosecuted, convicted, and sentenced to prison at a much higher rate than whites. One such racial minority is Native Americans. For a long time, very little attention has been paid to the issue of Native Americans and the criminal justice system, but recently researchers, policy makers, and legislators have been focusing on Native Americans and the criminal justice system. This chapter examines the nature and extent of the involvement of Native Americans in crime and the criminal justice system, including responses to issues of crime among Native Americans and policy implications.

BRIEF OVERVIEW OF NATIVE PEOPLE

Individuals who are referred to as Native Americans in the United States include American Indians, Eskimos (Inuits), and Aleuts. There are slightly more than 2 million (2,119,000) Native Americans (who identified themselves as such in the 2000 U.S. census), constituting 0.78% of the nation's population. They are divided into tribes, with great diversity among the tribes (Boomgaard, 2000).

Their historical and cultural roots date back thousands of years. When Europeans came to this country, there were approximately 10 to 12 million indigenous people living on the land that became the United States. The indigenous people were divided into numerous autonomous nations, each with its own highly developed culture and history. Politically,

149

the indigenous people were not weak, dependent groups of people but rather powerful equals. Over the years, they have been stripped of their resources and subjected to political and economical exploitation and cultural suppression (Ross, 1998).

Native Americans value harmony with nature and believe in protecting the land rather than destroying it for commercial and industrial purposes. They are present-oriented rather than future-oriented, and they believe that there is an interconnectedness of all things, living and nonliving. They value the extended family, and they place great emphasis on respect for their elders. They also view good health as the result of four elements: the physical, the mental, the emotional, and the spiritual (Joe & Malach, 1992).

In general, Native Americans consider their traditional culture and spirituality to be inseparable. Their spiritual beliefs are founded on the principle that all natural things are interconnected and that the land is the primary source of strength and life. Native spirituality is governed by the notion of the Creator (Great Spirit or God) as the ultimate being, with all other living things possessing a spirit. Humans are only one of the living things on earth and, as such, are required to respect the living creatures with whom they live. Each native culture uses mediums such as ceremonies, animals, symbols, and behavioral traits to demonstrate certain aspects of that particular culture's spirituality. The exact nature of these mediums usually varies from culture to culture and within different communities of the same cultural grouping (Benson, 1991).

Today, many Native Americans live on 283 Native American reservations in the mainland United States and in some 200 Inuit, Aleut, and Native American communities in Alaska (Boomgaard, 2000). Others live in marginalized areas of cities such as Los Angeles, Tulsa, Oklahoma City, San Francisco, and Phoenix (Utter, 1993). Native Americans still maintain their cultural heritage and their tribal customs (Joe & Malach, 1992). Native Americans on average have much higher unemployment rates, lower incomes, poorer housing, lower levels of schooling, and higher incidences of serious diseases and alcoholism than the national averages. Many Native American leaders feel that the urbanization of their population is destroying their culture because many young Native Americans have never seen their reservations or spoken their native language (Boomgaard, 2000).

NATIVE AMERICANS AND CRIME

The United States has long recognized Indian tribes as governments that exercise authority over their members and their territories.[1] The United States has granted Native Americans tribal rights to self-government. However, under the federal trust responsibility, the United States has provided felony law enforcement in most of Indian country since the 1880s through the Departments of Interior and Justice. Generally, the local governing authority on an Indian reservation is a tribal government or council. Jurisdiction over crimes committed on Indian land depends on several factors, including the identity of the victim, the identity of the offender, the severity of the crime, and where the crime was committed. Tribal governments have criminal jurisdiction over crimes committed by American Indians[2] in Indian country. Tribal authority to sentence offenders is limited to one year or less imprisonment and a $5,000 fine. Tribes generally share jurisdiction over felony offenses with the state, and serious felony offenses are under the jurisdiction of state or federal government authorities (U.S. Department of Justice, 2000a).

In an October 1997 report, the Justice Department's Criminal Division concluded that although most of the United States has witnessed a drastic reduction in serious crime over the past seven years, on Indian reservations crime was spiraling upward. Between 1992 and 1996, the overall American crime rate dropped about 17%, and homicides were down 22%. For the same period, however, the Bureau of Indian Affairs reported that murder rates on Indian reservations rose sharply. Some tribes have murder rates that far exceed those of urban areas. Other violent crimes by Native Americans parallel the rise in homicide (U.S. Department of Justice, 1997a).

In 1999, the Justice Department's Bureau of Justice Statistics issued what can be considered the first comprehensive analysis of Indians and crime, and the findings reveal a disturbing picture of American Indian involvement in crime as both offenders and victims. The study found that the arrest rate for alcohol-related offenses among American Indians (drunken driving, liquor law violations, and public drunkenness) was more than double that of the total population during 1996. However, the drug arrest rate was lower than that of other races. Almost four in ten American Indians held in local jails had been charged with a public order offense—most commonly driving while intoxicated (U.S. Department of Justice, 1999a).

American Indians are also victims of violent crimes at a disproportionate rate. The U.S. Department of Justice (1999a) found that American Indians experienced per capita rates of violence that are more than twice those of the general population. From 1992 through 1996, the average annual rate of violent victimization among Indians 12 years and older was 124 per 1,000 residents, compared with 61 for blacks, 49 for whites, and 29 for Asians. In seven of ten violent victimizations of Native Americans, the assailant was someone of a different race, a substantially higher incidence of interracial violence than that experienced by white or black victims. Among white victims, 69% of the offenders were white; similarly, black victims are most likely to be victimized by a black assailant (81%). For American Indian victims of rape and sexual assault, the offender is described as white in 82% of the cases (U.S. Department of Justice, 1999a).

Native Indians suffer 7 sexual assaults per 1,000 compared to 3 per 1,000 among blacks, 2 per 1,000 among whites, and 1 per 1,000 among Asians. American Indians also suffer the nation's highest rate of child abuse. American Indians were about 0.7% of murder victims from 1976 to 1996, but the rate has been declining since 1991, as has the murder rate for all groups. The only exception to this decline is the murder rates among American Indians aged 40 to 49, which has increased by 2.8%, and age 50 and older, which has increased by 12.7%. The murderer of an American Indian was most likely to be a non–American Indian (40%), in fact, most often white (33%). Although the "typical" murder victim was killed by a handgun, American Indian victims are most likely to be killed by a rifle, shotgun, or stabbing (U.S. Department of Justice, 1999a).

One of the major causes of criminal activity among Native Americans is drugs. Alcohol is more often a major factor in crimes committed by and against Native Americans than for other races. Seventy percent of Native Americans in local jails for violent crimes had been drinking when they committed the offense, nearly double the rate for the general population. In 55% of violent crimes against American Indians, the victim said the offender was under the influence of alcohol or drugs (U.S. Department of Justice, 1999a).

The increase in crime among Native Americans is also related to emerging gang violence and offenders returning to tribal communities after incarceration. Other causes include poor parental role models, dysfunctional families, broken-down communities, culture shock, and loss of spirituality, all of which are cited as contributing factors to the high number of Native Americans in the jails (Hayes, n.d.). Dysfunctional parents rear dysfunctional children. It is a vicious cycle, and it will take two or three generations to break the chain.

NATIVE AMERICANS AND THE CRIMINAL JUSTICE PROCESS

On any given day, an estimated 1 in 25 Native Americans 18 years old and older is under the jurisdiction of the nation's criminal justice system. This is 2.4 times the rate for whites and 9.3 times the rate for Asians but about half the rate for blacks (U.S. Department of Justice, 1999a).

Native Americans and Corrections

Native Americans are overrepresented as inmates, 1.1% of the total correctional population, which breaks down to 1.5% of federal inmates, 1.0% of state inmates, and 2.9% of local jail inmates (U.S. Department of Justice, 1999a). Nearly 12,000 American Indians were held in state or federal prisons on December 31, 1997. Excluding inmates held in 69 Indian detention facilities operated by the Bureau of Indian Affairs or tribal authorities, there were 492 sentenced inmates per 100,000 American Indians. Between 1990 and 1997, the number of American Indians in state and federal prison increased by 98%, with the rate for the males increasing by 95% and that of the females by 150% in 1997. The rate increased from 275 per 100,000 in 1990 to 492 in 1997; the rate for the males increased from 516 in 1990 to 905 in 1997, as the rate for females increased from 35 to 80 (U.S. Department of Justice, 1999b).

At midyear 1999, a total of 19,679 American Indians were in custody (U.S. Department of Justice, 2000a). There were 1,621 American Indians in jails on Indian reservations, and of these 84% of the inmates were males and 16% females; 75% had previous convictions. There were another 5,200 American Indians in local jails, with a rate of 247 per 100,000—more than three times as many American Indians in local jails as on Indian reservations. At midyear 1999, there were 11,123 American Indians in state prisons and 1,735 in federal prisons. Federal and state prison and jail authorities held 797 American Indians per 100,000 American Indians compared with 682 persons per 100,000 for the general population. The rate of incarceration for American Indians was about 15% higher than the national rate mid-year 1999 (U.S. Department of Justice, 2000b). There were another 26,234 under community supervision, on state or federal probation and parole, and on community supervision in Indian reservations. Overall, state, federal, local, and tribal authorities were supervising 45,913 American Indians. The majority of American Indians were sentenced to the community (26,234). American Indians account for just under 1% of the American resident population and about 1% of those in custody of jails or prisons (U.S. Department of Justice, 2000b).

Native American Women

Violence against American Indian women is particularly severe. The rate of violent crime experienced by American Indian women is nearly 50% higher than that reported by black males. The violent crime rate for Native American women during 1992–1996 was 98 per 1,000 females, a rate considerably higher than that found among white females (40) or black females (56) (U.S. Department of Justice, 1999a)

Native American women are also overrepresented as offenders, 1.3% of federal inmates and 1.2% of state inmates (U.S. Department of Justice, 1997b). Among American Indian women, the incarceration rate in 1998 was 80 per 100,000, 2½ times the rate among white women (U.S. Department of Justice, 1999b). South Dakota has an especially high percentage of Native American female prisoners in federal jurisdictions. In the South Dakota women's prison, which has 202 inmates, 66% of the inmates are white, 31% are Native Americans, and 3% are black (Lujan, 1995; South Dakota Advisory Committee, 2000).

Ross (1998) reported that, although Native Americans in Montana are only 6% of the state population, they constitute 25% of the total female prison population. She also found that landless Native American women were more likely to be criminalized and imprisoned than women from other racial and ethnic groups or other Native American women. Her study indicated that Native American women were given longer sentences than white women and that they were convicted more often for "male-type" crime than white women, which could account for the longer sentences. Lujan (1995) attributed the disproportionate incarceration rate of Native American women to racist stereotyping, labeling, paternalism, language and cultural differences, oppression, and unresolved grief over the genocide of Native Americans.

Native American and Death Penalty

Of the 6,139 inmates sentenced to death between 1973 and 1997, 52 or 0.8% were Native Americans. Between 1977 and 1999, five Native American men were executed; four died by lethal injection and one was electrocuted. At the end of 1999, there were 28 American Indians under sentence of death (U.S. Department of Justice, 2000c).

RESPONSES TO NATIVE AMERICAN CRIMES

Government Response

The federal government's response to crime among Native Americans has increased in recent years. Recognizing the severity of the problem of violent crime suffered by Native Americans, the Office of Justice Programs (OJP) administers several large grant programs that provide funding to American Indian tribes and tribal organizations to deal with crime. The OJP also encourages the coordination of resources at the tribal level to combat crime more effectively in tribal communities. In addition, OJP is working to ensure that tribal governments are included in efforts to improve access to and integration of criminal justice and information technology so that Indian tribes can more effectively combat crime in Indian country and share information among the various tribal justice components, as well as within and among jurisdictions. It encourages American Indian tribes to utilize federal resources to ensure coordination in designing effective communication and information-sharing systems (U.S. Department of Justice, 1997c).

The Office for Victims of Crime (OVC) provides direct assistance to crime victims in Indian communities. Its OVC activities among American Indians have included (1) the provision of emergency services for American Indian crime victims; (2) the establishment of victim assistance programs on reservations; (3) the establishment of programs to improve the investigation and prosecution of child sexual abuse cases in Indian country; (4) training and technical assistance for a variety of professionals who have responsibility for the identification, investigation, and prosecution of crimes, and the treatment of victims on American Indian reservations; (5) inclusion of American Indians as a category of victims that states may use in meeting their underserved requirement in Victims of Crime Act (VOCA) victim assistance programs; and (6) the dissemination of information about the availability of crime victim compensation programs. The Office of Victims of Crime has also established a special fund, the Federal Crime Victims Emergency Services Fund (the Emergency Fund), to provide emergency assistance to all victims of federal crime, including Native Americans. Upon request, funds are made available to U.S. attorneys' offices to address emergencies in which victims involved in federal prosecutions need services that are unavailable or inaccessible through other sources (Boomgaard, 2000).

To maximize the effectiveness of these programs, a variety of culturally appropriate training and technical assistance opportunities are available to American Indian tribes and tribal organizations. In addition, Bureau of Justice Assistance (BJA) funds such programs as Tribal Strategies against Violence, a tribal–federal partnership that empowers tribal communities through the development and implementation of a comprehensive reservation-wide strategy to reduce crime, violence, and substance abuse. Through the National Institute of Justice, studies on the effectiveness of OJP's programs on American Indian reservations and research into the causes of crime and violence examine the effectiveness of current efforts and provide for the development of innovative and responsive new programs (U.S. Department of Justice, 1997c).

Former president Clinton had directed the attorney general and the secretary of the interior to develop a plan to improve public safety and the criminal justice system in American Indian communities. Through the Indian Country Law Enforcement Improvement Initiative, these two agencies have been working together to promote effective law enforcement and public safety in American Indian communities. In fiscal year 2000, the Department of Justice (DOJ) provided $91.5 million for tribal law enforcement salaries and for equipment, training, construction of detention facilities, juvenile justice programs, tribal courts, research and evaluation, and federal law enforcement efforts (U.S. Department of Justice, 2000d).

In 1988, the first two tribal victim assistance programs were established in Michigan. There are now six active tribal programs in the state. Today, Arizona, California, Kansas, Minnesota, Montana, North Dakota, South Dakota, and Washington have established victim assistance programs primarily for Native Americans. These programs provide counseling, personal advocacy, therapy, assistance in filing compensation claims, and follow-up contact. Very few Native Americans knew that compensation programs were available to them. This lack of familiarity persisted even though eligible state compensation programs, which receive federal funds, must compensate victims of federal crime on the same basis as they compensate victims of state crimes. The OVC has been working with the National Organization of Crime Victims Compensation Boards to initiate a Native American outreach effort to inform victims of crime on American Indian reservations about compensation programs (Boomgaard, 2000).

The Native American Community Response

Crime is a local problem, and Native American communities also have a responsibility to prevent crime. Among the initiatives taken by Native Americans are tribal drug courts established by some tribes with combined resources from the Justice Department, the Indian Health Service (IHS), and the Bureau of Indian Affairs (BIA). Tribes are also trying to improve services for domestic violence victims and to improve the investigation and prosecution of violent crimes against women. Some Indian tribes have diverted tribal resources to improve public safety by investing in jails and detention facilities, as well as graduated sanctioning. Other Native American tribes have begun to enhance tribal justice practices and systems. Native American tribes throughout the nation are also returning to indigenous justice ways, such as peacemaking and circle sentencing. Others are combining Western approaches and indigenous justice ways. In short, tribes are developing response systems that accurately reflect their communities' problems and unique problem-solving methods (U.S. Department of Justice, 2000d).

POLICY IMPLICATIONS

There is a general consensus that poverty, lack of job opportunities, and an inadequate educational system have contributed to heightened levels of criminality. The efforts by the federal and state agencies are useful, but government needs to place more emphasis on eliminating the factors and conditions that adversely affect Native Americans. The government needs to implement more holistic and long-range services that will end marginalization and remove criminogenic conditions that predispose Native Americans to criminal behavior. The government should attempt to demarginalize Native Americans by providing social, economic, educational, and political opportunities and resources that will empower them. The government should improve the quality of life for Native Americans, especially those who reside in high-crime neighborhoods and are at risk of becoming criminals.

Criminal justice agencies should provide more outreach programs and liaisons for the Native American communities. Some police departments have outreach officers who work out of substations and become actively involved in the communities they serve. This approach is intended to minimize the cultural and social distance between law enforcement officers and minority communities and to break the "us versus them" mentality. More of these programs are needed in Native American communities, especially where there is a high level of tension between criminal justice agencies and Native American communities.

Despite the fact that minorities are overrepresented in the criminal justice system, many of the prevention and treatment strategies established are without any multicultural component that takes into account the social and cultural milieu in which offenders find themselves (Corley & Smitherman, 1994). Programs for Native Americans will be successful only if they incorporate the ideals and cultural framework of Native Americans. The federal and state governments also need to establish more culturally sensitive and appropriate rehabilitation, treatment, and spiritual programs for Native American offenders throughout the criminal justice system.

Discrimination undoubtedly plays a role in the arrest, prosecution, and sentencing of Native Americans, and the criminal justice system appears to have been ineffective in handling the Native Americans in its care. The systemic bias in the criminal justice system needs to be eliminated. This can occur if non–Native American criminal justice personnel at all levels of the system are trained to understand the Native American culture and to be sensitive to the needs of the Native Americans under their care. Another way to reduce the bias in the criminal justice system is to make criminal justice agencies representative of the communities they serve. Unfortunately, Native American professionals are underrepresented in all aspects of the justice system, even though many justice organizations have made special efforts to recruit Native Americans. States and the federal government, therefore, need to make a great effort to involve more Native American criminal justice professionals at all levels of the criminal justice system. It is critical that governments take immediate steps to eradicate racial bias from our criminal justice system.

Native Americans have the unique legal right to establish criminal justice organizations to provide services for their own nations. The Navajo Nation, for example, has its own police, courts, probation services, and peacemakers devoted to traditional justice practice (Perry & Neilsen, 2000). More programs with this type of approach are needed to deal with Native American offenders.

Generally, most major crimes fall within the federal jurisdiction, and misdemeanors are handled in tribal courts. Tribal courts have no criminal jurisdiction over non-Indians. In other words, a crime committed on a Native American reservation can be subjected to investigation by local law enforcement, consisting of tribal and/or BIA police, state troopers, or federal law enforcement personnel from the BIA or the FBI. In some cases, the difficulty of determining criminal jurisdiction, particularly when there may be concurrent jurisdictions, may result in untimely action or no action at all. For example, in cases involving Indian women, police may often ignore crimes of abuse on the pretext of jurisdictional uncertainties (National Sexual Violence Resource Center, 2000). This kind of jurisdictional confusion can obviously prevent the delivery of services to victims and the prosecution of perpetrators. Clearer guidelines and procedures are needed regarding the investigation and prosecution of crimes.

Native American communities should play a greater role in the prevention of crime among their members. They need to provide more educational, recreational, and service programs for their members. There is value in members of the Native American communities designing and operating their own services, such as battered women's shelters and rape crisis centers. Thus, Native Americans also need to increase the local services that are available to their people.

Many Native American programs utilize a restorative justice approach because they focus on preventing further occurrences of criminal justice behavior through resolving the underlying issues and "healing" the offender, victim, and community (Hudson & Galaway, 1996). These kinds of programs not only are the most culturally sensitive strategy for helping many Native American offenders and victims but also may ultimately be the most effective because restorative justice approaches have the potential to help resolve the large issue of marginalization that causes Native American individuals to come into conflict with the criminal justice system in the first place (Neilsen, 2000). Native Americans need to increase these programs in their communities as well.

FUTURE RESEARCH

The information available on crime justice and Native Americans clearly shows that they, like African Americans, are overrepresented in the criminal justice system. During the past decade, studies have been conducted to determine the treatment of racial and ethnic minorities in the criminal justice system. Some of the studies have concluded that racial bias, both overt and unconscious, continues to cause not only police but also prosecutors and judges to treat minorities differently and more harshly than whites. This occurs at every point in the criminal justice process, whether at the arrest, charging, bail, jury selection, or sentencing stage (American Civil Liberties Union, 1996). Other research indicates there is no discrimination but that minorities commit a disproportionate number of crimes. Most of the research, however, has been conducted on African Americans and Hispanics. There have been very few, if any, studies focusing on Native Americans. Future research needs to examine the extent to which racial discrimination contributes to the overrepresentation of Native Americans in the criminal justice system and whether the disproportionate number of Native Americans in the criminal justice system is the result of discrimination. It is imperative for researchers to determine whether Native Americans are arrested, prosecuted, and convicted based on their race.

The federal and state governments and community groups offer several programs, preventive and rehabilitative, to Native Americans. These programs need to be assessed for their effectiveness. Future research should determine if they have achieved their goals in preventing crimes.

Comparative studies on Native Americans need to be conducted. Most research on minority groups fails to take into consideration the diversity within minority groups, which is true of studies on Native Americans. Most of the research on Native Americans ignores tribal differences and neglects Eskimos (Inuits) and Aleuts. It is also important that researchers compare the processing of Native Americans through the tribal justice system and the federal and state criminal justice system. Finally, a comparative study of crime and criminal justice on Native People in the United States (Native Americans) and Canada (Aboriginal People) would be invaluable.

SUMMARY

Although Native Americans were the original inhabitants of this land called the United States, they have suffered years of discrimination and oppression. Historically, they suffered repeated economic exploitation of their land, forced migrations, depletion of life-sustaining herds, and exclusion from educational and business opportunities. As a result, most of them live in poverty, with a shorter life expectancy, higher infant mortality rates, less education, and fewer economic opportunities than the general population. They are also overrepresented at all levels of the criminal justice system. They have some of the highest arrest, prosecution, and incarceration rates in the United States. The widespread use of alcohol by Native Americans remains a debilitating legacy of colonization, and data indicate a positive correlation between alcohol use and crimes among Native Americans.

Although there has been some effort on the part of federal and state governments to address the problem of crime among Native Americans, more needs to be done. Native Americans have also tried to deal with problem of crime in their communities, but this is only the beginning. The problem of crime in Native Country should have a high priority for governments and the Native American community in general.

No one program or organization alone can effectively promote safer Native American neighborhoods. The active involvement of community residents, faith-based organizations, schools, and businesses, in partnership with criminal justice and mental health, social service, and drug treatment providers, is important in the prevention of crime among Native Americans. The criminal justice system (law enforcement, prosecution, courts, and corrections) must be responsive to the public safety needs of these communities and collaborate with other public, private, and community organizations to prevent crimes. What is needed is a holistic approach that would require comprehensive strategies, multidisciplinary partnerships, and collective commitment on the part of federal and state governments and the Native American communities to effectively address the problem of crime in the Native American communities.

DISCUSSION QUESTIONS

1.   Describe the responsibilities of government with regard to crime.

2.   What are the reasons for the high crime rate among Native Americans?

3.   What factors may be related to the disproportionate incarceration of Native American women?

4.   Discuss two federal programs designed to reduce crime among Native Americans.

5.   What is the response of the Native American community to crime among Native Americans?

NOTES

1.   Government documents use the term "Indian," so this term will be used in this chapter when government sources are used.

2.   The term "Native Americans" is the more acceptable term used to describe this group of people, but government documents often use the term "American Indians." Consequently, the term "American Indians" is used in the chapter only when government sources are used. In all other instances, the term "Native Americans" is used.

REFERENCES

AMERICAN CIVIL LIBERTIES UNION. (1996, February 26). Urges court to purge criminal justice system of racial bias. Available at: http://www.aclu.org/news/n022696b.html.

BENSON, G.F. (1991). *Developing crime prevention strategies in aboriginal communities.* Ottawa, Canada: Solicitor General of Canada. Available at http://www.sgc.gc.ca/EPub/Abo/e199112/e199112.htm.

BOOMGAARD, M. (2000, February 23). *Native Americans in the United States.* Washington, DC: U.S. Government Printing Office. Available at: http://www.bsos.umd.edu/cidcm/mar/usnatam.htm.

CORLEY, C., & SMITHERMAN, C. (1994). Juvenile justice: Multicultural issues. In J. Hendricks & B. Byers (Eds.), *Multicultural perspectives in criminal justice and criminology* (pp. 259–290). Springfield, IL: Charles C. Thomas.

HAYES, J. (n.d.). Native people and the justice system. *Windspeaker.* Available at: http://www.ammsa.com/classroom/CLASS3justice.html.

HUDSON, J., & GALAWAY, B. (1996). Introduction. In B. Galaway & J. Hudson (Eds.), *Restorative justice: International perspectives* (pp. 1–14). Monsey, NY: Criminal Justice Press.

JOE, J.R., & MALACH, R.S. (1992). Families with Native American roots. In E.W. Lynch & M.J. Hanson (Eds.), *Developing cross-cultural competency: A guide for working with young children and their families* (pp. 89–119). Baltimore, MD: Paul H. Brookes.

LUJAN, C. (1995). Women warriors: American Indian women, crime and alcohol. *Women and Criminal Justice, 7,* 9–33.

LUJAN, C. (1998). Or, "The only real Indian is the stereotyped Indian." In C.R. Mann & M.S. Zatz (Eds.), *Images of color, images of crime* (pp. 47–57). Los Angeles: Roxbury.

NATIONAL SEXUAL VIOLENCE RESOURCE CENTER. (2000). Sexual assault in Indian Country: Confronting sexual violence. Available at: http://www.nsvrc.org/indian.html.

NEILSEN, M.O. (2000). Stolen lands, stolen lives: Native Americans and Criminal Justice. In the Criminal Justice Collective of Northern Arizona University (Ed.), *Investigating difference: Human and cultural relations in criminal justice* (pp. 47–58). Boston, MA: Allyn and Bacon.

PERRY, B., & NIELSEN, M.O. (2000). Reinvestigating difference. In the Criminal Justice collective of Northern Arizona university (Ed.), *Investigating difference: Human and cultural relations in criminal justice* (pp. 271–286). Boston, MA: Allyn and Bacon.

ROSS, L. (1998). *Inventing the savage: The social construction of Native American criminality.* Austin, TX: University of Texas Press.

SOUTH DAKOTA ADVISORY COMMITTEE TO THE UNITED STATES COMMISSION ON CIVIL RIGHTS. (2000). *Native Americans in South Dakota: An erosion of confidence in the justice system.* Available at: http://www.usccr.gov/pubs/sdsac/ch1.htm.

U.S. DEPARTMENT OF JUSTICE. (1997a). *Sourcebook of criminal justice statistics, 1996.* Washington, DC: U.S. Government Printing Office.

U.S. DEPARTMENT OF JUSTICE. (1997b). *Correctional populations in the United States,1995.* Washington, DC: U.S. Government Printing Office.

U.S. DEPARTMENT OF JUSTICE. (1997c). *Office of Justice Programs partnership initiatives in Indian Country.* Washington, DC: U.S. Government Printing Office.

U.S. DEPARTMENT OF JUSTICE. (1999a). *American Indians and crime.* Washington, DC: U.S. Government Printing Office.

U.S. DEPARTMENT OF JUSTICE. (1999b). *Prisoners in 1998.* Washington, DC: U.S. Government Printing Office.

U.S. DEPARTMENT OF JUSTICE. (1999c). *Tribal youth program.* Washington, DC: U.S. Government Printing Office.

U.S. DEPARTMENT OF JUSTICE. (2000a). *Prison and jail inmates at midyear 1999.* Washington, DC: U.S. Government Printing Office..

U.S. DEPARTMENT OF JUSTICE. (2000b). *Jails in Indian country, 1998 and 1999.* Washington, DC: U.S. Government Printing Office.

U.S. DEPARTMENT OF JUSTICE. (2000c). *Capital punishment 1999.* Washington, DC: U.S. Government Printing Office.

U.S. DEPARTMENT OF JUSTICE. (2000d). *Office of Justice Programs fiscal year 2000 program plan.* Washington, DC: U.S. Government Printing Office. Available at: http://www.ojp.usdoj.gov/00progplan/00prog.txt

U.S. DEPARTMENT OF JUSTICE. (2001). *OVC fact sheet: Children's justice partnerships for Indian communities.* Washington, DC: U.S. Printing Office.

UTTER, J. (1993). *American Indians: Answers to today's questions.* Lake Ann, MI: National Woodlands Publishing.

SECTION IV
Juvenile Justice

12

Violent Offenses by Adolescent Girls on the Rise

Myth or Reality?

Dorothy Taylor and Luigi Esposito

❖

Recent studies have revealed a significant increase in violent crimes by adolescent girls. Although some researchers have claimed that these increases are actually illusory media representations, data show increases in violent crimes among adolescent girls between 1989 and 1993. A few researchers have sought to address the causes underpinning the growth in this segment of the juvenile and criminal justice systems. Unlike previous (gendered) interpretations that attributed violent female offending to presumably inherent female traits, such as innate tendencies toward emotional outbursts and loss of control, more recent studies have shown that violent crimes committed by adolescent girls are actually the result of a highly complex combination of factors, including victimization, substance abuse, unfavorable economic conditions, and dysfunctional family systems. Nevertheless, various gaps exist in this small stream of research: (1) the existence of structural differences (for example, unique patterns of organization and interaction) among minority communities that may lead to possible variations in outcomes when the foregoing considerations are taken into account and (2) a thorough examination of the underlying variegated cultural dynamics that may influence these possible racial and ethnic variations.

Although violent crime has plagued American society throughout its history, there is a dearth of literature on violent crimes committed by adolescent girls. For the most part, studies of female offenders have concentrated almost exclusively on criminal activities typically associated with feminine roles, such as shoplifting and various forms of sexual deviance. The result is that violent crime has been generally designated a male problem. In spite of the neglect, Acoca (1999) reports that girls and women make up the fastest growing segments of the juvenile and criminal justice systems. Although many researchers have questioned the validity of the increase, arguing that illusory media representations are at the heart of these so-called increases, there is little doubt that arrests of girls for violent crimes have increased substantially during the past 10 years.

It should come as no surprise that female delinquency is disproportionately representative of minority girls living in low-income communities. As is well known, distinct social dynamics (for example, the lack of jobs and of productive social networks) make these communities especially vulnerable to various types of street crimes (Hagan, 1994). For the most part, however, the issue of violence among adolescent girls has been dismissed as "rare" and thus unimportant. At most, a host of ethnographic studies (for example, Jankowski, 1991; Miller, 1975; C. Taylor, 1993) have been undertaken among minority female gang members, but even these studies have either ignored or not paid serious attention to these girls' experiential considerations in assessing their gang-related activities, including violent crime, focusing instead on comparing the female gang members with their male counterparts. As a result, the interpretations in many cases have shown a clear gender bias (see Chesney-Lind, 1997, pp. 46–55). On the positive side, however, these studies have revealed the societal conditions that promote crime among female gang members and offer some insights into these girls' unique life histories, social etiquette, and modes of interaction that often lead to violence.

This chapter discusses possible structural and processual contingencies that lead to variations in racial or ethnic outcomes regarding girls' violent offenses. Rather than attribute this problem to "inherent" female liabilities or cultural deficiencies, one can argue that the unique patterns of organization and modes of interaction—typical of low-income minority communities—that are conducive to violent crimes are *not* simply residual outcomes of the structural conditions of these communities (as many writers suggest) but are contingent on the various processes that reflect the meanings and experiential considerations that characterize these girls' daily lives. We hope that such an exploration will lead to more socially grounded solutions to the problem.

REVIEW OF THE LITERATURE

As mentioned earlier, violent crime has traditionally been understood as a male problem. When violent female offenders are studied, it is usually within the context of domestic violence, typically as a response to battering (Browne, 1987; see also Sommer & Baskin, 1994).

In 1999, female delinquency accounted for 17% of all juveniles arrested for violent crimes; 8% of juvenile arrests for homicide (murder or nonnegligent manslaughter); 9% for all juvenile arrests for robbery; 22% of juvenile arrests for aggravated assaults; and 30% of all simple assaults (Federal Bureau of Investigation, 2000). Furthermore, Poe-Yamagata and Butts (1996) found that girls are being arrested at a faster rate than boys for aggravated assaults, motor vehicle theft, arson, possession of a weapon, vagrancy, and curfew and loitering violations.

One source of delinquent data is self-report studies. A 1997 National Longitudinal Survey of Youth interviewed a representative sample of 9,000 youth who were between the ages of 16 and 18 at the end of 1996. This study found that 23% of the female juveniles in the study who had an official juvenile delinquency record were referred to the court for the first time at the age of 14, and 19% of them had their first referral at 19. According to the

Centers for Disease Control and Prevention's 1997 Youth Risk Surveillance System, 46% of females reported that they were in physical fights in school 12 months prior to the survey. In a survey conducted by Monitoring the Future (MTF), 47% of female seniors in high school reported that they had used an illegal drug in the previous year, and 25% had offered, sold, or given someone an illegal drug on school property in the past year (Snyder & Sickmund, 1999).

VIOLENT CRIME: GIRLS VERSUS BOYS

Is violent crime by adolescent girls actually on the rise, or are girls customarily pulled into the juvenile justice system for less serious offenses than are boys? One cannot dispute the accelerating entry of girls into the juvenile justice system (see Browne, 1987; Chesney-Lind, 1997, 1998; Hagan, 1994; Jankowski, 1991; C. Taylor, 1993). However, one must question whether girls and boys are evenly inclined to be disruptive, but girls are merely more likely to be arrested for this conduct because it violates society's stereotypical gender norms (Zaplin, 1998). Any attempt to comprehend this accelerating trend must start with an analysis of recent statistics. For example, Snyder (2000) reported a greater increase in the percentage of arrests of girls than boys between 1990 and 1999 in almost every offense category.

The official data indicate that between 1990 and 1999 arrests of juvenile females generally increased more (or decreased less) than male arrests in most offense categories. For example, arrests for girls for violent crimes between 1990 and 1999 increased by 93% for simple assault and 57% for aggravated assault but decreased 11% for robbery. The rate of arrests for juvenile males increased 35% only for simple assault; there were decreases in all other offenses, as shown in Table 12.1 (Federal Bureau of Investigation, 2000).

Official data also indicate that 355,337 arrests of girls under age 18 in 1999 represented 27% of the total juvenile arrests within that year. Table 12.2 lists the top ten crimes for which juveniles were arrested in the United States in 1999. The table shows that boys

TABLE 12.1 Percentage Change in Juvenile Arrests 1990–1999

Selected Serious Offenses	Female (%)	Male (%)
Murder and nonnegligent manslaughter	−39	−56
Robbery	−11	−17
Aggravated assault	57	−5
Other (simple) assaults	93	35
Weapons	44	−7
Burglary	−8	−34
Vandalism	28	−13

Source: Federal Bureau of Investigation. (2000). *Crime in United States, 1999.* Washington, DC: U.S. Government Printing Office.

TABLE 12.2   Top Ten Crimes for Which Youths under 18 Years Were Arrested in 1999

	Females (%)			Males (%)	
Offense	Number of Arrests	Percentage of All Female Arrests	Offense	Number of Arrests	Percentage of All Male Arrests
Larceny–theft	75,632	31	All other offenses*	164,551	10
All other offenses*	55,004	13	Larceny–theft	135,989	32
Runaways	47,867	100	Drug laws violations	86,226	18
Other assaults**	36,576	24	Other assaults**	83,116	16
Curfew and loitering law violations	30,456	100	Curfew and loitering law violations	68,927	100
Liquor law violations	27,304	35	Disorderly conduct	62,755	26
Disorderly conduct	24,673	33	Liquor law violations	60,692	22
Drug law violations	15,126	10	Vandalism	56,400	44
Aggravated assaults	7,948	16	Burglary	47,618	35
Vandalism	7,681	34	Runaways	32,909	100

Source: Federal Bureau of Investigation (2000). *Crime in United States, 1999.* Washington, DC: U.S. Government Printing Office.

*"All other offenses" includes all other nonindex offenses except traffic offenses of those listed in crime reports.
**"Other assaults" includes assaults that are not the "aggravated assaults" classified in the violent crime index.
"Other assaults" are classified under nonindex offenses.

and girls were arrested for the same offenses, except the girls' list has aggravated assaults and the boys' list has burglaries. A higher percentage of female delinquents were arrested for other assaults, vandalism, liquor law violations, and the all other offenses category than male delinquents. The arrests rate for larceny–theft was about the same for both males and females.

With regard to girls' involvement in serious and violent crimes, the arrest rate for girls in the Violent Crime Index escalated 40% between 1990 and 1999, compared with an increase of only 3% for boys (Federal Bureau of Investigation, 2000). Table 12.3 presents the percentage of girls arrested in the United States from 1990 to 1999 in five-year increments. It indicates the types of offenses girls predominantly committed and the changes in the types of offenses for which they were arrested in this period. For seven offenses, girls were at least 30% of the juvenile arrests in 1999: running away (59%), prostitution and commercialized vice (54%), embezzlement (48%), offenses against family and children (38%), forgery and counterfeiting (37%), larceny–theft (36%), and liquor law violations (31%). Table 12.3 shows a slow but steady increase in the percentage of female delinquent arrests over the ten-year period. Between 1990 and 1999, the percentage of overall juvenile arrest increased 7% and their portion of the total crime index arrests increased 7% as well.

TABLE 12.3   Female Proportion of Juvenile Arrests: 1990, 1995, 1999

Offense	Female Proportion of Arrests of Persons under age 18 (%)		
	1990	1995	1999
Total	**23**	**26**	**27**
Crime index total	**20**	**24**	**27**
Violent crime index	**12**	**15**	**17**
Murder and nonnegligent manslaughter	6	6	8
Forcible rape	2	2	2
Robbery	9	9	9
Aggravated assault	15	20	22
Property crime index	**22**	**26**	**29**
Burglary	8	10	11
Larceny–theft	28	32	36
Motor vehicle theft	11	15	16
Arson	10	12	11
Nonindex offenses	**24**	**26**	**30**
Other assaults	23	28	30
Forgery and counterfeiting	33	35	37
Fraud	30	26	29
Embezzlement	40	42	48
Stolen property	9	12	13
Vandalism	8	11	12
Weapons	6	8	9
Prostitution and commercialized vice	55	48	54'
Sex offenses (except prostitution and forcible rape)	7	7	8
Drug abuse violations	11	13	14
Gambling	5	5	4
Offenses against the family and children	35	37	38
Driving under the influence	14	16	17
Liquor law violations	28	29	31
Drunkenness	15	16	20
Disorderly conduct	20	25	28
Vagrancy	16	11	19
All other offenses (except traffic)	21	22	25
Curfew and loitering law violations	28	30	30
Running away	56	57	59

Data Sources: Federal Bureau of Investigation. (2000). *Crime in United States, 1999.* Washington, DC: U.S. Government Printing Office; Federal Bureau of Investigation. (1996). *Crime in United States, 1995.* Washington, DC: U.S. Government Printing Office; Federal Bureau of Investigation. (1991). *Crime in United States, 1990.* Washington, DC: U.S. Government Printing Office.

Their total violent crime index arrests increased 5%, total property index crime arrests increased 7%, and total nonindex offense arrests increased 6% as can be seen from the data in Table 12.3. Larceny–theft, embezzlement, and disorderly conduct caused the greatest increase in the arrest rate for girls between 1990 and 1999, with an 8% increase in each category.

Indeed, these national data attest to the increases in the extent and gravity of offenses by female adolescents. The issue of heated debate between politicians and researchers, however, is the actual underlying causes of these increases. For example, Acoca (1999) asked, "What influence do changing and often less tolerant family and social attitudes toward girls, shifts in law enforcement practices (particularly toward gangs), and the increasing availability of weaponry exert on girls' offending?" (p. 4). Furthermore, Chesney-Lind and Shelden (1992) questioned whether these recent trends are an anomaly, given girls' lower base rate of arrests and delinquency cases since the 1970s.

Homicide by Girls

Although juvenile homicides are overwhelmingly associated with boys, there has been an increase in girls' arrests for homicide nearly every year since 1984 (Office of Juvenile Justice and Delinquency Prevention, 1999). Heide (1999) argued that, even if this is the case, girls "are hardly responsible for the dramatic escalation in juvenile murder in the United States" (p. 13).

When girls commit murder, they are more likely than boys to murder family members or acquaintances (Rowley, Ewing, & Singer, 1987) and to use accomplices (Benedek & Cornell, 1989; Ewing, 1990; Heide, 1992), but unmarried girls who murder their babies usually act alone. Furthermore, girls are likely to carry out subordinate roles during gang-related homicides and felonies, usually involving male accomplices. Girls' motives for killing are related to psychological conflict, supporting boyfriends or significant others, and validating their allegiance to the gang (Ewing, 1990).

INTERACTION OF RACE AND GENDER

According to Sarri (1983), the interaction of race and gender plays a key role in decisions to dismiss charges against juveniles. She found that African American boys were more likely to be rigorously processed through the system, African American girls were more likely to get probation, white girls were more likely to be diverted from the system, and white boys were more likely to have the charges dropped. With regard to incarceration rates, Krisberg and Austin (1993) noted that African American boys and girls had the highest rates and Asian American boys and girls had the lowest.

The literature has reported many important racial differences in female delinquency (Chesney-Lind & Shelden, 1992; Heide, 1999; Krisberg and Austin, 1993; Zaplin, 1998). Official and self-report data have indicated that African American boys have the highest rates of involvement in delinquency, followed by white boys, African American girls, and white girls. For example, the racial composition of the juvenile population in 1999 was 79% white, 15% black, and 5% other races, with most Hispanics classified as white. In contrast, 57% of juvenile arrests for violent crimes involved white youth and 41% involved black youth. To a lesser extent, black youth were also overrepresented in juvenile property crime arrests, with 27% of these arrests involving black youth and 69% involving white youth (Snyder, 2000). Some studies (for example, Wolfgang & Figlio, 1985) report a rate for delinquency of African American girls that is close to that for white boys. Hindelang, Hirschi, and Weiss's (1981) earlier study of self-reported delinquency discovered that African American girls were much more likely to admit that they stole $50 or more and were involved in auto theft, aggravated assault, and robbery, whereas African American girls and white girls were almost equally likely to admit having been involved in burglaries. Hindelang and colleagues (1981) also reported that for two major offenses—aggravated assault and robbery—the rates for African American girls were closely associated with those for white boys (see Table 12.4).

The 1997 National Longitudinal Survey of Youth (referred to earlier) found that white males (95%) were less likely to be arrested than black males (13%) or Hispanic males (12%). Further, a greater proportion of black and Hispanic males than white males were arrested more than once. Equal proportions of white, black, and Hispanic females had ever been arrested. In addition, white, black, and Hispanic females were equally likely to have been arrested more than once (Snyder & Sickmund, 1999).

In the early 1980s, the juvenile homicide rate for black youth was four times the white rate. In 1993, the black rate peaked at nearly seven times the white rate. With a greater decline in homicides for blacks than whites between 1993 and 1997, the disparity between the rates for blacks and whites declined to a ratio of five to one. In 1997, the risk of being murdered is similar for boys and girls in their preteen years, but the risk was much greater for boys in their teenage years, especially for blacks. Overall, the murder risk for black juveniles in 1997 was about triple that of white juveniles. Most disparate among juveniles was the murder risk for 17-year-old blacks, which was seven times the rate for whites (45.96 per 100,000 versus 6.43 per 100,000) (Snyder, 2000). In 1997, 92% of murdered juveniles were killed by persons of their own race. The percentage of same-race killings was greater for blacks (94%) than for whites and declined as the age of the victim increases (Snyder & Sickmund, 1999).

TABLE 12.4   Race and Sex Differences for Selected Offenses

	Male (%)		Female (%)	
Offense	White	Black	White	Black
Theft ($50+)	16.5	17.3	1.7	6.5
Auto theft	9.7	7.3	0.8	1.7
Burglary	16.8	12.9	4.9	4.3
Aggravated assault	10.2	15.4	3.1	8.9
Robbery	4.1	7.9	0 .7	5.3

Based on self-report data.

Source: Hindelang, Hirschi, and Weiss (1981), Appendix B.

VIOLENCE IN JUVENILE CORRECTIONAL SETTINGS

Increasing violence among juveniles has become a national problem in schools, neighborhoods, and also correctional settings. Among the most critical problems in juvenile correctional institutions are gang activity and violent assaults on staff and other inmates (Willett,
1996). Because of the violence of youths in Texas correctional facilities, for instance,
administrators have acknowledged the need for continuous staff development and training
in management tools such as conflict resolution to deal with the unique problems of violent
youths (Allen & Simonsen, 1998).

To address this issue, the Office of Juvenile Justice and Delinquency Prevention
(OJJDP) awarded a competitive, cooperative agreement in 1995 for a three-year project to
the Illinois Institute for Dispute Resolution to develop, in concert with other established
conflict resolution organizations, a national strategy for broad-based education and training
in the use of conflict resolution skills (Howell, 1995). In 1997, the project conducted additional training sessions in conjunction with conferences of national educational, justice,
and youth-serving organizations (OJJDP, 1997).

Some researchers have found that violence occurs less frequently in female than in
male juvenile correctional facilities. According to Bowker (1980), violence seems to be
used mainly to establish dominance and subordination when nonviolent means fail.

EXPLANATIONS FOR THE INCREASE IN FEMALE DELINQUENCY

The data presented here clearly indicate that female delinquency has shown a steady
increase over the past several years. The question is, What are the possible explanations for
the increase? Some writers have argued that these increases are not new and can be traced
to the women's movement in the 1970s, which called for the eradication of female subordination and oppression. The general idea was that women were rebelling against their submissive roles, and their increased participation in violence was a clear indication of this
rebellion (see Chesney-Lind, 1997, pp. 34–35.) However, Chesney-Lind (1986) stated that
this phenomenon was actually grounded in the experiences of white, middle-class women,
not adolescent girls. More recently, research on violent female offenders has focused on
adolescent female gang members, most of whom are African American and Latinas from
low-income backgrounds and communities (Moore & Hagedorn, 2001).

As a result, the public's perception of female violent offenders has shifted from that
of middle-class, white battered women to African American or Latina adolescent female
gang members who are reputed to be just as vicious as their male counterparts. Chesney-
Lind (1997) has also pointed out that "when dramatic pictures of girls of color carrying
guns and wearing bandanas suddenly appeared in the popular media, there were very
few . . . studies to refute these images" (p. 2). Zaplin (1998) suggested that one result of the
increased media and political obsession with heinous crimes committed by juveniles has
been the endorsement by politicians and others of the death penalty for juveniles and the
greater likelihood of juvenile offenders being tried as adults.

Sommer and Baskin (1994) and Peters and Peters (1998), among others, found that
violence by adolescent girls is actually a lot more complex than was previously understood.
Specifically, various factors—including age, neighborhood, peers, and addiction—are cen-

tral to an adequate understanding of when and how adolescent girls become involved in violent street crime. Moreover, multiple configurations of these factors—at different points in time—result in different outcomes.

According to Taylor, Biafora, Warheit, and Gil (1997), family factors play a key role in female juvenile delinquency—more specifically, theft, vandalism, and major deviance (for example, assault and aggressive behavior). The primary objectives of their study of 503 African American, Hispanic, and non-Hispanic white adolescent girls attending public schools in Miami, Florida, were to determine the prevalence of 13 self-reported delinquent behaviors in the sample, to compare these rates among the three groups of students, and to explore the predictive influences of several family factors that correlate with delinquency. The researchers found that 37.5% of the sample engaged in one or more acts of serious delinquency, with African Americans reporting they had engaged in significantly more of these behaviors. The best predictors of theft and vandalism were low family pride and family substance abuse for Hispanics, low family communication for African Americans, and low family pride for non-Hispanic whites. Furthermore, the traditional family factors (for example, parental divorce and single female–headed households) that have been used repeatedly to understand delinquency by adolescent boys were not strong predictors of delinquency among these adolescent girls.

One clear implication of the study is that an integrated model is needed to gain a more thorough understanding of the problem. Fortunately, advances in criminological theory may serve as starting points. For example, a number of researchers (for example, Dunford & Elliott, 1984; Elliott & Huizinga, 1984; Fagan, Piper, & Moore, 1986) have attempted to integrate elements of strain, control, learning, and ecological approaches to study crime. However, even this integrative framework has its shortcomings. For instance, although Sommer and Baskin (1994) used it to develop "an integrated model of women's pathways into violent offending," this approach focuses mostly on outcomes and reduces process to specific variables across time. In effect, the interactional processes that underpin violent behaviors are circumscribed with clearly delineated standard, ethical, and cultural parameters that may have nothing to do with these girls' everyday lives (and everything to do with mainstream white, middle-class society).

Accordingly, what is needed is a more thorough analysis of the *processes* that lead to violent crimes among adolescent girls. Variables grounded in these girls' experiential knowledge must supplant those grounded in white, middle-class visions of the world. Moreover, more attention must be paid to how agency shapes and is shaped by the structural factors that are considered. How do these girls define their identities (whether gender or racial), situations, and behaviors? What are their motivations for engaging in violence? Are these motivations widespread or locally determined?

Because the increase in violent crimes is most pronounced among female minorities, researchers must also be careful not to fall into the trap of grounding research in "unfree spaces" and producing what Fine and Weiss (1996; see also Fine, 1994) referred to as a "colonizing discourse" when explaining their behaviors. That is, they must refrain from "othering" these minority females by emphasizing what the public considers "the exotic, the bizarre, and the violent" (Fine & Weiss, 1996, p. 261). Instead, researchers must seek to create "free spaces"—spaces unconstrained by mainstream understandings of crime and violence—where these young girls can voice their interests, identities, and concerns. Only by gaining entrée into this experiential region can researchers hope to develop a better understanding of the problem without reinforcing negative stereotypes that portray minorities as undesirable "others."

GENDER-SPECIFIC ADVOCACY: 21ST-CENTURY SOLUTIONS

Modifying the factors underlying girls increased entry into the juvenile justice system (for example, victimization and abuse: physical, sexual, and emotional) (Acoca & Dedel, 1998; Chesney-Lind & Shelden, 1992; Heide, 1999) demands a well-established approach that includes initiatives at the national, state, and local levels. Acoca (1999) suggested that "girls in and on the edge of the juvenile justice system represent one of the least-served juvenile justice populations" (p. 10). Moreover, because life circumstances commonly experienced by juvenile female offenders contribute to girls' commission of crimes (Acoca, 1999; Belknap & Hosinger, 1998; Chesney-Lind & Shelden, 1998), a main focus of legislative initiatives must be the elimination of violence toward women and girls, both outside and inside the criminal justice system. There are several ways to do so:

1. The United States should comply with international conventions and standards for the protection of children and ensure that its legislation and policies match these standards (Amnesty International, 1998).

2. The development and enforcement of federal standards pertaining to conditions of confinement must specifically identify and respond to the needs of girls (Acoca & Dedel, 1998, p. 11).

3. Congress should continue to support the Violence against Women Office and other federal child-serving offices that provide programs and services to at-risk and delinquent girls and women (Acoca, 1999, p. 10).

4. Federal and state partnerships should be formed to help communities develop a working blueprint for measurably reducing youthful offending (Howell, 1995, p. 4).

An excellent example of the results of a federal–state partnership is the Practical, Academic, Cultural Education (PACE) Centers for Girls, with several locations in Florida and California. These centers have identified girls who are in and on the edge of entering the juvenile justice system and are profiling this population. PACE is also active with state and local public and private organizations that serve adolescents and with the National Council on Crime and Delinquency (NCCD) in designing and developing a broad continuum of services for girls, their children, and their families (*PACE Newsletter,* 1999).

The National Girls' Caucus is an advocacy group initiated by PACE to focus national attention on the unique needs of girls in the juvenile justice system. It is the opinion of this organization that "although discussion regarding juvenile justice reform continues to take place at national, state, and local levels, at-risk girls continue to be misunderstood and underserved" (Ravoira, 1999). Many researchers (Maynard, 1996; Pipher, 1994; Tucker & Wolfe, 1997) reported that problems normally associated with adolescence are exacerbated for girls who are in crisis. Numerous problems faced by adolescent girls include the death of a parent or relative, sexual and physical abuse, domestic violence (as victims), high-risk sexual behaviors, incarceration of close family members, involvement in gangs, substance use and abuse, and unique health issues (Ravoira, 1999).

With the motto "a small group can create change" and their concern about the lack of services for girls in the juvenile justice system, the founding members of the National Girls' Caucus (including child advocates, policy makers, national authorities on gender issues, service providers, educators, legislators, judges, funders, religious leaders, parents, and girls) held their first meeting of the caucus in March 1993, with funding provided by the Valentine Foundation. Since the inception of this organization, more than 450 individuals and agencies in Florida and California have become actively involved. Their challenge is clear: to "ensure that the voices of girls in the justice system are heard" (Ravoira, 1999, p. 27).

CONCLUSION

This chapter discussed the characteristics of violent female offenders, including those who commit homicide. Although scholars and politicians continue to debate whether violent female crime is increasing, the concern about this problem that is being voiced in the United States by criminal justice practitioners, politicians, the media, and the public is legitimate. It is imperative that collective action be taken to make children the nation's focus, especially "the youngest and least visible female offenders—adolescent girls—and their children. . . . [G]iven the developmental and childbearing potential of these young women and the low risks they pose to their communities, addressing their needs offers the Nation its best hope of halting the intergenerational cycle of family fragmentation and crime" (Acoca, 1999, p. 1).

For the past 15 years, research has recorded the connection between high rates of domestic and family violence and the criminalizing of girls for minor offenses, such as running away from these abusive households. It is important that scholars continue to investigate the relationships between violent female offending and childhood abuse, mental health issues, and substance use and abuse. Delinquency-processing officials in the juvenile justice system and policy makers must be more knowledgeable about the connection between the victimization of adolescents and subsequent delinquency.

DISCUSSION QUESTIONS

1. Recent studies indicate that an estimated 28% of violent female offenders are juveniles. Do you think this figure is on the rise, or has gender received more attention in recent years? State your position.

2. Discuss the distinct social dynamics that contribute to adolescent female delinquency.

3. In what context do researchers usually study violent female offenders, and why?

4. What role does the interaction of race and gender play in judicial discretion to dismiss charges against juveniles? Give examples.

5. Describe some of the approaches suggested for modifying factors underlying girls' increased entry into the juvenile justice system.

REFERENCES

ACOCA, L. (1999). Investing in girls: A 21st century strategy. *Juvenile Justice 4*(1), 3–13.

ACOCA, L., & DEDEL, K. (1998). *No place to hide: Understanding and meeting the needs of girls in the California juvenile justice system.* San Francisco: National Council on Crime and Delinquency.

ALLEN, H.E., & SIMONSEN, C.E. (1998). *Corrections in America: An introduction.* Upper Saddle River, NJ: Prentice Hall.

AMNESTY INTERNATIONAL. (1998). Betraying the young: Human rights violations against children in the U.S. justice system. London, England: Author.

AMNESTY INTERNATIONAL. (1999). *Not part of my sentence: Violations of the human rights of women in custody.* London, England: Author.

BELKNAP, J., & HOSINGER, K. (1998). An overview of delinquent girls: How theory and practice failed and the need for innovative changes. In R.T. Zaplin (Ed.), *Female offenders: Critical perspectives and effective interventions* (pp. 31–59). Gaithersburg, MD: Aspen.

BENEDEK, E.P., & CORNELL, D.G. (1989). Clinical presentations of homicidal adolescents. In E.P. Benedek & D.G. Cornell (Eds.), *Juvenile homicide* (pp. 37–57). Washington, DC: American Psychiatric Press.

BOWKER, L.H. (1980). *Prison subcultures.* Lexington, MA: Lexington.

BROWNE, A. (1987). *When battered women kill.* New York: Free Press.

CENTERS FOR DISEASE CONTROL AND PREVENTION. (1995). National Conference on Violence Prevention. Atlanta, GA: Author.

CHESNEY-LIND, M. (1986). Women and Crime: The Female Offender. *Signs 12,* 78–96.

CHESNEY-LIND, M. (1997). *The female offender: Girls, women, and crime.* Thousand Oaks, CA: Sage.

CHESNEY-LIND, M. (1998). *Girls, delinquency and juvenile justice.* Belmont, CA: West/Wadsworth.

CHESNEY-LIND, M., & SHELDEN, R.G. (1992). *Girls, delinquency and juvenile justice.* Pacific Grove, CA: Brooks/Cole.

DRUG STRATEGIES. (1998). *Keeping score, women and drugs: Looking at the federal drug control budget.* Washington, DC: Author.

DUNFORD, F., & ELLIOTT, D. (1984). Identifying career offenders using self reported data. *Journal of Research in Crime and Delinquency 21,* 57–86.

ELLIOT, D., & HUIZINGA, D. (1984). *The relationship between delinquent behavior and ADM problems.* Boulder, CO: Behavior Research Institute.

EWING, C.P. (1990). *When children kill.* Lexington, MA: Lexington.

FAGAN, J., PIPER, E., & MOORE, F. (1986). Violent delinquents and urban youth: Correlates of survival and avoidance. *Criminology 24,* 439–471.

FEDERAL BUREAU OF INVESTIGATION. (2000). *Crime in the United States—1999.* Washington, DC: U.S. Government Printing Office.

FEDERAL BUREAU OF INVESTIGATION. (1985–1997). *Crime in the United States.* Washington, DC: U.S. Government Printing Office.

FINE, M. (1994). Working the hyphens: Reinventing self and other in qualitative research. In N. K. Denzin & Y.S . Lincoln (Eds.), *Handbook of qualitative research* (pp. 70–81). Thousand Oaks, CA: Sage.

FINE, M., & WEISS, L. (1996). Writing of "wrongs" of fieldwork: Confronting our own research/writing dilemma in urban ethnographies. *Qualitative Inquiry 2,* 251–275.

HAGAN, J. (1994). *Crime and disrepute.* Thousand Oaks, CA: Pine Forge Press.

HEIDE, K.M. (1992). *Why kids kill parents: Child abuse and adolescent homicide.* Columbus, OH: Ohio State University Press.

HEIDE, K.M. (1999). *Young killers: The challenge of juvenile homicide.* Newbury Park, CA: Sage.

HINDELANG, M.J., HIRSCHI, T., & WEISS, J. (1981). *Measuring delinquency.* Newbury Park, CA: Sage.

HOWELL, J.C. (Ed.) (1995). *Guide for implementing the comprehensive strategy for serious, violent and chronic juvenile offenders.* Washington, DC: U.S. Department of Justice, Office of Justice Programs, Office of Juvenile Justice and Delinquency Prevention.

JANKOWSKI, M.S. (1991). *Islands in the street: Gangs and American urban society.* Berkeley, CA: University of California Press.

KRISBERG, B., & AUSTIN, J.P. (1993). *Reinventing juvenile justice.* Newbury Park, CA: Sage.

MAYNARD, R.A. (Ed.). (1996). *Kids having kids: A Robin Hood Foundation special report on the costs of adolescent childbearing.* New York: Robin Hood Foundation.

MILLER, E. (1975). *Violence by youth gangs and youth groups as a crime problem in major American cities.* Washington, DC: U.S. Government Printing Office.

MOORE, J., & HAGEDORN, J. (2001). *Female gangs: A focus on research.* Washington, DC: U.S. Department of Justice, Office of Justice Programs.

OFFICE OF JUVENILE JUSTICE AND DELINQUENCY PREVENTION. (1999). *Juvenile justice.* Washington, DC: U.S. Department of Justice.

PETERS, S., & PETERS, S.D. (1998). Violent adolescent females. *Corrections Today, 60,* 28–29.

PIPHER, M. (1994). *Reviving Ophelia, saving the selves of adolescent girls.* New York: Ballantine.

POE-YAMAGATA, E., & BUTTS, J.A. (1996). *Female offenders in the juvenile justice system: Statistics summary.* Washington, DC.: Office of Juvenile Justice and Delinquency Prevention.

PRACTICAL, ACADEMIC, CULTURAL EDUCATION CENTER FOR GIRLS. (1999, December). *PACE Newsletter.*

RAVOIRA, L. (1999). National Girls' Caucus. *Journal of the Office of Juvenile Justice and Delinquency Prevention, 4*(1), 21–28.

RENNISON, C. (2001). Violence, victimization, and race, 1993–1998. Washington, DC: U.S. Department of Justice.

ROWLEY, J.C., EWING, C.P., & SINGER, S.L. (1987). Juvenile homicide: The need for an interdisciplinary approach. *Behavioral Sciences and the Law, 5,* 3–10.

SARRI, R. (1983). Gender issues in juvenile justice. *Crime and Delinquency, 29,* 381–398.

SICKMUND, M., SNYDER, H.N., & POE-YAMAGATA, E. (1997). *Juvenile offenders and victims: 1997 update on violence.* Washington, DC: U.S. Department of Justice and Delinquency Prevention.

SOMMER, I., & BASKIN, D.R. (1994). Factors related to female adolescent initiation into violent street crime. *Youth and Society, 25,* 468–489.

SNYDER, H.N. (2000). *Juvenile arrests 1998.* Washington, DC: U.S. Department of Justice Programs, Office of Juvenile Justice and Delinquency Prevention.

SNYDER, H.N. (2000). *Juvenile arrests 1999.* Washington, DC: U.S. Department of Justice Programs, Office of Juvenile Justice and Delinquency Prevention.

SYNDER, H.N., & SICKMUND, M. (1999). *Juvenile offenders and victims: 1999 national report.* Washington, DC: National Center for Juvenile Justice, Office of Juvenile Justice and Delinquency Prevention.

TAYLOR, C. (1993). *Girls, gangs, women and drugs.* East Lansing: Michigan State University.

TAYLOR, D.L., BIAFORA, F.A., WARHEIT, G., & GIL, A. (1997). Family factors, theft, vandalism and major deviance among a multi-racial/ethnic sample of adolescent girls. *Journal of Social Distress and the Homeless, 6*(1), 71–87.

TUCKER, J., & WOLFE, L. (1997). *Victims no more: Girls fight back against male violence.* Washington DC: Center for Women Policy Studies.

WILLETT, J. (1996). Programs and services. In H.E. Allen & C.E. Simonsen (Eds.), *Corrections in America: An introduction* (pp. 38–42). Upper Saddle River, NJ: Prentice Hall.

WOLFGANG, M.E., & FIGLIO, R.M. (1985). *Delinquency in a birth cohort.* Chicago: University of Chicago Press.

ZAPLIN, R.T. (1998). *Female offenders: Critical perspectives and effective interventions.* Gaithersburg, MD: Aspen.

13

The Impact of Gender on Juvenile Court Decisions

A Qualitative Insight

Charles J. Corley, Timothy S. Bynum, Angel Prewitt, Pamela Schram, and John Burrows

This research utilizes an ethnographic approach to examine the impact of gender on the processing of females through the juvenile system. To that end, various court personnel (for examples, referees, judges, both intake and probation officers) were interviewed, using a protocol analysis inquiring about the importance of various factors at different stages of the judicial process. Qualitative findings suggest that legal and extralegal factors are germane to the decision-making process and are framed within a social control context. More important, these data show that social control as perceived and operationalized by court officials varies in accordance with gender; that is, girls who were sexually active, promiscuous, expressive of negative attitudes, incorrigible, and labeled suspicious or deceptive in character were thought to need a higher level of social control than females who did not possess such traits. Thus, analyses suggest support for previous research that indicates that certain offenses are sexualized for adolescent girls and that stereotypes have an impact on formal decision-making processes.

INTRODUCTION

Stark (1990) suggests that women tend to bear the brunt of social control and that injustice in terms of gender relations does exist. Women were considered the backbone of civilization, and their inappropriate behavior aroused more negative responses from the social audience than men's inappropriate behavior (Freedman, 1981). Even in situations where gender bias did not exist, females thought it would. For example, Corley, Cernkovich, and

Giordano (1989) found that female adolescents thought their parents would be more upset with them if they shoplifted, came home late, dated too many persons, slept with someone, stole a car, or became pregnant than male adolescents who committed the same acts.

However, Corley and associates (1989) also found that school officials responded more leniently toward the indiscretions of female than to those of male adolescents. Findings such as these provide some support for the argument that the larger society uses a double standard of morality to exercise more control over females than over males.

The judicial system is a microcosm of the larger society. Previous research has shown that juvenile justice officials respond in one of two ways to the misdeeds of females who appear before them. One school of thought shows that female juveniles receive more punitive sanctions than male juveniles (Chesney-Lind, 1973; Klein, 1973; Curran, 1983). Meda Chesney-Lind (1977) asserts that the juvenile court is less tolerant of the offensive behaviors of female adolescents than of male adolescents. Moreover, Chesney-Lind suggests that this more punitive response can be incited by the sexualization of offenses by court personnel. Chesney-Lind maintains that offenses committed by female adolescents where there is the potential for sexual relations to occur prompt a harsher response from court officials toward females than similar offenses committed by adolescent boys. For instance, given the absence of supervision and the possibility of sexual relations to occur while truanting from home, a more negative response is directed toward female runaways than toward male runaways (Chesney-Lind, 1977).

By contrast, the chivalry perspective suggests that females are afforded less severe or more lenient treatment by criminal justice agencies than males. More specifically, the chivalry perspective suggests that criminal justice agencies take a protective posture toward women that affords them more lenient treatment. Moulds (1978) asserts that police officers and other law enforcement personnel have historically treated female offenders more leniently than male offenders. Thus, females are less likely to be arrested (Visher, 1983) and when arrested, are more likely to have their charges dropped than male suspects (Bernstein, Cardascia, & Ross, 1977).

However, this protective stance toward females is derived from culturally defined norms that differentiate between the sexes, and it is paternalistic in origin. Women have been defined as sexual beings whose primary purpose is to perform utilitarian functions in the home (Chesney-Lind, 1977). The arrest, subsequent removal, and exposure of females to criminal justice institutions could expose them to an environment detrimental to their role as mothers (Chesney-Lind, 1977). Because the juvenile court response toward female delinquency is paternalistic and based on societal norms and expectations, it can be either punitive or chivalrous, depending on the circumstances of the individual. Nonetheless, even the aforementioned less punitive response to female deviance is premised on "traditional gender-role expectations" that have higher standards for the behavior of females than for males.

Gender can affect juvenile justice processes primarily because the juvenile justice system (contrasted to the adult justice system) has never used a decision-making model requiring formal and explicit legal rationality (Platt, 1969; Horwitz & Wasserman, 1980). To do so would eliminate consideration of extralegal and social factors that might provide insight into the adolescent's behavior and may further suggest that the court has abandoned its attempt to provide individualized treatment and not punishment. Instead, the court operates on a model of substantive justice in which it is acceptable to use social background variables as a means to personalize treatment (Horwitz & Wasserman, 1980).

Moreover, social cognition researchers have identified two types of knowledge rela tive to criminal justice decisions: content and procedural. Lurigio and Stalans (1990) pro pose that content knowledge informs the decision maker of the relevance of events, persons, and systems, whereas procedural knowledge informs how a decision is to be made. However, Wyer and Gordon (1980) point out that socialization and experience in a domain shape both these types of knowledge. In addition, Wyer and Gordon (1982) suggest that decision makers use prior knowledge or representations of prior knowledge from memory to more effectively and efficiently derive decisions. These categorical representa tions (e.g., stereotypes) can include a label and defining features that are not interconnected or organized that bias interpretations and shape inferences and weighting of information in cases consistent with the stereotypic label (Wyer & Gordon, 1982). This tendency, com bined with a cognitive approach to stereotyping, suggests that stereotypes can be used to simplify complex judgmental tasks where the evidence is ambiguous (Tajfel, 1981).

It is the purpose of this research to examine decision making within the juvenile jus tice system, especially the influence of gender. To that end, this research examines the con tent of knowledge and information deemed relevant to decision makers and the context in which that information is framed. Moreover, an attempt is also made to determine whether categorical representations (that is, stereotypes) influence juvenile court decisions.

METHODOLOGY

This qualitative research emanates from a quantitative analysis of a sample of juveniles referred to court during 1990. These juveniles were representative of youths referred to court from across five counties within a Midwestern state. The selected counties were a geographical mix. Two of the five counties were highly urbanized (large sized), and three were a mixture of urban and suburban areas (medium sized). A random stratified sample of cases was tracked to examine juvenile justice court processes. The sample was 1,206 felony, 1,348 misdemeanor, and 532 status cases. Observations were made at major decision points (i.e., intake, detention, informal vs. formal processing, disposition, and placement).

The majority of females whose cases were found in juvenile court records were charged with status offenses. Yet, when the processing patterns of female status offenders were compared with those of female felony and misdemeanor offenders, higher percent ages were found of female status offenders experiencing formal hearings, wardship, deten tion, and out-of-home placement than females charged with more serious felony or misdemeanor offenses.

Given that the majority of females referred to juvenile court were status offenders who received more formal treatment than females charged with more serious misdemeanor or felony offenses, the authors wanted to understand why the court responded more for mally to female status offenders than to females charged with misdemeanor and felony offenses. To that end, an ethnographic investigation of the court's decision-making pro cesses was undertaken to provide insights into this dilemma.

Qualitative Data

Qualitative data are derived from personal interviews conducted with various juvenile court personnel (i.e., judges, referees, supervisors, intake staff, and probation officers) across five counties from a Midwestern state. In total, 94 interviews were conducted.

The overall objective of the interview process was to obtain an understanding of the pattern of each court's decision-making processes. To that end, questions focused on understanding legal and social factors deemed important to the decision maker for purposes of case processing, determination of sanctions, and placement. To further assist the research efforts, a status offense scenario (truanting from home) was presented to each court decision maker. Respondents identified factors that were important and commented about their impact on the decision-making process.

Sixteen three- by five-inch cards were laid in front of each interviewee for the scenario. On one side of each card was a category of information, and on the reverse were specific circumstances representative of a typical youth who may appear before the court charged with truanting from home. These categories and corresponding circumstances described the juvenile's age, race, prior offense record, length of time away from home, self-supportive activities while away from home, sexual behavior, school performance, attitude, co-offenders, substance abuse profile, living situation, criminal history of family, physical appearance, detection of signs of neglect or abuse, primary caregiver's occupation and income, and level of parental control.

Court staffs were free to make various comments about these categories and other noninclusive factors that could influence their decisions regarding the processing of a juvenile charged with truanting. In addition, procedural (formal vs. informal processing), dispositional, and placement decisions were recorded, as well as factors that contributed to these decisions. Although it was preferred that court personnel describe how the factors they identified affected specific stages of the justice process (intake, informal hearing, formal hearing and/or adjudication, disposition, and so forth), court personnel instead articulated how these factors affected decisions at intake and the general processing of cases either formally or informally.

FINDINGS

In general, court personnel expressed a preference that status offenders not be referred to juvenile court. Instead, they suggested that a social agency be designated to handle status offenders because these cases currently "take up" too much of the court's time. Court personnel believed that the juvenile court was already overburdened with the behaviors of more serious offenders and that the inclusion of less serious status offenders further strained court resources.

This attitude in part seems related to the amount of time juvenile courts allocate to investigating the juvenile who truants from home. Court personnel were less empathetic to youths charged with criminal offenses; they allotted less time to ascertaining why they engaged in criminal behavior and devoted more resources to investigating reasons for truanting. It was not uncommon for court staff to indicate they would interview the alleged runaway and obtain perceptions of the youth's home environment concerning truanting behaviors. For instance, a suburban referee commented:

> I always start with a verbal statement from the kid and look for any abusive situation. . . . I want to know why the kid left. . . . In their mind they may be taking justifiable action in leaving home. . . . Are they being encouraged to leave home by their peers because of a bad home situation?

Court staffs were particularly interested in ascertaining why female adolescents ran away from home. A suburban court intake worker noted:

> There are very few male runaways. . . . There has to be major bad stuff for a boy to leave home. . . . This is likely to be a neglect or abuse situation. . . . He may feel that running away beats being at home; at least no one is hitting him now. . . . Ninety percent of girls have sexual or physical abuse issues that are unresolved. . . . I'd say that every case I have seen involving a girl, without exception has included sexual abuse. . . . Neglect or child abuse frequently causes a kid to run. . . . The presence of a stepfather is a red flag that there may be sexual abuse going on.

They emphasized determining if the child (especially females) were truanting from a sexually abusive environment. Many interpreted a child's truanting from home as a "cry for help." However, it was not uncommon for court personnel to express a more empathetic or paternalistic attitude toward female runaways. Thus, female status offenders may spend more time in court than male status offenders because the court is attempting to act in the best interest of the female. To that end, a suburban referee further commented:

> The police are more paternalistic towards girls. . . . They are brought to court more often than boys for minor infractions. . . . By law we are ordered to do an investigation under the Child Protection Act if abuse or neglect is suspected. . . . You know eighty percent of these kids are abuse or neglect victims.

This perceived cry for help afforded the court the opportunity to intervene and provide what it perceived as necessary for the juvenile in question. For instance, an urban judge commented:

> Running away is a cry for help. . . . Locking these girls up is a way to help her. . . . I get hysterical at these types of cases and worry about these girls' personal risk of pregnancy and sexually transmitted diseases.

Throughout the interviews, court staff commented about the importance of knowing about the female status offender's sexual behavior. One urban court referee pointed out:

> With girls we do look at sexual behavior, but this is not brought up as an issue for boys. . . . I don't want to sound sexist, but promiscuity is a danger for girls.

Another judge from the same court elaborated on this sentiment, warning:

> If she gets pregnant, then she must drop out of school. . . . A boy can get a girl pregnant and still stay in school. . . . If the child is a sexually active runaway, then there is great cause for concern.

Yet another urban court intake officer spoke of the potential for sexually active girls to become further involved in other forms of deviant behavior. This court worker warned:

> There is a potential for prostitution among female runaways. Males are more likely to deal drugs in order to support themselves when away from home. . . . If there was prostitution, no way does this youth go home.

Court personnel's assertion that status offenders should receive attention or treatment from an entity other than the juvenile court seems to stem in part from the greater effort allocated to understanding why the juvenile is truanting from home. The court does not make a similar effort to understand why a juvenile engages in criminal behavior, and these cases do not consume as much time.

Although there was an effort to understand why the youth ran (for example, flight from an abusive or neglectful home or peer pressure), court personnel focused on the sexual behaviors of female runaways. Knowledge of the female's sexual behavior was said to be a potential indicator of abuse at home, risk of flight, risk of pregnancy, vulnerability to sexually transmitted diseases, and further involvement in criminal activity (for example, prostitution). Similar concerns were not expressed regarding the sexual behavior of males who ran away from home.

Family Issues and Female Truancy

Earlier research (Gottfredson & Hirschi, 1990; Hirschi & Gottfredson, 1993; Corley, Bynum, & Wordes, 1995) showed that the family is perceived as the primary institution responsible for controlling children. A juvenile's familial characteristics are important in determining how to handle an adolescent appearing before the courts. In regard to the impact of familial characteristics and truanting, court staff indicated that familial characteristics might be more important for females than for males.

Court staff expressed concern and alluded to differences between girls and boys regarding the devaluation of girls in comparison with boys by family members, the difficulties of controlling girls, the more negative attitudes maintained by girls than boys, and the extra efforts court staff undertake to protect themselves when interacting with females. For instance, a judge from a large urban metropolitan area responded, "Differences in treatment between girls and boys is not perpetuated by the court per se, but by the action of the family." This particular judge further articulated:

> Often the family does not value girls as much as boys. . . . Girls are underfoot and lipping off to the parents and parents often want to get them out of their hair. . . . Boys do stuff away from home.

A probation officer from a suburban area expressed similar sentiments:

> If a male and female are detained where the female is charged with running away and no other substantive charges and the male is charged with assault with intent to commit murder, the parents will say keep her but go to great lengths to get the boy released. . . . It is easier for the parents to deny the son's involvement since they are often not direct witnesses or victims of his actions.

Court personnel further suggest social control differences between males and females. Moreover, these perceived differences were said to affect treatment. Although caregiver control was important in all cases appearing before the court, the consensus was that control was particularly important for female adolescents. An urban probation officer said:

> I want to know if there is a family type relationship. . . . It doesn't have to be a mother and father, just a parental figure. . . . Does anyone have authority over this kid? This is particularly important for a girl running away.

Other court personnel felt that boys presented more of a challenge to parental authority and control than girls. For instance, an urban referee commented:

> I'd be easier on a female. . . . It is easier to address female delinquency with stern external male input or authority. . . . She would respond more to male authority than a boy would. . . . A father has more control over a daughter than a son.

In general, court personnel expressed more interest in understanding what contributed to the deviant behaviors of girls than in the deviant behavior of boys. This point was further clarified by court staff who believed not only that boys and girls should be treated differently by the court but also that courts principally present more of an empathetic or fatherly response to female status offenders. It was not uncommon for court staff to feel the same as the suburban probation officer who said:

> Generally, girls evoke more paternalistic responses to their delinquency than boys. . . . Girls might get into trouble or trouble gets into them. . . . Males are seen more as a leader in criminal behavior. . . . Females are believed to play a minor role in criminal behavior.

Sexuality, Social Control, and Attitude

Females who are sexually active were particularly troublesome to court personnel and evoked a different response from the court. Specifically, court personnel elaborated on difficulties the juvenile court and parent(s) encounter in attempting to control females who have become sexually active. For instance, a suburban referee commented:

> Sexually active girls are more sophisticated and more problematic. . . . Little girls that are sexually active are harder to keep at home and have more reasons to run.

There was also suspicion that females may be more likely to absent themselves from home than boys because of their involvement with boyfriends. An urban referee commented:

> But, girls who are sexually active can also be running because they have to have it [sex]. . . . They have not learned to stay away from bad relationships with boys that get them into trouble. . . . These girls are competing with the mother.

However, the primary issue involving sexually active female adolescents was control. Sexually active females were perceived to be in need of more external mechanisms of social control than non–sexually active females. To that end, an urban judge was adamant about what the court response should be toward females who are sexually active. Specifically, this judge felt:

> Generally females are status offenders. Those that are non–sexually active can be controlled at home. Girls that are sexually active compete with mom and are more difficult to control. The mother just cannot supervise and control them. . . . If there was prostitution in this runaway's case, no way does this youth go home.

Thus, sexually active females were particularly problematic because their sexual activity was evidence of a lack of social control that had to be restored by the court, parents, or both.

Court personnel also expressed higher levels of uneasiness when working with adolescent females than with males. To elaborate on the problematic aspects of working with females, a suburban probation officer responded:

> Girls are more disrespectful than boys, they're more emotional. . . . They're just nasty to work with. . . . I'd much rather work with boys than girls.

It was not uncommon for court staff to acknowledge that they preferred to work with boys rather than girls. Sentiments were expressed that suggest a stigma was attached to girls that was not attached to boys. A probation officer emphasized:

> If you are dealing with a little girl, they can be dumb. . . . You have to watch yourself when dealing with girls.

Court personnel (especially male staff) expressed annoyance regarding the additional protective measures believed necessary when interacting with females. For instance, an urban probation officer relayed:

> I always make sure to tell the supervisor when I'm seeing a female youth and for how long, just to cover myself from any alleged impropriety.

Additional measures court workers used to protect themselves from potential improprieties and allegations of inappropriate behavior when interacting with girls suggest court staff were more suspicious of the deviant behaviors (and motivations for those behaviors) of adolescent girls than those of adolescent boys. This outlook further contributes to a more negative perception of female adolescents than of male adolescents who appear in court charged with status offenses. Moreover, this more negative perception contributes to the greater likelihood that females who truant from home will receive more formalized treatment within the juvenile court than similarly charged males.

SUMMARY AND DISCUSSION

Gender has been identified as a factor that affects juvenile court decision making. This qualitative analysis of court personnel responses to a truanting scenario provides insights into why gender affects the decision-making processes of the juvenile court.

Court staffs were first and foremost interested in ascertaining whether a youth was running from a home environment that was abusive or neglectful. Court staff believed that the majority of adolescents (especially females) who truant from home experience some form of abuse, and they are committed to intervening on behalf of the child. However, truanting was not perceived as the same for male and female adolescents.

Matza (1964) commented that the juvenile court, in deciding how to handle youth who appear before it, relies heavily on the judgment of its personnel. Knowledge or information about legal and extralegal factors is important in that it enables the court to tailor its responses to meet the needs of individual youths. Gender influences decisions in part because the juvenile court attempts to tailor its sanctions. This study suggests juvenile court personnel perceive the social control needs of adolescent females differently from the social control needs of adolescent males.

Court personnel's perceptions that female adolescents, particularly those who are perceived to be sexually active, promiscuous, possessed of bad attitudes, incorrigible, suspicious, or deceptive, need higher levels of social control than adolescent males is in part predicated on categorical representations (i.e., stereotypical images) of women. For instance, the suggestion that promiscuity is a danger for girls suggests that court personnel ignore the fact that sexually promiscuous behavior can be dangerous to anyone who has unprotected sexual intercourse. Moreover, the court's obsession with the sexual behaviors of female truants sexualizes the offense for girls and places the juvenile court in the position of categorizing female adolescents as either good girls or bad girls.

However, institutions have engaged in these types of categorizations for centuries. Pomeroy (1975) suggests that cultures throughout the world have historically categorized women into "either-or" roles. In particular, women have been categorized as either "Madonnas," who are faithful, submissive, and nurturing, or "whores," who are the tempters of men (Pomeroy, 1975).

A female who is labeled "bad" is said to possess at least one of the following three character flaws: (1) She is indecisive and lacks moral fortitude, (2) she is promiscuous, or (3) she is irresponsible because she is loosening not only her morals and values but also those of her mate and descendants (Pomeroy, 1975). The findings of this study show that some court personnel believed that little girls could be dumb, which is stereotypical and suggests that females are not perceived as responsible individuals and subsequently that they are in need of a more formal response from the court.

If the criminal justice system is perceived to be a part of the larger society in which the categorization and stereotyping of women occur, then the criminal justice system is likely to reflect or perpetuate this outlook in its macro-level social control processes. Bodenhausen and Lichtenstein (1987) reported that when subjects face a complex judgmental situation, they use stereotypes (when available and relevant) as a way of simplifying the judgment. Specifically, a stereotype is used as a central theme around which evidence consistent with it is organized and information inconsistent with the stereotype is rejected.

Notwithstanding, the analysis suggests that categorizations of females (i.e., stereotypes) are frequently used by juvenile court personnel and affect juvenile court processes. Although court personnel admitted they respond differently to the indiscretions of male and female adolescents (which shows in the quantitative results), qualitative analysis shows that this difference is in part based on stereotypical images of females. This image is further conditioned by a girl's perceived level of sexual activity, promiscuousness, attitude, incorrigibility, and alleged suspicious or deceptive character. Possession of any or all of these traits can result in adolescent females having their cases handled in a more formal manner by court personnel who are seeking compliance with more socially acceptable, gender-based forms of behavior.

DISCUSSION QUESTIONS

1. What are the legal and extralegal factors that are relevant to the judicial decision-making process and in what context are they framed?

2. Discuss social control theory and its impact on perceived gender bias within the family.

3. Define content and procedural knowledge relative to criminal justice decisions. Give examples.

4. Defend the statement "larger societies use a double standard of morality to exercise more control over females than males."

5. What are the ethical arguments against categorizations of females, such as stereotypes, being frequently used by juvenile court personnel and their influence on juvenile court processing?

REFERENCES

AGETON, S., & ELLIOTT, D. (1974). The effects of legal processing on delinquent orientations. *Social Problems, 22,* 87–100.

ARNOLD, W. (1971). Race and ethnicity relative to other factors in juvenile court dispositions. *American Journal of Sociology, 77*(2), 211–227.

BARTON, W. (1976). Discretionary decision-making in juvenile justice. *Crime and Delinquency,* 470–480.

BERNSTEIN, I., CARDASCIA, J., & ROSS, C. E. (1977). Defendant's sex and criminal court decisions. In R. Alvarez et al. (Eds.), *Discrimination in organizations.* San Francisco: Jossey-Bass.

BISHOP, D., & FRAZIER. C. (1988). The influence of race in juvenile justice processing. *Journal of Research in Crime and Delinquency, 25*(3), 242–263.

BLACK, D., & REISS, A. (1970). Police control of juveniles. *American Sociological Review, 35*(1), 63–77.

BLACKWELL, J.E. (1985) *The black community: Diversity and unity* (2nd ed.). New York: Harper & Row.

BODENHAUSEN, G., & LICHTENSTEIN, M. (1987). Social stereotypes and information-processing strategies: The impact of task complexity. *Journal of Personality and Social Psychology, 32*(3), 871–880.

BODENHAUSEN, G., & WYER, R. (1985). Effects of stereotypes on decision making and information-processing strategies. *Journal of Personality and Social Psychology, 48,* 267–282.

BYNUM, T., WORDES, M., & CORLEY, C. (1993) *Disproportionate representation in juvenile justice in Michigan: Influence of race and gender.* Research supported by funding from the Michigan Committee on Juvenile Justice through the office of Contract Management—Grant Management Division.

CARTER, T.J. (1979). Juvenile court dispositions: A comparison of status and nonstatus offenders, *Criminology, 17*(3), 341–359.

CHEN, D.B., & HUDSON, J. (1981). Discretion in juvenile justice. In D. Fogel & J. Hudson (Eds.), *Justice as fairness: Perspectives on the justice model* (pp. 168–192). Boston: Anderson.

CHESNEY-LIND, M. (1973, Fall). Judicial enforcement of the female sex roles: The family court and the female delinquent. *Issues in Criminology, 8,* 51–63.

CHESNEY-LIND, M. (1977). Judicial paternalism and the female status offender: Training women to know their place. *Crime and Delinquency, 122,* 51–63.

CHESNEY-LIND, M. (1986). Women and crime: The female offender. *Signs: Journal of Women in Culture and Society, 12,* 78–96.

CHESNEY-LIND, M. (1991). Patriarchy, prisons and jails: A critical look at trends in women's incarceration. *Prison Journal, 71,* 51–67.

CHUNN, D., & GAVIGAN, S. (1988). Social control: Analytic tool or analytic quagmire. *Contemporary Crisis, 12,* 107–124.

CHUSED, R. (1973). The juvenile court process: A study of three New Jersey counties. *Rutgers Law Review, 26,* 488–539.

COHEN, L.E., & FELSON, M. (1979). Social change and crime rate trends: A routine activities approach. *American Sociological Review, 44,* 588–607.

COHEN, L.E., & KLUEGEL, J.R. (1979). The detention decision: A study of the impact of social characteristics and legal factors in two metropolitan juvenile courts. *Social Forces, 58*(1), 146–161.

CORLEY, C., BYNUM, T., & WORDES, M. (1995). Conceptions of family and juvenile court processes: A qualitative assessment. *Justice System Journal, 18*(2), 157–172.

CORLEY, C., CERNKOVICH, S., & GIORDANO, P. (1989). Sex and the likelihood of sanction. *Journal of Criminal Law and Criminology, 80*(2), 540–556.

CORLEY, C., & WORDES, M. (1993) *Disproportionate representation and processing of juveniles by race and gender: Genesee probate court.* Research supported by funding from the Michigan Committee on Juvenile Justice through the office of Contract Management—Grant Management Division.

CURRAN, D. (1983). Judicial discretion and defendant's sex. *Criminology, 21*(1), 41–58.

DALY, K. (1987) Structure and practice of familial-based justice in a criminal court. *Law and Society Review, 21*(2).

ELLIOTT, D., & AGETON, S. (1980). Reconciling race and class differences in self-reported and official estimates of delinquency. *American Sociological Review, 45,* 95–110.

EMPER, L., & STAFFORD, M. (1991). *American delinquency: Its meaning and construction.* Belmont, CA: Wadsworth.

ESHLEMAN, J.R. (1989). *The family: An introduction.* Boston: Allyn and Bacon.

FAGEN, J., SLAUGHTER, E., & HARTSTONE, E. (1987). Blind justice? The impact of race on the juvenile justice process. *Crime and Delinquency, 33*(2), 224–258.

FEINMAN, C. (1979). Sex role stereotypes and justice for women. *Crime and Delinquency,* 87–95.

FELD, B.C. (1993). *Justice for children: The right to counsel and the juvenile courts.* Boston: Northeastern University Press.

FELSON, M. (1986). Linking criminal choices, routine activities, informal social control, and criminal outcomes. In R. Clark & D. Cornish (Eds.), *The reasoning criminal.* New York: Springer–Verlag.

FENWICK, C. (1982). Juvenile court intake decision making: The importance of family affiliation. *Journal of Criminal Justice, 10*(6), 443–453.

FERDINAND, T., & LUCHTERHAND, E. (1970). Inner-city youth, the police, juvenile court and justice. *Social Problems 17,* 510–527.

FRAZIER, C., RICHARDS, P., & POTTER, R. (1983). Juvenile diversion and net widening: Toward a clarification of assessment strategies. *Human Organization, 42*(2), 115–122.

FREEDMAN, E. (1981). *Their sister's keepers: Women and prison reform in America, 1930–.* Ann Arbor: University of Michigan Press.

GOTTFREDSON, M., & HIRSCHI, T. (1990). *A general theory of crime.* Stanford, CA: Stanford University Press.

HILL, R. (1980). Black kids: White justice. *New Society, 24,* 174–175.

HINDELANG, M. (1978). Race and involvement in common law personal crimes. *American Sociological Review, 43*(1), 93–109.

HIRSCHI, T., & GOTTFREDSON, M. (1993). Rethinking the juvenile justice system. *Crime and Delinquency, 39*(2), 262–271.

HORWITZ, A., & WASSERMAN, M. (1980). Some misleading conceptions in sentencing research: An example and a reformulation in the juvenile court. *Criminology, 18*(3), 411–424.

HUNT, A. (1976). Perspectives in the sociology of law. In P. Carlen (Ed.), *The sociology of law,* (pp. 22–44). Keele, UK: University of Keele.

JOHNSON, R.E. (1986). Family structure and delinquency. *Criminology, 24*(1), 65–80.

KEMPF, K., DECKER, S., & BING, R. (1990). *An analysis of apparent disparities in the handling of black youth within Missouri's juvenile justice systems.* St. Louis, MO: University of Missouri–St. Louis.

KLEIN, D. (1973, Fall). The etiology of female crime: A review of the literature. *Issues in Criminology 8,* 3–30.

KLEIN, D. (1982). The etiology of female crime: A review of the literature. In B. Price & N. Sokoloff (Eds.), *The criminal justice system and women: Offenders, victims, workers,* (pp. 35–60). New York: Clark Boardman.

KORNHAUSER, R. (1978). *Social sources of delinquency.* Chicago: University of Chicago Press.

LIEBER, M. (1992). *Juvenile justice decision making in Iowa: An analysis of the influence of race on case processing in three counties.* Cedar Falls, IA: University of Northern Iowa.

LURIGIO, A., & STALANS, L.A. (1990). Thinking more about how criminal justice decision makers think. *Criminal Justice and Behavior, 17*(3), 260–267.

MATZA, D. (1964). *Delinquency and drift.* New York: Wiley.

MATZA, D. (1964). *Becoming deviant.* Englewood Cliffs, NJ: Prentice-Hall.

MEADE, A. (1973). Seriousness of delinquency, the adjudicative decision and recidivism: A longitudinal configuration analysis. *Journal of Criminal Law and Criminology, 64*(4), 478–485.

MOULDS, D. (1978). Chivalry and paternalism: Disparities of treatment in the criminal justice system. In S. Datesman & F. Scarpetti (Eds.), *Women, crime and justice* (p. 341), Boston: Anderson.

NAFFINE, N. (1987). *Female crime: The construction of women in criminology.* Sydney, Australia: Allen and Unwin.

NATIONAL CENTER FOR HEALTH STATISTICS. (1989). *Monthly Vital Statistics Report.* Washington, DC: Author.

PLATT, A. (1969). *The child savers.* Chicago: University of Chicago Press.

POMEROY, S. (1975). *Goddesses, whores wives, and slaves.* New York: Schocken.

POOLE, E., & REGOLI, R. (1980). An analysis of the determinants of juvenile court dispositions. *Juvenile and Family Court Journal, 31*(3), 23–32.

POPE C., & FEYERHERM, W. (1990) Minority status and juvenile processing. *Criminal Justice Abstracts, 22*(2), 327–336; 22(3), 527–542.

RAFTER, N. (1990). *Partial justice: Women, prisons, and social control* (2nd ed.). New Brunswick, NJ: Transaction.

REISS, A., JR. (1951). Delinquency as the failure of personal and social controls. *American Sociological Review, 16,* 196–207.

ROSIER, K.B., & CORSARO, W.A. (1993). Competent parents, complex lives: Managing parenthood in poverty. *Journal of Contemporary Ethnography, 22*(2), 171–202.

ROSS, E. (1969). *Social control.* Cleveland, OH: Case Western Reserve University Press.

SAMPSON, R.J. (1983). *The neighborhood context of criminal victimization.* Unpublished doctoral dissertation, State University of New York at Albany.

SAMPSON, R.J. (1986). Crime in cities: The effects of formal and informal social control. In A.J. Reiss & M. Tonry (Eds.), *Communities and crime.* Chicago: University of Chicago Press.

SAMPSON, R., & LAUB, J. (1993). Structural variations in juvenile court processing: Inequality, the under class, and social control. *Law and Society Review, 27*(2), 285–311.

SCARPETTI, F., & STEPHENSON, R. (1971). Juvenile court dispositions: Factors in the decision-making process. *Crime and Delinquency, 17,* 142–151.

SIEVERDES, C. (1973). *Differential disposition of juvenile offenders: A study of juvenile court labeling.* Unpublished doctoral dissertation, Mississippi State University.

SIEVERDES, C., SHOEMAKER, D., & CUNNINGHAM, O. (1979). Disposition decisions by juvenile court probation officers and judges: A multivariate analysis. *Criminal Justice Review, 4*(2), 121–132.

SKOGAN, W. (1986). Fear of crime and neighborhood change. In A.J. Reiss & M. Tonry (Eds.), *Communities and crime.* Chicago: University of Chicago Press.

SMART, C., & SMART, B. (1978). *Women, sexuality and social control.* London: Routledge & Kegan Paul.

STARK, W. (1976–87). *The social bond,* 5 vols. New York: Fordham University Press.

TAJFEL, H. (1981). *Human groups and social categories: Studies in social psychology.* New York: Cambridge University Press.

THORNBERRY, T. (1973). Race, socioeconomic status and sentencing in the juvenile justice system. *Journal of Criminal Law and Criminology, 64*(1), 90–98.

THORNBERRY, T. (1979). Sentencing disparities in the juvenile justice system. *Journal of Criminal Law and Criminology, 70*(2), 164–171.

TURNER, J., & HELMS, D. (1989). *Marriage and family: Traditions and transitions.* Orlando, FL: Harcourt Brace Jovanovich.

VISHER, C. A. (1983, February). Gender: Police arrest decisions and notions of chivalry. *Criminology, 21,* 5–27.

WELTER, B. (1973). The cult of true womanhood: 1820–1860. In J. Friedman & W. Shade (Eds.), *Our American sisters: Women in American life and thought,* (pp. 96–123). Boston: Allyn and Bacon.

WEST, C., & ZIMMERMAN, D. (1991). Doing gender. In J. Lorber & S. Farrell (Eds.), *The social construction of gender,* (pp. 7–12). Newbury Park, CA: Sage.

WORDES, M., BYNUM, T., & CORLEY, C. (1994). Locking up youth: The impact of race on detention decisions. *Journal of Research in Crime and Delinquency , 31*(2), 149–165.

WYER, R., & GORDON, S. (1982). The recall of information about persons and groups. *Journal of Experimental Social Psychology, 18,* 128–164.

ZATZ, M. (1987). The changing forms of racial/ethnic biases in sentencing. *Journal of Research in Crime and Delinquency, 24*(1), 69–92.

14

Weapons, Violence, and Youth: A Study of Weapon-Related Victimization among Urban High School Students

Zina T. McGee

This project examines victimization through firearms, knives, and other weapons among 500 African American high school students in the state of Virginia. To account for victimization patterns, attention is given to sociodemographic characteristics (including gender and grade level), exposure to guns and violence outside school, exposure to guns and violence in school, and personal violence-related activities that may place students at a greater risk of victimization. Relying on recent research examining victimization events, the study focuses primarily on the behavioral characteristics (such as arrest record, drug sales) of the students as potentially contributing factors to victimization. Special attention is paid to gender differences as factors that contribute to victimization experiences.

Despite the increase in research devoted to violent behavior among youth (for example, see Esbensen & Huizinga, 1993; Fagan, Piper, & Moore, 1986; Fagan, Piper, & Cheng, 1987; Fagan, Weis, & Cheng, 1990; Finkelhor, 1997), many studies have not effectively addressed the long-term effects of gun- and drug-related violence, particularly as it occurs within inner city areas and schools. Further, very little is known about the victims of such violence and the emotional disruption that may ensue. Although violence remains a defining characteristic of many cities, few researchers have explored the mental health and development of children and adolescents residing in chronically violent neighborhoods (see Farrell & Bruce, 1997; Farver & Frosch, 1996; Hill & Madhere, 1996; Sampson, 1998, for exceptions).

Research continues to indicate that many of the personal problems experienced by Black youth, in particular, originate in the social and economic structures of society, causing a direct impairment of their abilities to adapt to or modify their environment (Gibbs,

1988, 1989; Brookins, Peterson, & Brooks, 1997; Garbarino, 1996; Tobin & Gorman-Smith, 1997). Although research has focused on those exhibiting problematic behaviors in schools and communities, few have examined those who have coped with violence, poverty, discrimination, and other characteristics of chronic, stressful environments (Gibbs, 1998; Myers, Taylor, Alvy, Arrington, & Richardson, 1992). Issues of resilience, competence, and problem solving are rarely addressed in the literature pertaining to African American youth (McCubbin et al., 1998; Reynolds, 1998). Further, a majority of the studies that have addressed violence tend to emphasize the effects of media violence as opposed the chronic violence that many children and adolescents in this society encounter in their own lives (see Farver & Frosch, 1996). Epidemiologic surveys of mental health seldom include adequate samples of inner city Black youth, many of whom are subjected to the structural factors (i.e., unemployment, crime and violence, drugs) that enhance vulnerability to negative outcomes (Myers, 1989; Myers et al., 1992).

The current project addresses the relationships between victimization, development outcomes, personality factors, and coping strategies in African American adolescents in high-risk environments. Little is known about the levels of gun- and drug-related violence and subsequent victimization in inner city areas and schools. Further, few studies have examined the long-term effects of violence on youth victims, many of whom are African American. Media accounts of daily shootings in inner city neighborhoods and schools suggest that these areas are experiencing epidemic levels of antisocial behavior. It is assumed that youth who grow up within these violent conditions will be at a much greater risk for a broad range of problems, including crime, mental illness, chronic unemployment, poverty, and undereducation. However, few studies have systematically studied levels of real or perceived violence and fear of victimization among inner city youth, and fewer have determined the role of personality in people's ability to cope with these highly stressful environments. This project is designed to provide an understanding of the role of particular personality traits on coping strategies used by inner city Black youth over an extended period of time. Such an understanding will provide an empirical basis on which to develop and reinforce effective coping behaviors to offset the detrimental impact of growing up in such violent areas.

LITERATURE REVIEW

Violent Victimization

Recent school shootings in Arkansas, Oregon, and Colorado, where such events were markedly unexpected, have refocused the American public's attention on school crime and safety. For many, the problem of youth violence appears to be spreading beyond inner cities to suburbs (Lawrence, 1998; Kaufman et al., 1998). However, generalizable information about the effects of gun-related violence on child and adolescent development is relatively scarce. In both official records and self-report information, rates of violent victimization and offending have been increasing in the nation's schools over the past decade.

Recent studies have suggested that juveniles between the ages of 12 and 17 have the highest rates of victimization for both crimes of violence and crimes of theft (Snyder & Sickmund, 1997; U.S. Department of Education, 1998). In 1994, juveniles were almost three times as likely as adults to experience a crime-related injury, although the rates of injury that required hospitalization were similar. Further, personal crimes with juvenile victims occurred most often in school or on school property (Snyder & Sickmund, 1997; U.S. Department of Education, 1998). With regard to gun victimization, studies have also shown that a gun was used in 25% of serious violent offenses against juveniles in 1994. Nationwide, the prevalence of weapon carrying on school property is 8.5%, and 7.4% of students have reported being threatened or injured with a weapon on school property (Centers for Disease Control and Prevention, 1998). Overall, minority and male students are more likely to miss school because they feel unsafe and are more likely to carry guns. A significantly higher proportion of minorities and males are also more likely to report threats or injuries with weapons on school property (Centers for Disease Control and Prevention, 1998). Hence, research studies have persuasively demonstrated an increase in violence-related behaviors on school property, as evidenced in the numbers of juveniles reporting fear of victimization and subsequent gun ownership (for example, Chandler, Chapman, Rand, & Taylor, 1998).

These findings suggest the importance of the structural characteristics of communities and inner city areas that may enhance the likelihood of violence in inner city schools. The proposed relationship between schools and communities has led many to argue that schools no longer have distinct roles but are instead the products of a larger societal problem, one that is reflected in high-crime areas overpopulated with the poor and minorities (Elliott, Hamburg, & Williams, 1998; Davis, 1999; Lawrence, 1998). Similarly, researchers have implied that the presence of high-crime schools within high-crime communities intensifies the level of fear and apprehension experienced by many students (Tolan & Guerra, 1998; Sampson, 1998; Lawrence, 1998; Alvarez & Bachman, 1997). In many instances, conflict emerges as a product of the interdependence between the individual and social–contextual forces (Jessor, Donovan, & Costa, 1996; McDermott, 1983; Davis, 1999). Because this period of adolescence is generally marked by rapid change and growth, researchers have argued that destructive conflict among these youth will have special consequences developmentally (Tolan & Guerra, 1998, Jessor, Donovan, & Costa, 1996, Davis, 1999).

Violent Victimization and Youth Development

Although the dramatic increase in youth victimization on school grounds places the issue of gun violence within a larger social context, studies of the serious negative effects of violence on the mental health of American youth remain relatively scarce. Research continues to indicate that the experiences of children in schools reflect the availability and attitudes toward firearms within children's families and communities, and the serious impact of firearm injuries and violence on children and youth is reflected in self-reports of victimization and the extent to which they witness violent events (Shapiro, Dorman, Burkey, Welker, & Clough, 1997, 1998; Alvarez, 1997; Finkelhor, 1997; Kaljee, Stanton, Ricardo, & Whitehead, 1995; Warner & Weist, 1996). Thus, children who are exposed to violence as either victims or witnesses experience higher levels of depression, anxiety, and emotional distress, all of which can impair individual development (including self-esteem) and educational achievement (Jang & Thornberry, 1998; Shapiro et al., 1997, 1998). Kochenderfer and Ladd (1996), for example, found that the duration of children's victimization experiences was directly related to the extent of school adjustment problems. Egan and Perry

(1998), in a study of self-regard and victimization, found that the experience of being victimized decreased self-regard over time among a sample of youth. Similarly, studies have shown an increased connection between high levels of exposure to violence and indicators of poor adjustment, including depression, anxiety, and antisocial behavior (see Schwab-Stone et al., 1999).

Garbarino (1996), in a recent study of violence and youth, argues that the issue of violence is particularly problematic for inner city youth because of the trauma associated with community and school violence. In this regard, children and adolescents residing in war zones (such as areas plagued with gangs, crime, and drugs) are thought to be at a greater risk of psychological impairment because of continual exposure to a dangerous environment. In addition, research has emphasized the existence of unconscious forces (e.g., resistance to sleep, nightmares, dreams of fear) among youth living in environments characterized by fear (see Bell & Jenkins, 1991; Garabino, 1992, 1996; Kliewer et al., 1998a; Warner & Weist, 1996). Further, questions arise as to whether chronic exposure has an impact on desensitization and addiction to violence (Bowen & Chapman, 1996; DeHann & MacDermid, 1998; Garbarino, 1992, 1996).

With regard to mental health issues, additional studies based on children raised in communities where violence occurs have shown that direct encounters with violence (either as a victim or witness) increase the likelihood of experiencing anxiety, depression, social withdrawal, and difficulties in concentrating (Boney-McCoy & Finkelhor, 1995; Garbarino, 1996; Singer, Anglin, Song, & Lunghofer, 1995; Osofsky, 1995). Research has also suggested that traumatic events experienced prior to age 11 are three times more likely to result in posttraumatic stress disorder (PTSD) than those experienced after age 12. Further, issues of desensitization and addiction to danger are often raised in discussions of continual exposure to violence.

The Urban Stress and Mental Health Model developed by Hector F. Myers (1996; Myers et al., 1992) suggests that African American youth are particularly vulnerable because of stress-inducing factors, as well as factors relating indirectly to issues of oppression and racism (i.e., class oppression, proliferation of drugs, the use of violence to resolve interpersonal conflicts). Myers (1989; Myers et al., 1992) also argues that most socially distressing indicators of mental health problems among Black youth are the statistics reflecting the extent to which juvenile delinquency and violence have become a way of life. Research has suggested that during childhood, low socioeconomic status serves as one of many environmental factors that can contribute to delinquency and school dropout (McLoyd, 1998; Sampson, 1998; Tolan & Guerra, 1998). Therefore, the presence of "structural violence" in many communities can perpetuate systems of inequality, including poverty and unemployment, both of which can severely affect child development and influence behavioral problems among youth.

With regard to individual adaptation to violence, Sampson (1998) argues that although issues of childhood development are rarely addressed in the social science literature, structural factors such as poverty, violence, and residential instability can explain variations in crime and delinquency among youth. In this regard, delinquency emerges early in the life course, remains relatively stable over time, and is an important component to the empirical connection between the child health and development (Sampson, 1998). Although many youths are able to avoid problem behavior despite increased exposure to violence, research also suggests that a substantial number of "at-risk" youth are unable to adapt to such situations and are more likely to experience school failure and to participate in crime (see Simons, Johnson, Beaman, Conger, & Whitbeck, 1996; Elliott, Hamburg, & Williams, 1998). Thus, the behavior of children in and around schools is strongly influenced by social and psychological influences out of school, prompting many researchers to argue that the propensity for violence and involvement in delinquency is influenced by the desire of many youth to protect themselves from victimization by carrying guns (Davis, 1999; Mercy & Rosenberg, 1998; Lawrence, 1998; Vaughan et al., 1996).

In response to community and school violence, traits such as toughness and recklessness appear to exist in conjunction with extreme levels of fear (Garbarino, 1996). This is particularly problematic for younger children residing in "war zone" environments, many of whom are African American. Similarly, Gilligan (1991) argues that negative identity and low self-esteem are often products of racism and economic inequality, which in turn generate antagonism and aggressive behavior. Hostility and low self-esteem also lead to toughness and recklessness. Additionally, impairments in both school performance and intellectual development are viewed as the result of hostility and withdrawal of youth who have been continually exposed to violent situations (Garbarino, 1996). Many studies have also indicated significant changes in children's behavior, many of whom become more aggressive and hyperactive after a violent experience. In addition, difficulties in concentration often occur because of the intrusion of thoughts relating to violence. Escalating levels of violence are also considered to be the result of an association with drugs, gangs, and sophisticated weaponry in urban settings (Gilligan, 1991). The lack of legitimate economic and educational opportunities, coupled with the emergence of a powerful drug economy, further exacerbates the linkage between exposure to chronic community violence and stress reactions. Thus, research studies have clearly established a connection between increased exposure to violence and youth adaptation to stressful situations.

Coping Strategies and Personality Dimensions

Although few studies have examined the direct impact of urban violence on the mental health and development of African American youth, even less is known about coping strategies and adjustment. Osofsky (1995; Osofsky, Wewers, Hann, & Fick, 1993), in a discussion of the systems approach, argues that an understanding of childhood experiences should encompass the linkage between child and society. Additional emphasis is placed on social learning theory, whereby children learn to imitate what they see and experience. Therefore, exposure to domestic and community violence is thought to place children at a higher risk of becoming offenders as well as victims. Further, children's social and emotional adjustment is directly related to continued exposure to a dangerous environment. However, adjustment appears to be positively related to the presence of social support (e.g., parenting skills), regardless of the level of violence found within communities (Osofsky, 1995; Osofsky et al., 1993). Similarly, the absence of intrafamily conflict may serve as a buffer to exposure to community violence.

In one of the more extensive studies of community violence and coping strategies, Kliewer, Lepore, Oskin, & Johnson (1998) argue that violence has implications for school performance, social relationships, and the overall quality of a child's life. They emphasize global distress, depressive symptoms, and the extent to which social relationships moderate the associations between intrusive thinking and internalizing symptoms among inner city youth who have been exposed to violence. Results of their interviews with mothers and children indicate that children with high levels of violence exposure and inadequate social support had the highest levels of intrusive thoughts about violence, and further suggest that children cope better with violence when social support and opportunities to discuss violent experiences are present (Kliewer, Lepore, Oskin, & Johnson, 1998). In a related study, Kliewer and Kung (1998) found that higher levels of family adaptability protected inner city children from the impact of daily stressors that in turn cause negative outcomes such as behavior problems, anxiety, depression, and school difficulties. A third study examining predictors of threat perceptions in response to everyday situations revealed a relationship between threat perceptions and coping behavior, measured in terms of active, support seeking, distraction, and avoidance coping (Kliewer, Fearnow, & Walton, 1998). These findings suggest the importance of familial and social patterns that may influence the coping strategies used by inner city youth to protect themselves from daily stressors and chronic violence.

With regard to adjustment, studies have indicated that there is no single source of resilience or vulnerability, but the impact of environmental influences plays an integral role in this process (Hill & Madhere, 1996; Farrell & Bruce, 1997; Steele et al., 1999; Schwab-Stone, 1999; Stiffman, Hadley-Ives, Elze, Johnson, & Dore, 1999; Reynolds, 1998). Studies of coping strategies and behavior problems among inner city youth have suggested that reliance on avoidant or emotion-focused coping is associated with distress and behavior problems, whereas problem-focused or active coping is associated with positive behavioral outcomes. Further, differences in adjustment are considered to be the results of an interaction between personality variables and societal pressures. Thus, problems in personality development can have a severe impact on psychological resilience, including responses to community violence. Studies of the "big five" personality traits have stressed the identification of psychological factors that relate to distinctive individual characteristics. These factors include individual interpretations of experiences and emphasize issues of adaptiveness as people attempt to cope with life stressors (National Advisory Mental Health Council, 1995). Research conducted by McCrae and Costa (1986), for example, not only suggests that the influences of stressful situations on the choice of coping mechanisms can affect adaptational outcomes, but also addresses the selection of certain personality dimensions as influencing coping. By classifying traits into three broad domains (i.e., neuroticism, extraversion, openness to experience), the authors have been able to explore several facets, including anxiety, depression, assertiveness, feeling, and actions.

Many of the same factors classified in the Revised Personality Inventory have been used to address the linkage between personality and coping. For example, in a study of personality differences and coping among female nursing students, Parkes (1986) found that individuals with high neuroticism scores responded less adaptively to demanding circumstances and were more vulnerable to emotional distress than those with low scores. Her results further indicated that individuals with high neuroticism and low extraversion showed poorer adaptation to severe life stress and that the coping strategies adopted by introverts and extraverts were differentially influenced by the level of social support available. Sanderson and Clarkin (1994), in a study of the personality dimensions and treatment planning, found that clients using internalization as a coping style exhibited low extraversion and high neuroticism and were more likely to suffer from anxiety and depression. However, individuals who externalized as a means of coping exhibited high extraversion, low neuroticism, and low conscientiousness and were more likely to engage in defensive, impulsive behavior (Sanderson & Clarkin, 1994). Studies such as these suggest the importance of examining personality differences with regard to specific stressful events and the way in which individuals perceive and respond to them.

With regard to childhood and adolescent experiences, adaptation to a serious environment may be influenced by a buffering model, whereby high degrees of conscientiousness, agreeableness, and emotional stability may serve as moderators to important coping responses. Extraversion, in particular, has been linked to direct and problem-focused modes of coping with stressful situations. Studies have shown that extraverts often engage in support seeking and are more likely to report fewer problems and lower levels of psychological strain (see Amirkham, Risinger, & Swickert, 1995). Researchers have also argued that the agreeableness dimension is particularly useful in studies of development because it addresses the frequent and intense expression of negative emotions and can be used to predict behavior problems and academic achievement (see Graziano, 1994; Graziano, Jensen-Campbell, & Finch, 1997; Victor, 1994). Items relating to neuroticism (i.e., anxiety) and openness to experience (i.e., actions) dimensions may also serve as moderators of coping responses to life stressors, including those addressing victimization experiences.

Because of the negative reaction of the American public to any suggestion that social and economic outcomes of racism are the major determinants of urban violence, there is little chance that our nation will quickly mobilize to remove these barriers to physical and mental well-being. Therefore, a study of personality differences that lead to variations in the ability to cope among urban minority youth within these "war zone" environments will contribute significantly to the development of these abilities that will allow individuals to avoid many of the negative life outcomes described in previous paragraphs. Until sufficient attitude change occurs in the larger social structure to overhaul the social and economic realities of this society, we must discover the individual characteristics and traits that safeguard youth from the personal horrors of violence and allow them to build healthy lives.

RESEARCH STUDY

Findings of this study are based on the results of a three-year research effort to estimate the extent of violent victimization among inner city youth in Virginia. This report discusses the effects of victimization on mental health status and is designed to provide information on inner city violence to educators, policy makers, researchers, and others dedicated to restructuring the lives of youth placed at risk by societal conditions. More important, the findings reflect the social and economic problems that many youth face in inner city areas, as well as the need for increased intervention in the lives of youth at risk of community and school-related violence.

Research Design and Method

A violent victimization survey was modified to assess traumatic experiences among minority youth in urban areas. The initial survey was developed by previous researchers examining the degree to which inner city youth are victimized by threat of or actual firearm attack. Additional statements pertaining to issues of mental health status were derived from previous studies (Garbarino, 1996), particularly as they relate to posttraumatic stress disorder. Hence, the survey items were designed to examine the linkage between violent victimization and indicators of traumatic responses.

The analyses reported are based on responses to self-administered questionnaires completed by 500 youth, primarily between the ages of 12 and 17 in the state of Virginia. Census tract data were utilized to obtain a stratified sample selected from various school, church, and community organizations that service youth in urban areas. In all cases, program directors viewed the topic of guns and violence among students as highly politically charged. Students who participated in the youth organizations attended inner city high schools that had experienced firearm incidents in the recent past and had likely encountered gun-related violence (as victims, perpetrators, or bystanders) out of school. The survey was introduced to students as a regional study of firearms and violence among youth. Surveys were administered to 10 to 20 students at a time by research assistants.

Analyses of response consistency were conducted. For example, respondents who did not believe that American society is violent should not have responded to the next item that addresses the causes of violence in society. Ten such items were examined in a similar manner. Inconsistent responses averaged 1.3%, with a range of 0.6% to 2.8%. Respondents were scored for their number of contradictory answers. Respondents received scores between 0 and 10. Less than 2% scored above 2; no score exceeded 5.

Analysis and Findings

Table 14.1 presents a selection of results from the study. Automatic and semiautomatic handguns were the weapons of choice among students who reported carrying a gun in transit to or from school (5% of all respondents). The largest proportion of those who carry guns cited protection as the primary cause (13% of those carrying guns). The findings also indicate that most types of guns are readily accessible to juveniles.

Regarding access, 21% of the students reported that they could obtain a gun with no trouble at all. The results presented in Tables 14.2 and 14.3 reveal that more than two-thirds of the sample expressed an awareness of friends and other students who carry guns and other weapons to school. Furthermore, many of the students grew up in families where gun carrying was prevalent and in neighborhoods where drug and gun trafficking occurred (46% and 54%, respectively). Similarly, these students were frequently threatened and victimized by violence. Preliminary findings also indicate that exposure to violence has a significant impact on mental health status, particularly symptoms of posttraumatic stress disorder. Results show that a significant number of students have experienced difficulty at home and at school as a result of exposure to violent events. More than two-thirds of the students reported anxiety or depression as a result of violence. The issue of unconscious distress also emerged, as many students expressed problems relating to nightmares and dreams about violence. These findings are consistent with earlier studies that documented impairment in school performance and intellectual development, both of which are due to hostility and withdrawal experienced by youth who have been continually exposed to violent situations (see Garbarino, 1996; DeHann & MacDermid, 1998; Farrell & Bruce, 1997; Hill & Madhere, 1996; Schwab-Stone et al., 1999).

The results presented in Table 14.4 further indicate that a significant proportion of these youth have also been involved in personal violence-related activities. With regard to

TABLE 14.1   Youth Crime and Victimization

	Total (%)	Male (%)	Female (%)	N
Access to guns with little trouble	21	24	17	492
Gun ownership/semiautomatic	5	8	2*	490
Purpose for carrying gun/protection	13	16	9*	485
Threatened with a gun	13	14	13	485
Threatened with a knife	12	14	11	478
Threatened with other weapon	13	17	9*	482
Shot at with a gun	6	8	4*	473
Stabbed with a knife	6	6	5	475
Injured with other weapon	8	10	6	478
"I have had trouble studying because of violence"	48	49	47	491
"I have had dreams or nightmares about violence"	43	40	46	489
"I have felt anxious or depressed about violence"	46	44	48	489
"I have been afraid to go outside of my home because of violence"	25	22	28	493

*Gender differences are statistically significant at the .05 level.

TABLE 14.2   Exposure to Guns out of School

	Total (%)	Male (%)	Female (%)	N
Are there any handguns in your home?	25	24	26	481
Does gun and drug dealing occur in your neighborhood?	54	50	59*	492
Gun carrying among family members	46	52	40*	490
Gun carrying among friends	37	40	34*	493
"I have seen someone shot"	37	41	33*	487
"I have seen a murdered body"	33	38	28	489

*The relationship described is statistically significant at the .05 level.

gender differences, the findings are consistent with previous studies that have noted significantly higher rates of violence and victimization among males. Further preliminary analyses have revealed high intercorrelations between the items addressing exposure to guns out of school, exposure to violence in school, personal violence–related activities, violent victimization, and symptoms of posttraumatic stress disorder. Thus, the results show the

TABLE 14.3   Peers, Weapons, and Exposure to Violence in School

	Total (%)	Male (%)	Female (%)	N
Do any kids in your school carry guns with them to school?	31	31	30	493
Other kids known personally by the respondent who have been victimized by guns	29	24	35	467
Other kids known personally by the respondent who have been victimized by knives	29	26	33	469
Other kids known personally by the respondent who have been victimized by other weapons	23	23	24	461
Is there a lot of violence in your school?	29	34	24*	481
Have you felt unsafe while you were in school?	9	7	11	472

*Gender differences are statistically significant at the .05 level.

usefulness of the violent victimization survey to assess levels of victimization, violence, and fear among inner city students.

Personality measures were derived from a modified version of Lewis Goldberg's 100 Synonym Clusters (Goldberg & Rosolack, 1994). Words were eliminated that were not understood by adolescents or that had a low correlation with the bipolar (opposite) paired word. Thus, 50 of the strongest words were included, each of which addressed at least one of the "big five" factors (Graziano, 1994; Graziano et al., 1997). Adolescents were asked to rate themselves on a scale of self-concept measures. Items were scored on a five-point scale ranging from 1 ("strongly disagree") to 5 ("strongly agree").

With regard to coping responses as moderated by the "big five" model, the study used Halstead, Johnson, and Cunningham's (1993) version of the Ways of Coping Checklist (WCCL). Adolescents were asked to identify a violent event that occurred within the past month and then to identify the specific coping strategy they used in response to that situation. Special attention was paid to coding stressful events based on violent incidents. Coping responses were read to the participants as they rated items on a four-point scale (1, "does not apply or not used" to 4, "used a great deal"). An exploratory factor analysis was utilized to determine common themes. Items directed toward coping responses among adolescents included problem focused, social support, wishful thinking, and avoidance.

In an effort to create scaled items reflecting the "big five" model, responses were combined into five factors: Extraversion, Openness to Experience, Agreeableness, Conscientiousness, and Emotional Stability (Neuroticism). Because of the small number of items (8 to 14 per dimension) and low reliability coefficients for Extraversion and Emotional Stability ($\alpha = .59$ and $\alpha = .69$ respectively), an explanatory principal components analysis was

TABLE 14.4   Personal Violence-Related Activities

	Total (%)	Male (%)	Female (%)	N
Respondent has been arrested or picked up by the police	22	30	12**	483
Respondent has stolen something worth more than $50	22	25	19	486
Respondent has used a gun to commit a crime	6	9	3	484
Respondent has used some other weapon to commit a crime	8	10	6	479
Respondent has been involved in drug dealing (selling and/or buying)	18	23	11*	484
Respondent has used alcohol	34	35	34	483
Respondent has used drugs (crack, cocaine, and/or heroin)	6	5	6	482
Respondent has carried a gun to school	6	7	5	490
Respondent has carried a gun out of the home	10	14	6*	488
Respondent has gotten into fights (% many times)	14	14	13	487

*Gender differences are statistically significant at the .05 level.
**Gender differences are statistically significant at the .001 level.

conducted, and five independent constructs were created, including (1) a blended factor of high extraversion, low agreeableness, and low conscientiousness; (2) a low agreeableness and low conscientiousness factor; (3) a high openness to experience factor; (4) a low extraversion factor (introversion); and (5) a low emotional stability factor. Although all five elements exist within this structure, questions arise as to whether a representative five-factor structure exists.

Table 14.5 presents data linking relationships among personality, coping, and development outcome among youth victims. A subsample of youth ($N = 315$) who had either seen a violent event, been threatened with a weapon, or been attacked with a weapon was selected from the larger sample of 500 subjects. Bivariate correlations were then computed among the youth who had been exposed to violence to examine the relationship between coping, personality, and development outcome. With regard to the latter measure, items addressing delinquency, anxiety, and school acceptance were included. Results in Table 14.5 suggest that youth who score high on extraversion and low on agreeableness and conscientiousness (blended factor) are more likely to engage in negative behaviors (that is, gun carrying, drug dealing, criminal activity with a gun, and drug usage) as developmental outcomes and are less likely to engage in coping strategies such as problem focused, social support, and wishful thinking ($r = -.204$, $-.151$, and $-.156$, respectively). Results further

TABLE 14.5 Zero-Order Correlations Examining Personality, Coping, and Development Outcome among Youth Victims

	1	2	3	4	5	6	7	8	9	10	11
1. Factor score 1		.004	.087	.010	-.021	-.204**	-.151	-.156	-.094	.296**	.403**
2. Problem focused			.617**	.440**	.338**	-.204**	-.172**	.059	-.047	-.030	.037
3. Social support				.468**	.215**	-.189***	-.137*	.078	-.083	-.092	.065
4. Wishful thinking					.486**	.011	-.034	.090	-.031	-.110	.029
5. Avoidance						.125*	.058	.080	.041	.016	-.063
6. Gun carrying home and to school							.658**	.127*	.567**	.448**	-.039
7. Involvement in drug dealing								.235**	.416**	.369**	-.076
8. Anxiety/depression									.052	.192**	-.015
9. Crime with a gun or other weapon										.416**	.567**
10. Drug usage											-.010
11. "I am a good student"											

Factor score 1—high extraversion, low agreeableness, low conscientiousness.

*p < .05.
**p < .001.

indicate that problem-focused coping and social support coping relate more to resilience in that youth employing these strategies are less likely to carry guns ($r = -.204$ and $-.172$, respectively) and engage in drug dealing ($r = -.189$ and $-.137$, respectively). Additionally, avoidance is linked to maladaptivity, in that youth employing this coping strategy are more likely to have carried a gun ($r = -.125$).

DISCUSSION AND CONCLUSION

Findings of this research project suggest a linkage between coping, personality, and development among African American youth exposed to danger. They also suggest the need for further exploration of additional measures of coping, personality, and development to enhance the strength of these associations. These analyses are based on a race-homogeneous design consisting of data collection from African American youth residing in areas plagued by violence and crime. With regard to social class, research indicates that low socioeconomic status serves as one of the many environmental factors that can contribute to the use of violence to resolve conflicts (Myers, 1989; Myers et al., 1992). Further, studies have shown significant differences between personality descriptors among middle-class and lower-class African Americans. Mueller and Parcell (1981) argue that the first step in cross-cultural comparisons in child development is to examine patterns of development in different groups. African American and white middle classes appear similar in attitudes, contrary to the attitudes of those found within lower classes. Further, in an effort to understand the powerful influence of environmental factors, Mueller and Parcell (1981) developed the cultural ecological model that focuses primarily on the issue of human competence within the African American community. Emphasis is placed on adult techniques for child rearing and the search for attributes necessary for child growth and development. Within this context, elements of support seeking and personality development are discussed with regard to parent-child relationships. Thus, the present study aimed to examine the adjustment and coping experiences of lower-income minority youth with interpersonal violence and to develop personality profiles of these youth in an effort to understand the impact of negative environmental influences on individual adolescents. Parental occupation–based measures were utilized as a primary indicator of socioeconomic status (see Mueller and Parcell, 1981).

Mueller and Parcell (1981) argue that the validity of research involving American minorities is often impaired by the rejection of the cultural context of minority experiences and viewpoints. Additionally, they suggest that a major consequence of racism is the misrepresentation of the minority experience through acceptance of common myths and stereotypes. The authors point toward the importance of situationally relevant factors (e.g., unequal education, structured inequality) as opposed to person-centered characteristics (e.g., aggression, intelligence) in an effort to better understand problematic situations that American minorities face. Within this context, they argue that minorities should be allowed to interpret their own experiences, lending additional support to interpretative validity in social science research. The instruments utilized in this study were a series of questions relating personal experiences of violent events, adjustment outcomes, coping strategies, and personality dimensions. Future research should continue to explore the linkage between these factors as they relate to African American youth violence.

DISCUSSION QUESTIONS

1. Describe the Urban Stress and Mental Health Model.

2. Discuss the social learning theory.

3. What is response consistency?

4. Describe the "big five" model.

5. What is a race-homogeneous design?

REFERENCES

ALVAREZ, A., & BACHMAN, R. (1997). Predicting the fear of assault at school and while going to and from school in an adolescent population. *Violence and Victims, 12,* 69–86.

AMIRKHAM, J.H., RISINGER, R., & SWICKERT, R. (1995). Extraversion: A hidden personality factor in coping? *Journal of Personality, 63,* 189–212.

BARON, R.M., & KENNY, D.A. (1986). The moderator-mediator variable distinction in social psychological research: Conceptual, strategic, and statistical considerations. *Journal of Personality and Social Psychology, 51,* 1173–1182.

BELL, C.C., & JENKINS, E.J. (1991). Traumatic stress and children. *Journal of Health Care for the Poor and Underserved, 2,* 175–185.

BONEY-MCCOY, S., & FINKELHOR, D. (1995). Psychological sequelae of violent victimization in a national youth sample. *Journal of Consulting and Clinical Psychology, 63,* 726–736.

BOWEN, G.L., & CHAPMAN, M.V. (1996). Poverty, neighborhood danger, social support, and the individual adaptation among at-risk youth in urban areas. *Journal of Family Issues, 17,* 641–666.

BROOKINS, G., PETERSON, A., & BROOKS, L. (1997). Youth and families in the inner city: Influencing positive outcomes. In H. Walberg, O. Reyes, & R. Weissberg (Eds.), *Children and youth: Interdisciplinary perspectives* (pp. 45–66). Thousand Oaks, CA: Sage.

CENTERS FOR DISEASE CONTROL AND PREVENTION. (1998). Youth risk behavior surveillance— United States, 1997. *CDC Surveillance Summaries.* MMWR 1998 (August 14):47 (No.SS–3).

CHANDLER, K.A., CHAPMAN, C.D., RAND, M.R. & TAYLOR, B.M. (1998). *Students' reports of school crime: 1989 and 1995.* Washington, DC: U.S. Departments of Education and Justice.

COLL, C., CRNIC, K., WASIK, B., JENKINS, R., GARCIA, H., & MCADOO, H. (1996). An integrated model for the study of developmental competencies in minority children. *Child Development, 67,* 1891–1914.

COSTA, P.T., & MCCRAE, R.R. (1992). *Revised NEO personality inventory (NEO PI R) and NEO five-factor inventory (NEO-FFI).* Odessa, FL: Psychological Assessment Resources.

DAVIS, N.J. (1999). *Youth crisis: Growing up in the high-risk society.* Westport, CT: Praeger.

DEHAAN, L.G., & MACDERMID, S. (1998). The relationship of individual and family factors to the psychological well-being of junior high school students living in urban poverty. *Adolescence, 33,* 73–89.

DORNBUSCH, S.M., RITTER, P.L., LEIDERMAN, P.H., ROBERTS, D.F., & FRALEIGH, M.J. (1987). The relation of parenting style to adolescent school performance. *Child Development, 58,* 1244–1257.

EGAN, S.K., & PERRY, D.G. (1998). Does low self-regard invite victimization? *Developmental Psychology, 34,* 299–309.

ELLIOTT, D.S., HAMBURG, B., & WILLIAMS, K.R. (1998). Violence in American schools: An overview. In D.S. Elliott, B.A. Hamburg, & K.R. Williams (Eds.), *Violence in American schools: A new perspective* (pp. 3–30). Cambridge, MA: Cambridge University Press.

ESBENSEN, F., & HUIZINGA, D. (1993). Gangs, drugs, and delinquency in a survey of urban youth. *Criminology, 31*, 565–589.

FAGAN, J., PIPER, E., & CHENG, Y. (1987) Contributions of victimization to delinquency in inner cities. *Journal of Law and Criminology, 78*, 586–613.

FAGAN, J., PIPER, E., & MOORE, M. (1986). Violent delinquents and urban youth. *Criminology, 24*, 439–471.

FAGAN, J., WEIS, J., & CHENG, Y. (1990). Delinquency and substance use among inner city students. *Journal of Drug Issues, 20*, 351–402.

FARRELL, A.D., & BRUCE, S.E. (1997). Impact of exposure to community violence on violent behavior and emotional distress among urban adolescents. *Journal of Clinical Child Psychology, 26*, 2–14.

FARRELL, A.D., DANISH, S.J., & HOWARD, C.W. (1992). Risk factors for drug use in urban adolescents: Identification and cross-validation. *American Journal of Community Psychology, 20*, 263–286.

FINKELHOR, D. (1997). The victimization of children and youth. In R.C. Davis, A.J. Lurigio, & W.G. Skogan (Eds.), *Victims of crime* (pp. 86–107). Thousand Oaks, CA: Sage.

GARBARINO, J. (1996). Youth in dangerous environments: Coping with the consequences. In K. Hurrelmann & S. Hamilton (Eds.), *Social problems and social contexts in adolescence: Perspectives across boundaries* (pp. 269–290). New York: Aldine de Gruyter.

GIBBS, J. (1989). Black adolescents and youth: An update on an endangered species. In R. Jones (Ed.), *Black adolescents.* (pp. 32–46). Berkeley, CA: Cobb and Henry.

GILLIGAN, C. (1991). *Meeting at the crossroads: Women's psychology and girls' development.* Cambridge, MA: Harvard University Press.

GOLDBERG, L., & ROSOLACK, T. (1994). The big five structure as an integrative framework: An empirical comparison with Eysenck's p-e-n model. In C. Halverson, G. Kohnstamn, & R. Martin (Eds.), *The developing structure of temperament and personality from infancy to adulthood* (pp. 56–87). Mahwah, NJ: Lawrence Erlbaum.

GRAZIANO, W.G. (1994). The development of agreeableness as a dimension of personality. In C. Halverson, G. Kohnstamm, & R. Martin (Eds.), *The developing structure of temperament and personality from infancy to adulthood.* (pp. 76–98). Mahwah, NJ: Lawrence Erlbaum.

GRAZIANO, W.G., JENSEN-CAMPBELL, L.A., & FINCH, J.F. (1997). The self as mediator between personality and adjustment. *Journal of Personality and Social Psychology, 73*, 392–405.

HALSTEAD, M., JOHNSON, S., & CUNNINGHAM, W. (1993). Measuring coping in adolescents: An application of the Ways of Coping Checklist. *Journal of Clinical Child Psychology, 22*, 337–344.

HARTER, S. (1988). *Manual for the self-perception profile for adolescents.* Denver, CO: University of Denver.

HARTER, S., WATERS, P., & WHITESELL, N.R. (1998). Relational self-worth: Differences in perceived worth as a person across interpersonal contexts among adolescents. *Child Development, 69*, 756–767.

HILL, H.M., & MADHERE, S. (1996). Exposure to community violence and African American children: A multidimensional model of risks and resources. *Journal of Community Psychology, 2*, 26–43.

JANG, S.J., & THORNBERRY, T.P. (1998). Self-esteem, delinquent peers, and delinquency: A test of the self-enhancement thesis. *American Sociological Review, 63*, 586–598.

JESSOR, R., DONOVAN, J., & COSTA, F. (1996). Personality, perceived life chances and adolescent behavior. In K. Hurrelmann & S. Hamilton (Eds.), *Social problems and social contexts in adolescence: Perspectives across boundaries* (pp. 219–234). New York: Aldine de Gruyter.

KALJEE, L.M., STANTON, B., RICARDO, I., & WHITEHEAD, T. (1995). Urban African American adolescents and their parents: Perceptions of violence within and against their communities. *Human Organization, 54,* 373–382.

KAUFMAN, P., CHEN, X., CHOY, S.P., CHANDLER, K.A., CHAPMAN, C.D., RAND, M.R. & RINGEL, C. (1998). *Indicators of school crime and safety, 1998.* Washington, DC: U.S. Departments of Education and Justice.

KLIEWER, W., FEARNOW, M.D., & MILLER, P.A. (1996). Coping socialization in middle childhood: Tests of maternal and paternal influences. *Child Development, 67,* 2339–2357.

KLIEWER, W., FEARNOW, M.D., & WALTON, M.N. (1998a). Dispositional, environmental, and context-specific predictors of children's threat perceptions in everyday stressful situations. *Journal of Youth and Adolescence, 27,* 83–100.

KLIEWER, W., & KUNG, E. (1998). Family moderators of the relation between hassles and behavior problems in inner-city youth. *Journal of Clinical Child Psychology, 27,* 278–292.

KLIEWER, W., LEPORE, S.J., OSKIN, D., & JOHNSON, P.D. (1998). The role of social and cognitive processes in children's adjustment to community violence. *Journal of Consulting and Clinical Psychology, 66,* 199–209.

KOCHENDERFER, B.J., & LADD, G.W. (1996). Peer victimization: Cause or consequence of school maladjustment? *Child Development, 67,* 1305–1317.

LAWRENCE, R. (1998). *School crime and juvenile justice.* New York: Oxford University Press.

LENGUA, L.J., & SANDLER, I.N. (1996). Self-regulation as a moderator of the relation between coping and symptomatology in children of divorce. *Journal of Abnormal Child Psychology, 24,* 681–702.

McCRAE, R.R., & COSTA, P.T. (1986). Personality, coping, and coping effectiveness in an adult sample. *Journal of Personality, 54,* 385–405.

McCUBBIN, H.I., FLEMING, W.M., THOMPSON, A.I., NEITMAN, P., ELVER, K.M., & SAVAS, S.A. (1998). Resiliency and coping in "at-risk" African-American youth and their families. In H.I. McCubbin, E.A. Thompson, A.I. Thompson, & J.A. Futrell (Eds.), *Resiliency in African-American families* (pp 287–328). Thousand Oaks, CA: Sage.

McDERMOTT, J. (1983). Crime in the school and in the community: Offenders, victims, and fearful youth. *Crime and Delinquency, 29,* 207–282.

McGEE, Z.T. (1996). The violent victimization survey. In R. Jones (Ed.), *Handbook of tests and measurements for black populations* (pp. 613–620). Hampton, VA: Cobb and Henry.

McLOYD, V. (1981). The impact of economic hardships on black families and children: Psychological distress, parity, and socioemotional development. *Child Development, 61*(2), 311–346.

McLOYD, V.C. (1998). Socioeconomic disadvantage and child development. *American Psychologist, 53,* 185–204.

MERCY, J.A., & ROSENBERG, M.L. (1998). Preventing firearm violence in and around schools. In D.S. Elliott, B.A. Hamburg, & K.R. Williams (Eds.), *Violence in American schools: A new perspective* (pp. 159–187). New York: Cambridge University Press.

MILLER, L.S., WASSERMAN, G.A., NEUGEBAUER, R., GORMAN-SMITH, D., & KAMBOUKAS, D. (1999). Witnessed community violence and antisocial behavior in high-risk, urban boys. *Journal of Clinical Child Psychology, 28,* 2–11.

MUELLER, C.W., & PARCELL, T.L. (1981). Measures of socioeconomic status: Alternatives and recommendations. *Child Development, 52,* 13–30.

MYERS, H.F. (1989). Urban stress and mental health in black youth: An epidemiological and conceptual update. In R. Jones (Ed.), *Black adolescents* (pp. 123–154). Berkeley, CA: Cobb and Henry.

MYERS, H.F., TAYLOR, S., ALVY, K.T., ARRINGTON, A., & RICHARDSON, M.A. (1992). Parental and family predictors of behavior problems in inner-city black children. *American Journal of Community Psychology, 20,* 557–576.

NATIONAL ADVISORY MENTAL HEALTH COUNCIL. (1995). *Basic behavioral science research for mental health: A national investment.* Washington, DC: U.S. Department of Health and Human Services.

OSOFSKY, J.D. (1995). Children who witness domestic violence: The invisible victims. *Social Policy Research Report, 9,* 1–16.

OSOFSKY, J.D., WEWERS, S., HANN, D.M., & FICK, A.C. (1993). Chronic community violence: what is happening to our children? In D. Reiss, J.E. Richters, M. Radke-Yarrow, & D. Scharff (Eds.), *Children and violence* (pp. 54–69). New York: Guilford.

PARKES, K.R. (1986). Coping in stressful episodes: The role of individual differences, environmental factors, and situational characteristics. *Journal of Personality and Social Psychology, 51,* 1277–1292.

REYNOLDS, A.J. (1998). Resilience among black urban youth: Prevalence, intervention effects, and mechanisms of influence. *American Journal of Orthopsychiatry, 68,* 84–100.

REYNOLDS, C.R., & RICHMOND, B.O. (1997). What I think and feel: A revised measure of children's manifest anxiety. *Journal of Abnormal Child Psychology, 25,* 15–21.

RICHTERS, J.E., & MARTINEZ, P. (1993a). The NIMH community violence project: i, Children as victims of and witnesses to violence. In D. Reiss, J.E. Richters, M. Radke-Yarrow, & D. Scharff (Eds.), *Children and violence* (pp. 2–23). New York: Guilford.

RICHTERS, J.E., & MARTINEZ, P. (1993b). The NIMH community violence project: ii, Children as victims of and witnesses to violence. In D. Reiss, J.E. Richters, M. Radke-Yarrow, & D. Scharff (Eds.), *Children and violence* (pp. 24–35) New York: Guilford.

ROBINS, R., JOHN, C., & CASPI, A. (1994). Major dimensions of personality in early adolescence: The big five and beyond. In C. Halverson, G. Kohnstamm, & R. Martin (Eds.), *The Developing structure of temperament and personality from infancy to adulthood.* (pp. 267–292). Mahwah, NJ: Lawrence Erlbaum.

ROSENBLATT, J.A., & FURLONG, M.J. (1997). Assessing the reliability and validity of student self-reports of campus violence. *Journal of Youth and Adolescence, 26,* 187–202.

SAMPSON, R. (1998). The embeddedness of child and adolescent development: A community-level perspective on urban violence. In J. McCord (Ed.), *Violence and childhood in the inner-city.* (pp. 31–77). New York: Cambridge University Press.

SANDERSON, C., & CLARKIN, S. (1994). Use of the NEO-PI personality dimension in differential treatment planning. In P.T. Costa & T.A. Widiger (Eds.), *Personality disorders and the five factor model of personality* (pp. 219–236). Washington, DC: American Psychological Association.

SANDLER, I.N., TEIN, J., & WEST, S.G. (1994). Coping, stress, and the psychological symptoms of children of divorce: A cross-sectional and longitudinal study. *Child Development, 65,* 1744–1763.

SCHWAB-STONE, M., CHEN, C., GREENBERGER, E., SILVER, D., LICHTMAN, J., & VOYCE, C. (1999). The effects of violence exposure on urban youth. *Journal of the American Academy of Child and Adolescent Psychiatry, 38,* 359–368.

SHAKOOR, B.H., & CHAMBERS, D. (1991). Co-victimization of African American children who witness violence: Effects on cognitive, emotional, and behavioral development. *Journal of the National Medical Association, 83,* 233–238.

SHAPIRO, J.P., DORMAN, R.L., BURKEY, W.M., WELKER, C.J., & CLOUGH, J.B. (1997). Development and factor analysis of a measure of youth attitudes toward guns and violence. *Journal of Clinical and Child Psychology, 26,* 311–320.

SHAPIRO, J.P., DORMAN, R.L., BURKEY, W.M., WELKER, C.J., & CLOUGH, J.B. (1998). Youth attitudes toward guns and violence: Relations with sex, age, ethnic group, and firearm exposure. *Journal of Clinical and Child Psychology, 27,* 98–108.

SIMONS, R.L., JOHNSON, C., BEAMAN, J., CONGER, R.D., & WHITBECK, L.B. (1996). Parents and peer group as mediators of the effect of community structure on adolescent problem behavior. *American Journal of Community Psychology, 24,* 15–171.

SINGER, M.I., ANGLIN, T.M., SONG, L., & LUNGHOFER, L. (1995). Adolescents' exposure to violence and associated symptoms of psychological trauma. *Journal of the American Sociological Association, 273,* 477–482.

SNYDER, H., & SICKMUND, M. (1997). *Juvenile offenders and victims: A national report.* Washington, DC: Office of Juvenile Justice and Delinquency Prevention.

STEELE, R.G., FOREHAND, R., ARMISTEAD, L., MORSE, E., SIMON, P., & CLARK, L. (1999). Coping strategies and behavior problems of urban African-American children: Concurrent and longitudinal relationships. *American Journal of Orthopsychiatry, 69,* 182–193.

STIFFMAN, A.R., HADLEY-IVES, E., ELZE, D., JOHNSON, S., & DORE, P. (1999). Impact of environment on adolescent mental health and behavior: Structural equation modeling. *American Journal of Orthopsychiatry, 69,* 73–86.

TOBIN, P., & GORMAN-SMITH, R. (1997). Families and the development of urban children. In H. Walberg, O. Reyes, & R. Weissberg (Eds.), *Children and youth: Interdisciplinary perspectives* (pp. 67–91). Thousand Oaks, CA: Sage.

TOLAN, P.H., & GUERRA, N. (1998). Societal causes of violence against children. In P.K. Trickett & C.J. Schellenbach (Eds.), *Violence against children in the family and community* (pp.195–210). Washington, DC: American Psychological Association.

U.S. DEPARTMENT OF EDUCATION, NATIONAL CENTER FOR EDUCATION STATISTICS. (1998). *Violence and discipline problems in U.S. public schools: 1996–97.* Washington, DC: Author.

VAUGHAN, R.D., McCARTHY, J., ARMSTRONG, B., WALTER, H.J., WATERMAN, P.D., & TIEZZI, L. (1996). Carrying and using weapons: A survey of minority junior high school students in New York City. *American Journal of Public Health, 86,* 568–572.

VICTOR, J. (1994). The five factor model applied to individual differences. In C. Halverson, G. Kohnstamm, & R. Martin (Eds.), *The developing structure of temperament and personality from infancy to adulthood* (pp. 46–86). Mahwah, NJ: Lawrence Erlbaum.

WARNER, B.S., & WEIST, M.D. (1996). Urban youth as witnesses to violence: Beginning assessment and treatment efforts. *Journal of Youth and Adolescence, 25,* 361–377.